RECONSTRUCTING
STRANGELOVE

For Carl,
and the rest of us
P.O.E.

RECONSTRUCTING STRANGELOVE

INSIDE STANLEY KUBRICK'S 'NIGHTMARE COMEDY'

MICK BRODERICK

WALLFLOWER PRESS

LONDON & NEW YORK

A Wallflower Press Book
Published by
Columbia University Press
Publishers Since 1893
New York • Chichester, West Sussex
cup.columbia.edu

Wallflower Press® is a registered trademark of Columbia University Press

A complete CIP record is available from the Library of Congress

ISBN 978-0-231-17708-5 (cloth : alk. paper)
ISBN 978-0-231-17709-2 (pbk. : alk. paper)
ISBN 978-0-231-85100-8 (e-book)

Columbia University Press books are printed on permanent
and durable acid-free paper.
Printed in the United States of America

Cover image:
Stanley Kubrick lines up a shot in the War Room set of *Dr. Strangelove*.
Publicity still © Columbia Pictures 1964.

Contents

Acknowledgements

My sincere thanks go to Katharina Kubrick for helping me start the ball rolling on this project a couple of years after Stanley's all-too-premature passing. Katharina provided entrée to the family and the then, as yet uncatalogued, archive. Christiane Kubrick was a gracious host for my two-week visit to Childwickbury in April 2005, kindly facilitated by her brother and Stanley's executive producer and estate executor, Jan Harlan. It was a delight to sit in the Kubrick family library surrounded by scores of *Dr. Strangelove* boxes, filled with files and photographs. Christiane also provide me with a fascinating and lengthy interview, and Katharina later added some childhood recollections.

My great appreciation is also extended to the son of novelist Peter George, David, and his wife Lorraine, for their hospitality in Hastings on a few short visits during the course of the research and writing. Peter George's eldest daughter Sara also kindly offered her memories of the period. I am similarly grateful to the son of author Terry Southern, Nile, and his mother Carol, who found time for me to visit both of their homes in the US for interviews.

Other Kubrick collaborators generously offered their recollections over the years, including early career Kubrick producing partner/director James B. Harris; Stanley's career-long attorney Louis C. Blau; *Lolita* and *Dr. Strangelove* editor Anthony Harvey; *Strangelove* and *A Clockwork Orange* titles, trailer and cut-up artist Pablo Ferro; and Kubrick's long-time personal assistant Tony Frewin.

Richard Daniels, the Stanley Kubrick Archivist, University of the Arts London Archives and Special Collections Centre, has been everything you want a specialist archivist to be – highly knowledgeable, curious and enthusiastic about all things Kubrickian. Other custodians of the Archive who helped with my enquiries during my peripatetic London visits over the years include: Wendy Russel (Archives Assistant,) Sarah Mahurter (Manager, University of the Arts London Archives and Special Collections Centre), Sarah Cox (Assistant Archivist) and Naomi Crede (Archives Assistant). My thanks also to the Kubrick Archives and University of the Arts London for duplicating images, and especially to Jan Harlan for granting me reproduction permission. Special thanks also to David George for access and permission to use images from the Peter George Archive. Filmmaker David Naylor very kindly shared interview transcripts early on of other Kubrick collaborators from his anniversary edition DVD documentary *Inside Dr. Strangelove*. A shorter version of chapter five was first published in the Tatjana Ljujic, Richard Daniels and Peter Krämer edited collection, *Stanley Kubrick: New Perspectives* (Black Dog), revised here with thanks.

Yoram Allon, Commissioning Editor at Wallflower Press, has remained remarkably steadfast and good-humoured during my protracted delays, as has Meredith Howard at Columbia University Press. Thanks also to designer Elsa Mathern for her canny cover work conjuring Pablo Ferro's *Strangelove* title style.

Institutional support came in the form of two sabbatical study leaves approved by my former School of Media, Communication & Culture, and current School of Arts at Murdoch University. AMK (alt.movies.kubrick) administered by Rod Munday both in internet and social media form provided the gateway for my initial outreach to the Kubricks in 2002 and AMK has continued to be a source of wisdom and online resourcing. Fellow AMKer, *Village Voice* film critic Bilge Ebri, also lent his support early to promote the project, as did Toby Miller more recently in a lengthy podcast highlighting the research. Other correspondents who provided, or otherwise offered, assistance include Curtis Tsui from the Criteron Collection, and biographers Rhys Lloyd and Lee Hill. Jonathan Parfrey, former executive director of Physicians for Social Responsibility (LA) and now heading US not-for-profit NGO, Climate Resolve, has provided decades of informative banter and deep insight on matters nuclear and cinematic. The lovely Christine Spiegel has been a stalwart companion during the past two years of manuscript work.

The wonderful National Security Archive (NSA) at Georgetown University remains a formidable repository of declassified nuclear documentation drawn from both sides of the 'Iron Curtain'. William Burr's resolute Cold War scrutiny has been at the vanguard of endless Freedom of Information (FOI) requests that have released thousands of pages of preciously secret material, shedding light on nuclear security matters past and present. The NSA's director of communication, Lauren Harper, also provided expert advice on the FOI request and appeals processes of the FBI and CIA, although both agencies responded too late for any detailed inclusion here.

Michelle Morrison and, in particular, Gwen Velge assisted with timely endnote formatting and citation assistance, while Erin Hawley generously helped with the initial auditing of the thousands of *Strangelove* papers from Childwickbury. Good friend and perennial collaborator on matters atomic, Bo Jacobs, turned his nuclear gaze to the unpublished manuscript, as did my frequent screen co-producer and co-writer, Stuart Bender. I'm especially grateful to Stanley Kubrick Archivist Richard Daniels who diligently provided important feedback at short notice. I thank them all for their incisive and astute comments. Needless to say I remain entirely responsible for the content and any matters of inaccuracy that may have — inevitably — slipped through the cracks.

But I'd like to hold off judgement on a thing like that until all the facts are in.

Mick Broderick
Perth, Western Australia
July 2016

Dr. Strangelove Timeline

1945

- President Roosevelt dies in office 12 April. Fifteen-year-old Stanley Kubrick's photo of a despondent newspaper vendor is sold to *Look* magazine for $25, appearing in 26 June issue.
- Kubrick completes his formal education at Taft high school.
- First atomic detonation, code named 'Trinity', near Alamagordo in New Mexico, 16 July.
- Hiroshima and Nagasaki destroyed by atomic bombs 'Little Boy' (uranium gun) and 'Fat Man' (plutonium implosion), respectively killing 140,000 and 70,000 Japanese on 6 and 9 August. Tens of thousands more die in the following months.
- Soviet Union declares war on Japan, invading Manchuria same day as the Nagasaki attack. Japanese Emperor announces surrender via radio on 14 August. Formal surrender occurs 14 September aboard the *USS Missouri*.

1946

- Winston Churchill delivers his 'Iron Curtain' speech in Missouri, 5 March.
- Kubrick graduates from Taft high school in January.
- Kubrick contributes multiple photo essays as an 'informal' apprentice photographer for *Look* magazine from April to November.
- A-bombs 'Able' and 'Baker' detonated at Bikini Atoll in the South Pacific in early July. Due to the high levels of radioactivity affecting the surrounding ships, test shot 'Charlie' is cancelled.

1947

- Kubrick promoted to staff photographer at *Look*, 7 January.
- 5 August issue of *Look* features a cover photo with credit by Stanley Kubrick.
- Kubrick obtains a private pilot's certificate, 15 August.

1948

- Kubrick marries 'high school sweetheart' Toba Metz on 29 May and moves to Greenwich Village.

1949

- Kubrick's photo essay 'Prizefighter' published in *Look* in January.
- First Soviet Atomic device exploded, 'First Lightning' (RDS-1, aka 'Joe-1'), in Kazakhstan on 29 August.
- Kubrick resigns from *Look* to concentrate on filmmaking, November.

1950

- Top Secret National Security Paper (NSC-68) mandates 'massive retaliation' as US policy, April.
- Kubrick produces his first film, the documentary short *Day of the Fight,* based on his earlier *Look* article, sold to RKO-Pathe for $4,000.

1951

- *Day of the Fight* opens 26 April in New York, supporting the feature drama *My Forbidden Past.*
- Kubrick films *The Flying Padre* for RKO-Pathe, based on his earlier *Look* article.

1952

- First American thermonuclear detonation, 'Ivy-Mike', at Enewetak Atoll, with a yield over ten megatons (Mt) of TNT equivalent explosive force, vapourises two small islands.
- Kubrick produces, directs, photographs and edits his 'one-man' feature *Fear and Desire*, filmed over five weeks, with sound post-synchronised.
- Kubrick hired for second unit filming on the *Omnibus* Abraham Lincoln television series.

1953

- Kubrick commissioned to make short colour film, *The Seafarers,* for the International Seamen's Union.

- *Fear and Desire* released 31 March.
- First Soviet H-bomb (RDS-6s, aka 'Joe-4') detonated with a 400 kiloton yield, 12 August.
- Katharina (Kubrick) born to Christiane Harlan and Werner Bruhns, December.

1954
- Fifteen-megaton American thermonuclear 'Castle-Bravo' test at Bikini Atoll spreads to fallout across 7,000 square miles of the Pacific, contaminating Marshall Islanders, American service personnel and the crew of a Japanese fishing vessel, 1 March.
- Nationwide 'Operation Alert' exercises commence, where the Federal Civil Defense Administration simulate three nuclear bombs striking NYC. The drills continued amidst increasing public protest until cancelation in 1962.

1955
- Kubrick's second feature film, *Killer's Kiss,* released in New York, 22 November.

1956
- Kubrick's third feature *The Killing*, starring Sterling Hayden, and produced by James B. Harris, released by United Artists, 20 May.

1957
- SAC stages a B-52 airborne alert, trialed to enable nuclear-armed bombers to circle the globe on permanent rotation 24 hours a day.
- Eisenhower permits 'Top Secret' predelegation of nuclear weapons use by lower echelon commanders, without requiring his direct executive approval, May.
- *Paths of Glory* released by United Artists, 25 December.

1958
- Kubrick marries actor-artist Christiane Harlan who remains his life-long partner up to his death on 7 March 1999.
- Soviet Union unilaterally announces a halt to nuclear testing in March.
- Kubrick spends six months developing *One Eyed Jacks* with Marlon Brando, May to late-November.
- Peter George publishes *Two Hours to Doom* (UK), November.
- Harris-Kubrick acquire screen rights to Vladimir Nabokov's *Lolita*.

1959
- Kubrick family moves to Beverly Hills while Stanley develops a number of projects.

- Kubrick hired by producer-star Kirk Douglas for *Spartacus* in mid-February.
- Paperback edition of Peter George's *Red Alert* published in USA by Ace Books, March.
- Daughter Anya born in April.
- Harvey Wheeler's short story 'Abraham'59 – A Nuclear Fantasy' published in *Dissent* (Winter).

1960

- Kubrick and Nabokov meet at Universal Pictures to discuss approaches to *Lolita*, March.
- Daughter Vivian born in August.
- Pentagon develops the Single Integrated Operational Plan (SIOP) to launch over 3,000 nuclear warheads against the Soviets, China and Warsaw Pact countries.
- Former RAND Corp. strategist, Herman Kahn, publishes *On Thermonuclear War.*
- *Spartacus* premiers in Hollywood, 19 October.

1961

- *Lolita* developed and produced.
- Berlin Crisis escalates from June to October, with the border closed and the Berlin Wall under construction in August.
- Kubrick makes arrangements, on and off, for travel to Australia with his family between August 1961 and August 1962.
- Soviet nuclear moratorium ends, and 50Mt 'Tsar bomba' detonated four weeks later on 30 October.
- Kubrick and Harris read *Red Alert* and begin developing *Edge of Doom* in early October.
- Kubrick writes to Peter George, 4 November.
- Harris-Kubrick obtain rights to *Red Alert* via Sig Shore in late December.

1962

- George travels to New York to work on treatments/scripts with Kubrick and Harris, January–March.
- Concerns are raised by George and Kubrick over possible plagiarism by *Fail-Safe* authors Wheeler and Burdick, May.
- Kubrick interviewed (unpublished) by Terry Southern for *Esquire* magazine, March.
- *Lolita* released in USA, 12 June.
- Kubrick-George script renamed and registered as *Dr. Strangelove*, May.
- *Fail-Safe* widely serialised in American newspapers, October.
- Cuban Missile Crisis occurs during 14–28 October. For the first time US nuclear forces are placed at DEFCON 2 nuclear alert, one level away from war.

- Kubrick cables Terry Southern with offer of eight weeks work commencing 7 November
- Second unit photography commences across the Arctic Circle (Iceland, Greenland, Canada) in November.

1963
- Studio principal photography commences at Shepperton Studios, 28 January.
- *Fail-Safe* plagiarism suit announced by Kubrick, George and Columbia Pictures, February.
- Peter Sellers injures ankle requiring replacement role for Major Kong (by Slim Pickens), April–May.
- *Strangelove* post-production May–October.
- Limited Test Ban Treaty signed by US, USSR and UK, August.
- President Kennedy assassinated in Dallas, the day *Dr. Strangelove* is due to be previewed, 22 November.

1964
- *Dr. Strangelove* begins general domestic release by Columbia Pictures, 29 January
- Kubrick and George publish letters refuting publicity claims that Terry Southern is the 'author' of *Dr Strangelove*, August.
- *Time* magazine features Peter Sellers as Dr Strangelove on the cover of its 'Nuclear Issue', 25 September .
- Sidney Lumet's film version of *Fail-Safe* in general release, 7 October.
- Rod Serling's teleplay *A Carol for Another Christmas*, updating Dickens' novel to a nuclear age parable, featuring Sterling Hayden and Peter Sellers, aired on CBS, 24 December.

1965
- *Dr. Strangelove* nominated for four Oscars and seven BAFTA Awards, (wins four BFTAs).
- *Journey to the Stars/2001* commences development.
- James B. Harris's directorial debut, the nuclear thriller, *The Bedford Incident*, released by Columbia Pictures, 11 October.

Glossary

AEC Atomic Energy Commission

BADS The Bomb Alarm Display System

CIA Central Intelligence Agency

CINCSAC Commander in Chief, Strategic Air Command

ECM Electronic Counter Measures

EDSs Environmental Sensing Devices

ICBM Intercontinental Ballistic Missile

IRBM Intermediate Range Ballistic Missile

JCAE Joint Committee on Atomic Energy

JCS Joint Chiefs of Staff

NATO North Atlantic Treaty Organization

NORAD North American Air Defense Command

NSA National Security Archive

NSAM National Security Action Memorandum

PAL Permissive Action Link

PGA Peter George Archive

TMR Two Man Rule

TPC Two Person Concept

TSC Terry Southern Collection

RAND Research and Development (Corporation)

SAC Strategic Air Command

SAM Surface to Air Missile

SIOP Single Integrated Operational Plan

SKA Stanley Kubrick Archive (University of the Arts London)

SKPC Stanley Kubrick Papers (Childwickbury)

SLBM Submarine Launched Ballistic Missile

SSB Single Side Band (radio)

Stanley Kubrick's Atomic Antecedents

This book is premised upon the assumption that anyone reading it will have already viewed *Dr. Strangelove,* or have a working knowledge of the film. This book is not devoted to a close textual reading of the film, or a cineaste's analysis of the aesthetics of the movie. There are scores of such works on the subject available as monographs, biographies, book chapters, journal articles, blogs and documentaries, many cited in this book's bibliography. While by no means the last word on *Strangelove* (there are still volumes to be written), I have endeavoured to do justice to the more than five thousand pages of primary material gleaned from various archives. I draw principally from accessing *Strangelove* production files and correspondence kept initially at the director's Childwickbury home and later donated to the Stanley Kubrick Archive at the University of the Arts London Archives and Special Collections Centre. Naturally, not every aspect of Kubrick's intensely researched studio production can be covered in this one book. Hence, my focus has been narrowed to chart the initial impetus and cultural-political context of Kubrick's approach to the subject matter, following the evolution of the creative collaborations that begat a work that remains a landmark of twentieth-century artistry.

It is not clear precisely when filmmaker Stanley Kubrick began studying 'the thermonuclear dilemma'. Certainly by 1958 it was known that Kubrick had been 'intrigued by the threat' of nuclear war.[1] According to dance archivist and *Killer's Kiss* (1955) choreographer, David Vaughan, Kubrick had discussed his fears of nuclear attack while living on the Lower East Side of Manhattan in the mid-1950s. Kubrick began dating dancer Ruth Sobotka and soon moved into her East 10th Street apartment, which Vaughan had previously shared. The choreographer remembers Kubrick 'really had a paranoia about the possibility of New York being obliterated by an atomic bomb. I remember at one point he wanted to go live in Australia because it was the place least likely to be the victim of an atomic bomb attack.'[2]

Few Americans, let alone resident New Yorkers, harboured any illusion that downtown Manhattan would be a primary bulls-eye in any future atomic attack upon America.[3] Indeed, within a few months, the triumphalist rhetoric greeting war's end and Allied victory in the Pacific was becoming increasingly muted. Thoughts turned towards what the weapon, if obtained by America's enemies, might do to a major metropolis. Images from Occupied Japan showed mostly structural and material effects of the Hiroshima and Nagasaki attacks. Few images or newsreel sequences in those early post-war years concentrated on the human consequences or ongoing suffering from the Atom bombings and official reports frequently downplayed the effects of radiation, whether immediate of intergenerational.[4]

Growing from mid-teens into adulthood in New York would have exposed Stanley Kubrick to a wide range of nuclear culture influences. These include newspapers, pulps and pictorial magazines such as *Life* and *Look*, the latter magazines Kubrick undoubtedly followed as a budding professional photographer in order to keep up with current affairs and hone his photographic skills. Working for *Look* from April 1946 exposed Kubrick to the world of photojournalism and New York was at its centre.[5] *Look*'s chief rival and competitor was Henry Luce's *Life*. Both of these weekly and fortnightly pictorials devoted considerable space to reports on aspects of the atomic age throughout the Cold War, though they approached the topic from different vantages.

Look ran a vast amount of topical articles on the atomic age – before and during Kubrick's tenure as a photographer – from lightweight pieces to sober analyses of strategy and science. These include 'Youth Ponders an Atomic Future' (January 1946); an atomic attack scenario, 'In one night forty cities could be wrecked, and forty million Americans killed' (March 1946); Nagasaki bomb damage (May 1946); 'Your future in the atomic age', as told by J. Robert Oppenheimer and an accompanying article with the Strangelovean title 'Peace on Earth, dream or possibility?' (December 1946); 'When will Russia have the atomic bomb?' (March 1948); 'Doodles by the members of the United States Atomic Energy Commission' (March 1948); and 'Atom proof city, safe from atomic bombs' (October 1948). After Kubrick had resigned from *Look* to pursue his filmmaking ambitions, other editions of relevance in the lead-up to *Dr. Strangelove* included feature stories on General Curtis E. LeMay and the Strategic Air Command (January 1952); Russian 'atomic bomb supremacy' (June 1952); 'Hiroshima after the atomic bomb' (cover story August 1955); atomic accidents in the USA (September 1957); nuclear submarines and 'atomic-warhead missiles' (May 1958); nuclear bomb fallout (April 1960); 'The great fall-out shelter panic' (December 1961); and the special issue 'Secret', revisioning Hiroshima and Nagasaki bombings (August 1963). Although Kubrick's assignments rarely involved atomic science or its military application, he did capture Columbia University's enormous nuclear cyclotron, under construction at the time, in *Look*'s 11 May 1958 issue.[6]

From August 1945 the city of New York had become instantly synonymous with the development of the first atomic bomb. Cryptically using the wartime project's code name, US President Harry Truman's personal diary ominously described 'Manhattan' appearing over the Japanese homeland.[7] Previously innocuous names such as the 'Manhattan Engineering Works', the 'Manhattan Project' and the 'Manhattan District' soon connoted state secrets, big science and atomic annihilation. From the day after the bombing of Hiroshima was announced, imagery of a future atomic attack on New York City became widespread. On 7 August the New York daily newspaper *PM* displayed a graphic entitled 'Here's What Could Happen to New York in an Atomic Bombing', depicting in silhouette the devastating effects of a detonation occurring at Battery Park, obliterating downtown, with an 'area of concussion' expanding past Central Park and up to 104th Street.[8] A few days later, after the follow-up atomic destruction of Nagasaki, James Reston summarised the uneasy implication in *The New York Times*: 'in that terrible flash 10,000 miles away, men here have seen not only the fate of Japan, but have glimpsed the future of America'.[9]

The sentiment was echoed by radio broadcasters such H. V. Kaltenborn who warned of the Frankenstein-like capacity of the new weapon, assuming 'with the passage of only a little time, an improved form of the new weapon can be turned against us'.[10] Radio also featured programmes such as *The Fifth Horseman* (1946), depicting just such a scenario. In July 1946 writer-producer Arnold Marquis employed Hollywood stars such as Henry Fonda and Glenn Ford in a fiction series to help promote United Nations efforts to control nuclear energy. One episode featured William Bendix, in docu-drama form, graphically narrating an atomic attack on New York by 'nation X', with multiple, more powerful A-bombs being used 'all at once'.[11]

As with newspapers and radio, pictorial magazines entertained stories of New York under atomic assault. In November 1945 *Life* published 'The 36 Hour War', depicting the rubble surrounding the New York Public Library after a nuclear attack.[12] In 1946 *Mechanics Illustrated* deployed concentric circles of destruction over an illustration of Manhattan, while *Fortune* ran a fictional story called 'Pilot Lights of the Apocalypse', imagining a devastating attack on major US cities. That same year a *Reader's Digest* article entitled 'What the Atom Bomb Would Do to Us' invited readers to imagine what would happen if an atomic bomb was dropped directly onto the Empire State Building. Similarly, *Collier's* magazine graphically illustrated the devastation befalling 'an A-bomb blasted New York'.[13] In a bizarre photo-montage attempting to demonstrate the benign

'Healed by atomic power', full-page image from *Collier's* magazine, 3 May 1947, p. 14.

properties of atomic energy, *Collier's* ran a full-page colour image (3 May 1947) of a para- plegic man standing, having left his wheelchair, smiling and surrounded by a mushroom cloud. The image resonates uncannily with Doctor Strangelove's final ascendency at the conclusion of Kubrick's film, seemingly aroused from his confinement by the Doomsday Machine's detonation.

After the Soviet bomb was announced in September 1949 American magazines returned to representations of New York City as primary target for the enemy's new bomb. In 1950 *Collier's* headlined an issue 'Hiroshima USA', with an arresting cover painting by Chesley Bonestell. The feature article used several apocalyptic Bonestell im- ages showing Manhattan obliterated by simultaneous atomic strikes. In October 1950 *Time* profiled the Chairman of the New York State Civil Defense Commission, Lucius Clay, for its cover story, juxtaposed against a mushroom cloud towering above the Empire State Building.[14]

As a child growing up in the Bronx, Stanley Kubrick loved going to the movies. During his years at Taft high school Kubrick spend a great deal of time at two local cinemas,

Loew's Paradise and the RKO Fordham; he visited the movies twice a week to see double features.[15] It was a pattern set at an early age and continued throughout much of his teens and twenties. As David Vaughan relates, he often joined Kubrick and his girlfriend Ruth Sobotka (later his wife) at the movies in the mid-1950s 'all the time' because

> Stanley wanted to go to *every* movie. We used to go to terrible double-features on 42nd Street simply because Stanley wanted to see everything that was being put out. […] He was *obsessed* with going to see every film and was very critical … he would just see everything, that was all he really wanted to do.[16]

The trio would also frequent the Museum of Modern Art to watch European and Asian art films, something Kubrick continued pursuing well into his twenties.

Within a year of the 1949 Soviet A-bomb test, Hollywood productions began show-casing scenarios of a catastrophic future war. Arch Oboler's post-holocaust feature *Five* (1951) depicted a former Empire State Building employee ruefully describing New York's destruction. The same year a future, post-holocaust New York was presented in *Captive Women* (1951), set in the decaying structure of Manhattan one thousand years after an atomic war, where the island is populated by rival tribes including 'the Mutates' and 'the Norms'. The stridently anti-communist *Invasion USA* (1953) featured patrons of a downtown New York bar collectively believing that they are under nuclear attack while shoddy special effects intercut with newsreel footage luridly displayed the A-bombing of Manhattan. By decade's end, *The World, The Flesh, and the Devil* (1959) portrayed a trio of post-holocaust survivors wandering the deserted, but undamaged Manhattan, ready to repopulate the planet as a mixed-race à trois. In the Cold War comedy *The Mouse that Roared* (1959), a tiny European principality 'invades' New York during a citywide nuclear alert exercise and acquires a revolutionary Q-bomb, holding America ransom (see chapter two). Following the shock launch of Sputnik, *Rocket Attack USA* (1961) capitalised on fears of an American-Soviet 'missile gap' and depicted a nuclear-armed ICBM launched against New York.

American television of the period also entertained narratives of nuclear annihilation wrought upon America, especially New York. Based on author Judith Merill's *Shadow on the Hearth*, the Motorola TV Hour broadcast *Atomic Attack* (1950) on ABC. The live melodrama featured a suburban New York housewife hearing that Manhattan has been obliterated by an H-bomb, fearing her commuter husband has been killed. Edward Murrow's civil defence documentary *One Plane, One Bomb* (1953), broadcast repeatedly in the 1950s, simulated a nuclear attack on New York and called for civilian volunteers to act as aircraft spotters. As a precursor to many themes raised by *Dr. Strangelove*, John Frankenheimer's live televi-sion production of Rod Serling's 1956 script 'Forbidden Area', for *Playhouse 90*, employed docudrama realism. The play presents a Soviet sleeper agent planted inside a crucial SAC base, sabotaging B-52 bombers prior to a Russian sneak attack. The plot is discovered by a joint military and civilian think-tank and the imminent threat averted. In the White House the Navy Chief demands that the US President order him to sink the stalled Russian fleet, despite the Soviet Premier ordering a complete force stand down and withdrawal. The Air Force Chief immediately concurs, displaying the hawkish military mentality later motivating *Dr. Strangelove*'s Generals Ripper and Turgidson (see chapters two and four):

> Sir, you've got a lock on 'em – ground, sea and air. You can hit them where they live, safely. We caught their fleet at sea; their planes must be massed on their bases. All we have to do is proceed according to plan. We can smear every base, every industrial complex, once and for all. We can eliminate them, now and forever. This is self-preservation, sir. Our children can live, in peace.

During the decade newsreels and live TV broadcasts of the annual *Operation Alert* civil defence exercises regularly showed preparations for an attack by 'five or more H-bombs' on Manhattan. Television advertising funded by civil defence authorities featured local New York residents imploring their fellow citizens to build family bomb shelters. However, episodes of Rod Serling's seminal series *The Twilight Zone* – such as the 'The Shelter' (September 1961) and 'One More Pallbearer' (January 1962) – dramatised the folly of constructing private bomb shelters in the thermonuclear era, whether deep under a Manhattan skyscraper or in outer suburban New York.

As Nathan Abrams has convincingly argued, Stanley Kubrick can be usefully, and perhaps fundamentally, considered a post-war 'alternative New York Jewish intellectual'.[17] The crucible for this sensibility was forged in Greenwich Village, where the young photographer and neophyte filmmaker lived with his first wife Toba Metz from 1948. A key aspect of this tradition is the comedic impulse and the capacity to deploy satire as acceptable social criticism.[18] Kubrick's intellectual mentors and contemporaries in this domain included Jules Feiffer, Joseph Heller, William Gaines and Lenny Bruce. Indeed, as Abrams and others demonstrate, both Feiffer and Heller were initially approached to work on the comic script version(s) of *Dr. Strangelove*.[19] However, it was possibly Paul Krassner and *The Realist* magazine that had the most evident, though more indirect, influence on the film. According to Tony Frewin, within a day or two of taking on the role of Kubrick's runner and long-term personal assistant, the director gave him a copy of *The Realist* to read and enjoy. Kubrick had been acquainted with the magazine since its launch in late 1950s.

Examining back copies reveals a remarkable socio-political correspondence anticipating Strangelovian satire and black comedy. The 'Survival' column by Harold Fowler in October 1958, for example, refers to Mao Tse-Tung's threat that any A-bomb used on

China will be met with an equivalent US city destroyed, a policy echoed by the Soviets.[20] Fowler describes the current 'missile gap', noting that in a few years 'our underground Minute Man Missiles' will be 'dead-man triggered to destroy Russia even if not an American were left alive to push their buttons'. The commentary uncannily prefigures Peter George, Herman Kahn and Stanley Kubrick's concepts of a Doomsday Device. Unlike Ambassador De Sadesky's 'reliable source', identified as *The New York Times* (see chapter two), for Kubrick it may well have been Krassner's *The Realist*. Not only does Fowler's column presage the Doomsday Machine but forecasts the idea of 'surrender' versus the 'sacrifice' of US cities, similar to the city-swap plot in both *Fail-Safe* and some treatments and versions of the *Dr. Strangelove* script (see chapters one and three). Echoing Kubrick's own mounting concerns, the December 1958 editorial of *The Realist* describes a New Jersey attorney and family of five moving to New Zealand 'to escape the dangers of the Bomb' while noting, ironically, that the *Australian Journal of Biological Sciences* had recently reported 'heavy radioactive contamination of sheep and cattle in that area'.[21] The editorial continues by lampooning a television commercial 'selling' fallout shelters and civil defence.[22]

In advance of General Turgidson, a November 1959 article in *The Realist* on the 'King Kong Defense System' talks satirically of 'clobbering' the commies, using cheaper than Atlas ICBM 'King Kong missiles'.[23] The same issue features a Jules Fieffer cartoon center-spread depicting a psychotherapy patient lamenting his apathy: 'Years ago I got aroused on Atomic Holocaust! But not now [its] Brinksmanship! Gunboat diplomacy!' Adjacent to the King Kong missile article is a short piece concerning Dr. L. Harrison Matthews, the Director of the London Zoological Association, who whimsically advocates nuclear war as a means to reduce overpopulation – wiping out a third of humans – leaving 'a useful amount of elbow room for the survivors, provided it wasn't too irradiated'.[24] *Strangelove* resonances continue on page eleven with a satirical quote from 'the US Army's leading civilian scientist', Wernher von Braun (see chapter two) and another article about escaping off-planet until the radiation diminishes after nuclear war – although according to an American general the war may be fought from the moon, using warheads buried deep in lunar mine shafts. The same issue includes a *Meet the Press* quote from 'inventor of the H-bomb', Dr. Edward Teller, stating that fallout dangers are over-exaggerated.[25] *The Realist*'s February 1960 issue prints a previously unpublished letter by Steve Allen to a Catholic newspaper rebuffing 'The Smear Against SANE', the National Committee for a Sane Nuclear Policy and its Hollywood office. Allen mentions 'socially-conscious actors' such as Keenan Wynn and many others doing public good, who are not 'Pink' despite the accusations of communist sympathies.[26] Years later after the critical success of *Dr. Strangelove*, Kubrick politely declined SANE's offer of the Eleanor Roosevelt Peace Award, which went instead to rival producer Max E. Youngstein for *Fail-Safe*.[27]

Little wonder that when Kubrick dived headlong into the disturbing research on nuclear war that he began strategising how he and his family might avoid or minimise the impact of their exposure to a global thermonuclear confrontation.[28] Stanley had met and married Christiane Harlan in 1958 while he was in Germany making *Paths of Glory*. Kubrick's third wife features as the sole female in the film, paraded before Colonel Dax's (Kirk Douglas) dirty and disheveled company of French troops, granted a momentary break for R&R away from the front-line trenches. During the troubling geopolitical events of the late 1950s and early 1960s Kubrick and his young family (with Christiane's daughter Katharina and two additional girls born eighteen months apart, Anya in 1959 and in Vivian 1960), the family had shuttled across Europe and North America, during and in between Kubrick's direction of *Spartacus*. The Kubricks next travelled to the UK for the filming of Vladimir Nabokov's controversial novel *Lolita*. The Harris-Kubrick deal with Associated Artists to bankroll the movie took advantage of the Eady Plan, a scheme that entitled foreign production companies to substantial financial concessions if a film was shot using at least 80% British crew.[29] Throughout the production Kubrick lived with his family in central London. At that time, Britain had developed its own independent nuclear deterrent and had an arsenal of scores of atomic and nuclear bombs, missiles and tactical weapons mostly aimed at Soviet cities.[30] The UK also hosted a large array of American military and communication and intelligence facilities, making the island nation an exceptionally dense target for Soviet attack, with multiple nuclear bulls' eyes centring on London and the neighbouring countryside.[31]

With the tensions in Berlin subsiding again into a tense stand-off, *Lolita* finished shooting and Anthony Harvey attended to the edit with Kubrick. It was during this period and relative hiatus that Kubrick and Harris began looking for a new project. As outlined in greater detail in the following chapter, during the Berlin scare Kubrick seriously contemplated travelling to Australia, partly to explore production opportunities but principally to depart the northern hemisphere before nuclear war broke out. The family obtained entry visas in their passports, something that puzzled his daughter Katharina later on in life. When she questioned her mother, Christiane, about the visa, she confirmed that they all had come *very* close to leaving.[32] Christiane Kubrick remembers conversing with her husband about 'how England would certainly get it, and the fall-out'.[33] Stanley felt they were 'typical of people ... in denial'. He confided to her, 'we're just as stupid as those people who didn't leave Germany in time' to avoid the genocidal Nazi regime. Regardless of the imminence of the nuclear threat, Christiane thought the idea of buying passage to Australia was 'grotesque'. She was glad her husband ultimately relinquished the plan, 'because we would have had to share a bathroom' on the cruise ship! The episode remains a source of incongruous amusement for Christiane, noting 'on the day that he said that, the major crisis was already over'.[34]

This episode offers an intriguing insight into the director's palpable and rational nuclear fears, something he faced head-on domestically and intellectually. Developing what became *Dr. Strangelove* helped to personally exorcise these concerns via the artifice of narrative cinema, subversively producing a cultural polemic that has touched generations. In the chapters that follow I concentrate on the historical data as material evidence to justify my claims or to dispute and clarify the assertions of others. The conventions of such scholarship often deter from enabling an otherwise ebullient, discursive appraisal of this work of comic genius. Nevertheless my hope is that I have captured the essence of Kubrick's approach and the purity of his artistic vision without becoming too rhetorically turgid.

NOTES

1   Allison Castle, Jan Harlan and Christiane Kubrick, *The Stanley Kubrick Archives* (Köln: Taschen, 2008), 534.
2   Vaughan in Vincent Lobrutto, *Stanley Kubrick: A Biography* (New York: D. I. Fine Books, 1997), 93.
3   See Mick Broderick and Robert Jacobs, 'Nuke York, New York: Nuclear Holocaust in the American Imagination from Hiroshima to 9/11', *The Asia-Pacific Journal* 10, no. 11/6 (2012); http://apjjf.org/2012/10/11/Robert-Jacobs/3726/article.html.
4   See Kyoko Hirano, 'Depiction of the Atomic Bombings in Japanese Cinema During the US Occupation Period', in *Hibakusha Cinema*, ed. Mick Broderick (London: Kegan Paul International, 1996); Abé Mark Nornes, 'The Body at the Center – the Effects of the Atomic Bomb on Hiroshima and Nagasaki', ibid.
5   See Philippe Mather, *Stanley Kubrick at Look Magazine: Authorship and Genre in Photojournalism and Film* (Bristol, UK: Intellect, 2013), 26–8, 41–7.
6   See image in ibid., 40.
7   Truman quoted in Robert H. Farell, 'Truman at Potsdam', *American Heritage*, June/July 1980, 42.
8   Anon, 'Here's What Could Happen to New York in an Atomic Bombing', *PM*, 7 August 1945, 7.
9   James Reston, *The New York Times*, 12 August 1945.
10 Kaltenborn quoted in Paul Boyer, *Fallout: An Historian Reflects on America's Half-Century Encounter with Nuclear Weapons* (Columbus: Ohio State University Press, 1998), 7.
11 See Christopher D. Geist, 'Arnold Marquis' "the Fifth Horseman": Documentary Radio as Popular Criticism' (Bowling Green State University, 1975).
12 Anon, 'The 36 Hour War: The Arnold Report Hints at the Catastrophe of the Next Great Conflict', *Life*, 19 November 1945, 27.
13 See Robert Littell, 'What the Atom Bomb Would Do to Us', *Reader's Digest*, May 1946, 125; Robert De Vore, 'What the Atomic Bomb Really Did', *Collier's*, 2 March 1946, 19.
14 'Civilian Defender Clay', *Time*, 2 October 1950, 2.
15 Lobrutto, *Stanley Kubrick: A Biography*, 11.
16 Vaughan in ibid., 93.

17 Nathan Abrams, 'An Alternative New York Intellectual: Stanley Kubrick's Cultural Critique', in *New Perspectives on Stanley Kubrick*, ed. Tatljana Ljujic, Richard Daniels and Peter Krämer (London: Black Dog, 2014), 62–81.

18 See Geoffrey Cocks, *The Wolf at the Door: Stanley Kubrick, History, and the Holocaust* (London: Peter Lang, 2004).

19 Ibid., 72.

20 Harold Fowler, 'Survival', *The Realist*, no. 3 (1958): 18; http://ep.tc/realist/03/13.html.

21 Paul Krassner, 'Yes, Virginia Is a Sanity Clause', ibid., no. 5: 1.

22 Ibid., 2.

23 Anon, 'King Kong Defense System', *The Realist*, no. 13 (1959): 9; http://ep.tc/realist/13/09.html

24 Ibid., 10; http://ep.tc/realist/13/10.html

25 Ibid., 12; http://ep.tc/realist/13/12.html

26 Steven Allen, 'The Smear against Sane', *The Realist*, no. 15 (1960): 9-10; http://ep.tc/realist/15/10.html

27 Donald Keys letter to Kubrick, 9 July 1964, SKPC.

28 On North American nuclear refugees migrating to Australia and New Zealand, see P. Anna Johnson's memoir *Australia Years: the Life of a Nuclear Migrant*, where she claims to have met many of the 'thousands' of like-minded Americans who left in the early 1960s.

29 Paul Duncan, *Stanley Kubrick: Visual Poet 1928–1999* (Köln: Taschen, 2003), 76.

30 See Ken Young, 'A Most Special Relationship: The Origins of Anglo-American Nuclear Strike Planning', *Journal of Cold War Studies* 9, no. 2 (2007): 5–31.

31 According to documents released by the UK National Archives, by the early 1970s the UK government drew up a top secret list of 106 cities, towns and bases across the country seen as 'probable nuclear targets' noting London would be subjected to two-to-four H-bombs of up to five megatons each. See Rob Edwards, 'UK government's secret list of "probable nuclear targets" in 1970s released', *The Guardian*, 6 June 2014; https://www.theguardian.com/world/2014/jun/05/uk-government-top-secret-list-probable-nuclear-targets-1970s.

32 Katharina Kubrick interviewed by the author, November 2015.

33 Christiane Kubrick interviewed by the author, April 2005.

34 Ibid.

CHAPTER ONE

The Road to *Strangelove*: From *Red Alert* to *The Delicate Balance of Terror* and Beyond

The development of what ultimately became the *Dr. Strangelove* script was a lengthy and convoluted process. It was by far the most complex writing assignment that Kubrick had undertaken up to that point, including the massive re-writing of Nabokov's overlong screenplay with James B. Harris and the unplaced efforts under Harris-Kubrick Pictures.[1] Due to the fluid working arrangements and the competing, often parallel project development, the complete chronology and quantified outputs during this period are difficult to establish definitively. Kubrick's papers and production files (mostly donated to the University of the Arts London Archives and Special Collections Centre) do allow for a substantial reconstruction of these events, aided by the materials kept by David George and the few surviving *Strangelove* items held by Nile Southern (and the literary deposit at the New York Public Library).

The Stanley Kubrick Archive holds copious undated notes, script fragments, re-writes, miscellaneous drafts and multiple notecards, many in the director's distinctive handwriting, some with annotations by George, and many typed, that are difficult to date accurately despite attempts at cross-referencing. Conflicting lists of possible actors are detailed, often without assigned roles. Characters' names change inexplicably and some are shunted about across script drafts, while others return to their original designation or with slight modification. Hence, some of what follows in this chapter is speculative, a best guess at a calendar of events in the development process. As this book endeavours to demonstrate, Kubrick's overall working methods were expanded, refined and consolidated during *Dr. Strangelove*. His deliberate embrace of improvisation and opportunity during rehearsal enabled creative contributions from cast and crew to improve the script and narrative perspective (see chapters two and five). Chief amongst these developments was Kubrick's construction of the film while editing – a process where entire sequences were pragmatically jettisoned if they did not match the tone of the film or were otherwise considered superfluous.

As noted in the Introduction, Kubrick had been concerned by the potential (mis)use of nuclear weapons for years. His musing on the thermonuclear dilemma became an infectious one. He ploughed through Herman Kahn's *On Thermonuclear War* (1960) and passed it onto Harris, who became 'involved in the same concerns'. The producer recalls it was

> pretty sophisticated in terms of how it explained everything. Stanley had already read the thing several times and was an expert on it as he always becomes on any new subject that takes his fancy.[2]

From October 1961 to January 1963, Kubrick continued to develop and revise a range of nuclear scenarios, initially working with producer-partner Harris, then *Red Alert* author Peter George, and lastly with Terry Southern. Within the first three months a serious nuclear thriller had emerged based on George's novel. Harris-Kubrick Pictures secured a production deal with Seven Arts. However, Kubrick soon changed his mind. He trusted his instinct not to abandon nagging reservations that compelled him to see the inherent, comic absurdity of the nuclear era. After announcing the change towards 'nightmare comedy' to George and Harris, Seven Arts promptly rescinded the deal. Kubrick regrouped and worked on satirical script treatments with George, while still retaining the 'serious' version as a working option. A fortuitous meeting with Terry Southern, who had come to interview Kubrick about *Lolita* for *Esquire* magazine, led to a later invitation by the director to engage Southern for approximately eight weeks in late 1962 in order to sharpen the dialogue and bring hipster Southern's unique talent for the absurd and grotesque into play.

As outlined in the Introduction, although the director had been concerned with the perils of the nuclear age since the early 1950s, and had contemplated migrating to Australia for a number of years, it wasn't until after he had completed his post-production and distribution commitments on *Lolita* that he seriously turned his mind to the subject. When Stanley cast Christiane in *Paths of Glory* in 1957 she already had a young daughter (Katharina, born in 1953) from her marriage to German actor Werner Bruhns. Christiane had spent a good deal of time as an actor and performer in Berlin and knew the city well. In 1961 when the second Berlin crisis emerged (following the Allied air-lift in 1948) it seemed as though a conflict might erupt between NATO, East Germany and the Soviets, and possibly escalate to all-out thermonuclear war. The year before, tensions between Khrushchev and Eisenhower had peaked over the shooting down of a U-2 spy plane overflying Russia. An irate Soviet Premier cancelled his offer to Eisenhower to visit Moscow to discuss disarmament and publicly paraded captured American pilot, Francis Gary Powers, in a subsequent 'show trial'.[3] Berlin remained a geopolitical irritant and unresolved matter for Soviets as East German citizens increasingly sought refuge in the West, rejecting the communist system.

With a new President in the White House, Khrushchev met Kennedy in Vienna in June 1961 but the leaders' meeting began frostily and quickly deteriorated towards impasse. The next day Khrushchev demanded that JFK solve the 'Berlin problem' by year's end. Kennedy responded, 'It's going to be a cold winter'.[4] Khrushchev had previously issued an ultimatum to Eisenhower in 1958 and secretly decided in July 1961 to close the East German boarder in order to prevent the large flow of communist refugees entering the West. On 13 August, East German border guards began restricting such movements, a mass transit that had risen to over a thousand per day.[5]

Within 24 hours construction began on concrete walls at key Berlin check-points. East German soldiers were ordered to shoot anyone who attempted to defect. That same day, after meeting with staff at the Australian embassy in London, Kubrick sent a letter of thanks for the working lunch to discuss his possible residency options.[6] A week later amid increasing tensions in Berlin, Kubrick wrote to his attorney, Louis Blau, advising him that he was planning to return to New York the next month, noting that he was 'trying to come up with a worthwhile project to do'.[7]

The idea of becoming a southern hemisphere nuclear refugee was likely taking hold. On 24 August the Kennedy administration issued a 'solemn warning' at 'aggressive' Soviet moves to prevent Allied access to West Berlin. By the end of August the Soviet Union suddenly abandoned its self-imposed nuclear test moratorium by detonating a nuclear weapon. They continued to explode on average at least one atomic or thermo-nuclear device every day throughout September and October. The Soviets also withdrew from tripartite (US/UK/USSR) talks aimed at establishing a limited test ban treaty. Troubled by international financial affairs, on 5 September Kubrick wrote to his to legal advisors with concerns that an associate might empty one of his bank accounts and travel to 'a non-extradition treaty country and live out the rest of their lives in wealth and safety from the H-bomb'.[8] The correspondence suggests that Kubrick's strongly held nuclear concerns were becoming manifest in the filmmaker's day-to-day business.

Throughout early October Kubrick continued to liaise with Australian authorities about his proposed visit. He wrote to Australia House in London to obtain tourist visas for himself and his family 'for the dual purpose of having a vacation and scouting loca-tions in Australia for a film project which I am considering'.[9] The London office of the Bank of New South Wales advised him that he would face no penalty if 'remitting capital funds from Australia should you decide not to stay there on a permanent basis'. The bank also provided him with two letters of introduction to be used in Australia. Due to meet Embassy officials for an interview on 4 October, Kubrick raised the question about how he might prove that his permanent place of abode was outside Australia since he didn't 'own a home in America'.[10]

The following day Kubrick visited Alastair Buchan at the Institute for Strategic Studies in London. Although Buchan was dismissive of Kubrick's ambitious idea to make a film on the possibilities of nuclear war and the procedures that the US had in place to prevent unauthorised attack, Buchan gave Kubrick a copy of *Red Alert*.[11] Already immersed in the scholarship of the nuclear age, and having read Kahn's *On Thermonuclear War*, Peter George's novel hit a nerve. From there things moved quickly. Harris and Kubrick spent the next few weeks working on ideas for adapting the novel into a film; their working title was *Edge of Doom*.[12] In a letter dated 25 October 1961, headed 'Intended Screen Play Revisions for the Novel "Red Alert"', Harris and Kubrick outlined the broadest possible scope for the proposed movie.[13] The document was later sent to American authors Eugene Burdick and Harvey Wheeler, while politely declining their offer of rights to the early, pre-publication draft of their forthcoming novel *Fail-Safe* (see chapter three).[14]

Throughout October Kubrick continued to liaise with various Australian authorities regarding his 'idea of taking up permanent residence', seeking tax advice on precedents by visiting American actors whose previous tax exemptions were being challenged in the Australian High Court. A Sydney-based tax consultant advised Kubrick that, while any future ruling would not adversely affect him personally, 'the tax position of actors and actresses who might join your project may well turn on' the court's decision.[15] It is impossible to tell from the remaining correspondence what that project was. It may well have been the nuclear narrative he felt so impelled to produce. Having filmed in the USA on both the east and west coasts, in Germany, Spain and the UK, the prospect of relocating to film in Australia was far from fanciful. Stanley Kramer had recently spent the summer of 1959 filming the post-nuclear drama *On the Beach* on location in Melbourne with Gregory Peck, Ava Gardiner, Fred Astaire and Anthony Perkins. Other US studio films and British features were made in Australia at the time, including *The Sundowners* (Fred Zinnerman, 1960) with Deborah Kerr, Robert Mitchum and Peter Ustinov; *Summer of the Seventeenth Doll* (Leslier Norman, 1959) with Ernest Borgnine, Anne Baxter and Angela Lansbury; and *The Siege of Pinchgut* (aka *Four Desperate Men*) (Harry Watt, 1959) starring Aldo Ray and Heather Sears. There was plenty of technical talent in Australia for any such undertaking, recently confirmed by several US and UK productions. As Kubrick remarked:

> Except for natural locations unique to a particular part of the world, pictures can be made anywhere good craftsmen can work. Atmosphere is created by the film-makers, not by the location or the studio.[16]

397 Castle Drive
Englewood Cliffs
New Jersey

November 4, 1961

Dear Mr. Bryant,

Though I am informed your name is Peter George I shall write to your pen name until otherwise advised.

First of let me tell you who I am; I am a film director ("Paths of Glory", "Spartacus", "Lolita"). I've been in England for over a year and returned to New York only last week, expecting to contact you here. Your agent Mr. Merridith corrected that assumption.

Be that as it may, I read "Red Alert" some weeks ago and enjoyed it immensely. I've been wrapped up in Brodie, Kissenger, Kahn, Morgenstern for quite some time and found your book to be the only nuclear fiction I'd come across that smacked of knowledge.

Letter from Kubrick to Peter George, 4 November 1961, page 1 of 3. (Peter George Archive)

By the end of October 1961, the Soviet Union exploded a massive 50Mt thermo-nuclear bomb ('Tsar bomba'), impressively delivered by aircraft, high above the Novaya Zemlya archipelago in the Arctic. The device was reported to be upgradable to 100Mt. It remains the largest nuclear detonation ever conducted. The CIA evaluated the explosion as an unambiguous attempt to intimidate the Kennedy administration into capitulation over Berlin, attempting to force America into accepting Khrushchev's December dead-line for Western withdrawal.

Having recently moved back to New York, Kubrick hand wrote a modest, three-page introductory letter to Peter George on 4 November 1961 outlining his background as a filmmaker and his admiration for *Red Alert*.[17] Kubrick notes that the book is just the prop-erty he had been looking for, save two caveats that rendered it 'unusable'. Firstly:

Why, if the Russians had built a Doomsday Machine, would they have kept it a secret? After all its purpose would have partly been to prevent such an unauthorised action. They should have advertised it!

Reading this note one can almost hear Doctor Strangelove's high-pitched declamation to the Soviet Ambassador 'Vy didn't you tell zee vorld, eh?!' Kubrick continues with his second reservation:

In the tender international situation you can't imply an American President refrains from turning an unauthorised attack into an all-out attack simply because the Doomsday Machine renders it impractical – even if it might be true.

Kubrick affirms that these two misgivings make 'an otherwise completely plausible situation unreal'. Regardless, the filmmaker commends George for the knowledge he displays and the accuracy of the technical details. He calls the plot dramatic and believable, finding the book suspenseful and exciting. There is no record of George's reply but during the next five weeks, Kubrick and Harris continued to work on adapting the novel and the filmmakers set about acquiring the rights, engaging Sig Shore from Video Artists in New York to act as an intermediary. Kubrick wrote to George again on 28 November expressing his delight that 'we have worked everything out', and enquiring about the author's imminent trip to New York, offering to help with preparations for such.[18] In reply George took up that offer for assistance in finding accommodation, somewhere nearby Stanley, noting he planned to arrive on 16 December.[19] This was a remarkable commitment demonstrating significant trust between both parties given the rights to the novel had not yet been formally secured.

On 13 December Shore offered George's Fifth Avenue literary agent, Scott Meredith, $5,000 for in perpetuity rights, other than publication rights, with an immediate option for 12 months, extendable to 24 months. Shore gave Meredith a week to consider the proposal.[20] On 22 December Meredith agreed to $3,500 cash for rights on behalf of his client, except publication, and Shore confirmed acceptance on 26 December.[21] The same day, Eugene Burdick submitted an outline and partially completed version of *Fail Safe* to Harris-Kubrick Pictures for the 'potential purchase of motion picture rights'.[22]

Peter George first contemplated the 'idea for the story' in late 1956, around the time of the 'Suez fiasco', on his way back to the UK from Hong Kong.[23] Later while on duty with the RAF (probably in early 1957 at Pucklechurch near RAF Filton) he spotted a British V-bomber flying low overhead. George casually commented to a fellow airman that it might be on its way to start World War III: 'Supposing that chap went mad and suddenly flew off to drop his bombs on Russia.'[24] At the time his aside seemed neither here nor there, merely an amused distraction with a tinge of black humour, but it slowly stimulated an idea about the 'possibility of war by accident or lunacy', one that proved irresistible for the part-time author. George later began to develop the concept and the 'idea for the book slowly germinated'.[25] In December 1956 he met with his publisher Tom Boardman Jnr, and outlined his concept, involving

> The possibility of bombers being launched by some means, and which could not be recalled, and the possibility that it they reached their target and destroyed it during a time of peace, it might become necessary to accept an equivalent nuclear retaliation.[26]

While expressing interest, Boardman suggested George first concentrate on completing two other works, so the author set about working on *Red Alert* later, finalising his draft in February 1958. Boardman 'hawked' the book around in America where literary agent Scott Meredith secured a paperback sale with Ace Books. The following year the film rights option was sold to a producer named Kessler.[27]

Peter George was the son of a Welsh schoolmaster and won a scholarship to Hereford Cathedral School but the outbreak of World War II war prevented him from attending university. After joining the RAF as a volunteer he served as a navigator on Beaufighters and Mosquitos and saw action against the Nazis. At the end of the war he was demobbed, but remained a reservist, and undertook night school (English Honours) at Exeter.[28] He was later called up when the Korean War commenced and then decided to remain in the service, taking a commission with the RAF. He was stationed in Hong Kong (September 1954 to December 1956) where he studied Chinese. He subsequently returned to the UK and worked at various bases in Britain, including Neatishead during 1959–60, until he resigned his commission in 1961 to pursue writing full-time.[29]

While George worked during the Cold War at a secret UK radar facility on the east coast of Britain he was certainly not a spy nor an intelligence officer, as has been claimed by many writers.[30] Nor was he an 'active' (or otherwise) member of CND, as his eldest daughter Sara has confirmed, despite multiple imputations in print over the years.[31] George did not believe in unilateral disarmament but desired 'disarmament of all kinds'. At the time of *Strangelove*'s release he described his political orientation as 'progressive Liberal' noting to the *Daily Worker*, 'I am not a Communist and certainly not a Tory ... if I think the Liberal will let the Tory in, I vote Labour'.[32] A prudent and practical man, as an author immersed in nuclear strategy and military matters, he decided to move his family to Hastings, 100km south of London, on the coast. The relaxed seaside location provided the writer with what he felt was an essential component for Cold War life – large sandstone caves nearby that could provide protection from fallout in any nuclear attack on Britain.[33]

Some have speculated that George took his own life after writing *Commander-1*, his post-holocaust follow-up book to *Red Alert*, and the *Dr. Strangelove* novelisation, disappointed at the marginal critical reception, and profoundly depressed by his immersion into the visceral, fictional world of nuclear survivalists.[34] However, Sara George, who was in her late-teens when her father committed suicide in 1966, feels these presumed motivations are both confected and inaccurate. George had been a heavy drinker throughout his service career and battled alcoholism later in life. He was hospitalised several times during the period and was ultimately advised, at the famous Maudsley hospital in London, that it would take him two years as an in-patient to 'dry out' and to treat his evolving psychoses. It was two years, Sara acknowledges, that her father no longer had. George was effectively given six months to live due to cirrhosis of the liver. Guns had also become a disquieting feature in the George household as the author battled his illnesses, sometimes answering a door knock with shotgun in hand.

At the point of developing *Dr. Strangelove* a couple of years earlier, Christiane Kubrick recalls Peter George was very ill. 'He had serious stomach problems – he didn't live very much longer. You know, it was quite apparent when we met him that he wouldn't live long.'[35] Christiane understood that her husband's collaborator was suffering from advanced liver damage, and that George was well aware of the implications. He 'couldn't eat at all – and he would lace his drink, milk with whiskey. It's too sad. Nice man. You know, from way back you could see ... he was even to the end a very nice man. Hugely intelligent.'[36]

George was formally employed by Harris-Kubrick Pictures from 7 January to 28 April but stayed on as a paid technical advisor.[37] After arriving in New York his first assignment was to produce a prose treatment based on his book, breaking up the script, scene by scene, which he wrote from 15 to 25 January 1962. He compiled over a hundred brief scenes with a framing plot device that is substantially different from *Red Alert*. The treatment opens with a B-52 flying over New York City on Christmas Eve. A family watching television prepares to send their two children off to bed. The narrative shifts between such scenes of domesticity to the routine functions of the nuclear bomber crew heading towards their target, operations inside NORAD and SAC headquarters and the Pentagon. Unidentified operatives in the Arctic jam the early warning radars across North America and Russian planes are detected nearing the USA. An attack warning is immediately initiated and the US President orders a full civilian alert be proclaimed. The Americans anticipate multiple Soviet missile launchings long before their bombers arrive. In the Pentagon's War Room, the President meets assembled NATO representatives and the Soviet Ambassador. He orders the 'Go code' for an equivalent number of SAC bombers to move towards their targets. Fears of a Soviet missile strike on America, which would initiate 'all-out war', lead to capital cities across Europe undertaking civilian alert measures.

The Russian Ambassador, 'a suave man of the world', assures the President there is no first-strike against the USA and in dialogue with the Soviet Premier the President orders a recall code. A few B-52s are struck by Soviet missiles, after information on the planes' defence systems and target locations is reluctantly provided by the Pentagon. Doubts as to the veracity of the recall code are expressed by the featured bomber crew. From SAC headquarters the Commander informs the President that three of the bombers have failed to acknowledge the recall, suggesting technical problems may be the cause. Inside one damaged B-52, the radioman is dead and his equipment shattered. The Captain maintains a low flight path just prior to bombing their target, an ICBM base near the city of Tobolsk. This is the sole remaining American plane. If the bomber reaches its primary and secondary targets the Soviet Premier bluntly demands two American cities be destroyed in retaliation. The President reluctantly agrees to the city swap 'conditional on actual destruction of Russian cities'. The Premier notes that a Soviet submarine off the US coast will launch a missile to annihilate the town of Plattsburg, leaving the President virtually no time for evacuation. On the bomb run, moments before dropping his thermonuclear weapon, the Captain experiences grave doubts – all the ICBMs are still on their launch pad, they've not seen any other nuclear explosions in-flight, the recall code may have been genuine... In the final seconds, he aborts the bombing and banks the plane away from the target. When confirmation reaches the War Room everyone 'bursts into animated and slightly hysterical hilarity'. The scene is intercut with the family in New York who have been fearing the worst, watching events on television. The treatment ends with a personnel change of shift at SAC headquarters and the President and Premier exchanging messages: 'We end not on a note of agreement, but at least of necessity for agreement made more urgent than ever by the events of the night.'[38]

With George in New York working diligently on a variation of *Red Alert* and superpower tensions easing in Berlin, Kubrick wrote to the Bank of New South Wales in Sydney advising that his trip to Australia has been postponed ('but not abandoned') and transferring half of the funds in the Australian account to an American bank.[39] The single greatest flashpoint for escalating that conflict had already passed on 30 October when US and Soviet forces directly confronted each other at Checkpoint Charlie, the same time as the 'Tsar bomba' detonation. Both sides deployed tanks, with gun turrets aimed at each other and separated by less than 100 metres. The stand-off was precipitous and lasted sixteen hours. The American general in charge was instructed to avoid confrontation while Kennedy opened a back-channel to Khrushchev 'in order to defuse what had blown up'.[40] It worked, and one by one the tanks withdrew from both sides.

At some point while in New York Kubrick made George aware of *Fail-Safe*, then still in draft form. In late January, Kubrick had also discovered Burdick's short story 'Abraham 59, A Nuclear Fantasy', penned under the nom de plume F. B. Aiken, and alerted his

SAC's underground command post, circa 1961. (US National Archives)

attorney. With Kubrick's help and advice George was encouraged to sue for plagiarism, an option he carefully pursued in the following months (see chapter three).

By mid-February 1962, a number of typed script fragments emerged based on George's treatment where the simmering Berlin crisis is still prominent.[41] In one example, after NORAD picks up deliberate radar-jamming from an Eskimo village, the US Tepee early warning system detects 'mass missile launchings in the Soviet Union' and the 'shit hits the fan'.[42] A series of brown photofax pages are annotated by George and Kubrick with the final pages of this version depicting a lone, damaged and burning B-52 (named 'The Big John') seconds away from dropping its nuclear weapon.[43] The Captain remains hesitant but finally accedes. With only seconds remaining the burning plane explodes, apparently absolving the Captain of committing the act, but the pre-armed bomb nevertheless ignites on impact.[44]

In late February a first draft of the script, *The Delicate Balance of Terror,* adopted the ubiquitous acronym style (*D.B.O.T.)* so prevalent amongst RAND Corp. and other military-industrial complex discourse. This version included notes about an animated 'prologue' concerning 'the effects of thermonuclear war', and a 'documentary of SAC scrambles' along with hand-written notes listing potential actors' names, from Richard Basehart to Dane Clark.[45] Writing on his favourite yellow foolscap stationery, Kubrick's War Room dialogue included detailed prognostications of retaliatory versus first strike attacks, discussing the difference (pre-Turgidson) between 150 million and five-to-ten million Americans killed. The Pentagon political banter is Kahnian in style, covering 'assurance' rates for the strategic targeting of the military (counterforce) versus cities.[46]

A second copy of the same script includes public domain research materials featuring two large photos – one of the Big Board display at SAC headquarters, the other of the coloured SAC phones used to issue the 'Go-code'.[47] Annotations by Kubrick reveal the writer-director wanting to foreground the importance of the 'Berlin crisis' as a framing device for the narrative, proposing a montage of newsreels to 'dramatize' the events. He pondered 'can we, aught we, go to flashbacks? Should we use vignettes?' As a political thriller Kubrick notes 'great sympathy must be built for President' and his nuclear targeted, city-swap decision must be 'beyond criticism or doubt'. Other characters such as Air Force General Richter are similarly treated sympathetically, suggesting his strident motivation may stem from losing a brother at Pearl Harbor. As with the original treatment and George's book, communication between the President and Soviet Premier is conducted by telex, not by phone, something that would actually occur during the Cuban Crisis. A dedicated 'hot-line' was only installed between the superpowers nearly a year later, and after they had signed the Limited Test Ban Treaty in August 1963. According to a White House statement, the new hotline would 'help reduce the risk of war occurring by accident or miscalculation'.[48] Less vulnerable to interception and more reliable than regular trans-Atlantic phone calls, *The New York Times* reported:

> Kennedy would relay a message to the Pentagon via phone, which would be immediately typed into a teletype machine by operators at the Pentagon, encrypted and fed into a transmitter. The message could reach the Kremlin within minutes, as opposed to hours.[49]

The red phone at SAC's underground operations centre, 1959.
(US National Archives)

In reality, there never was a dedicated telephone 'hotline' as depicted in numerous movies yet Kubrick was canny to capitalise on this development and branded his film a 'hot-line comedy'.[50] There were, however, as his bound script depicted, special red and gold phones used by SAC and the Pentagon to communicate by voice in times of extreme emergency. The gold phone connected the SAC Commander with Washington and the red phone could be used to issue orders to SAC bases around the world.[51]

A 52-page onionskin treatment by George dated 22 March 1962 revised his January version. Instead of introducing a couple in New York, this scenario opens in one of SAC's married officers' quarters. An Air Force Major and his wife watch a CBS *Report to the Nation* programme titled 'The Building of a Crisis' while their two young daughters are playing nearby. The TV special edition details a chronology of geopolitical incidents based around the continuing Berlin crisis from March through April, including the Soviet Union's detonation of a massive H-bomb of 300Mt, but reportedly upgradable to 600Mt, anticipating the actual 'Tsar bomba' detonation in October 1962. Peace protesters stage a sit-down in Trafalgar Square in London while anti-communist protestors take control of Madison Square Garden in New York. British fighters down a Soviet jet that was interfering with a commercial flight. The Soviet Premier visits the United Nations but his attempted assassination in New York ends in dire recrimination. The remaining narrative conforms to much of the earlier treatment except the story concludes with the damaged B-52, 'Big John', escorted by a Soviet jet which has communicated the Wing's recall code. While the B-52 concurs, the crew cannot disarm the bombs due to electrical and mechanical damage from Russian ground- and air-based attacks. With two H-bombs set to ground burst upon impact, the plane is running out of fuel and dangerously close to population areas. All aboard are concerned that a combined 50Mt surface detonation will create a vast swathe of deadly fallout.

In his BFI monograph on *Dr. Strangelove*, Kubrick scholar Peter Krämer has successfully demarked this range of the script development and its shifting emphasis across versions, evolving from the straight thriller variously titled as *The Delicate Balance of Terror*, *Red Alert* (and *Edge of Doom*) through to the satirical *The Rise of Dr. Strangelove* and, finally, *Dr. Strangelove: or How I Learned to Stop Worrying and Love the Bomb*.[52] As Krämer notes, from March to June 1962, Kubrick moved away from the entirely serious approach based on George's novel and the earlier script/treatments, towards a comic tack. This shift embraced the paradoxical absurdities of abstractly counting megadeaths, concepts of overkill, planning for underground survival, and a 'Doomsday Machine', which was first mentioned in George's novel (and possibly inspiring Herman Kahn) but not evident in the initial screenplays. According to Krämer, Kubrick (and to some degree George) increasingly drew on the genocidal legacy of Nazism to satirise the horrendous consequences of nuclear war:

For a Jewish-American film-maker of the early 1960s it would have been difficult to think about nuclear war without also thinking of the specifically Jewish 'holocaust'. Hence any attempt to deal with those responsible for bringing about a nuclear holocaust evoked the Nazi past.[53]

Elsewhere in the archive Kubrick has a single note card that reads 'Toynbee – Challenge and Response' alluding to the British philosopher's treatise that, historically, civilisations collapse once their leaders no longer respond creatively to challenges; instead resorting to nationalism, xenophobia, militarism and protecting the interests of a despotic elite.[54] Toynbee maintained that such civilisations 'die from suicide, not by murder'.

There are also several undated handwritten notes by Kubrick concerning his philosophical approaching to such subjects as comedy in the nuclear age. One item states:

> The serious writers of the 20th century have taken themselves too seriously. The comic spirit has been lacking; comic vision of life. Cynicism, loss of spiritual values, 2 world wars, the communist disillusionment, psychoanalysis has forced the 20th century writer to keep his hero uninvolved, detached, burdened with problems of relating to life. Withdrawal, asceticism, coolness or at least madness seemed the only path open. If the modern world could be summed up in a single word it would be absurd. The only truly creative response to this is the comic vision of life.[55]

Similarly, an undated handwritten document outlines Kubrick's intentions for the film:

1. To demonstrate that amoral technical efficiency and ruthlessness cannot prevent an accident from occurring
2. Once occurring an accident tends to accelerate
3. Your choice at the end is the garrison state or war
4. The absurdity of 'Logic'
5. To satirize government dependent on Scientific advice
6. To reveal facts about the deterrent
7. To be heretical[56]

By April Kubrick concentrated less on the conventional aspects of the script, instead developing concepts for the fresh, satirical slant. The director later recalled he held back on his initial temptation to the create a comic treatment from the start:

> my idea of doing it as a nightmare comedy came in the early weeks of working on the screenplay. I found that in trying to put meat on the bones and to imagine the scenes

fully, one had to keep leaving things out of it which were either absurd or paradoxical in order to keep it from being funny; and those things seem to be close to the heart of the scenes in question.[57]

Prior to Peter George's involvement, working late into the wee hours on the script treatment, Kubrick and Harris found themselves occasionally 'getting a little silly, a little giddy'.[58] Fatigued and bordering on hysterics, the two started laughing at the potentially comic, and seemingly inappropriate opportunities provided by the scenario. What would happen if the occupants of the War Room became hungry? In the middle of the crisis, would they get take-out from a nearby deli, with an apron-wearing waiter taking orders from the Joint Chiefs? According to Harris, he and Kubrick quickly checked themselves: '"Do you think that this could really be a comedy?" "Nah, I don't think so, it's too risky. We'd have to sustain the humour for two hours. I mean how are we going to do that".'[59]

The idea of a nuclear age satire or black comedy on film was hardly unique, though it took Kubrick's resolve to see a nuclear black comedy finally realised. Earlier attempts failed to materialise. In 1947 writer James Agee approached his friend Charlie Chaplin to develop a biting comedy about the new atomic age.[60] As film critic of *The Nation*, Agee had been a strong supporter of Chaplin's second talking picture, *Monsieur Verdoux* (1947), now regarded as one of the great black comedies of the twentieth century. Two years after the bombing of Hiroshima and Nagasaki and a couple of years before the Soviet Union detonated its first atomic device, Agee had developed an eighty-page, untitled treatment, later dubbed *The Tramp's New World*, set in the ruins of post-holocaust New York. It starred Chaplin's endearing, and now elderly, Tramp. Originally planned as a 'silent' film with sound effects and a musical score, Agee positioned the Tramp as a benevolent leader of dishevelled survivors who live in individualist, utopian squalor, where past sexual and racial divisions have been abolished. When a group of survivor scientists emerge from an underground bunker, having been entirely dependent upon a malfunctioning computer, the inevitable disparities between the two groups lead to a dialectical clash of these remnant 'civilisations'.[61] The idea was tossed about for over a year but Agee and Chaplin could not agree on a meaningful approach, so they eventually dropped the project. Despite the impasse, in one of his final screen appearances a decade later Chaplin returned to nuclear themes and Cold War paranoia in *A King in New York* (1957).

While Chaplin and Agee were considering abandoning their comic treatment, Aldous Huxley crafted a bizarre screenplay-novel, *Ape and Essence* (1948), set after a nuclear war has poisoned the northern hemisphere. The text is Joycean in abstraction but cynical and darkly humourous in design, and in the form of a 'discovered' film scenario.[62] Topically introduced by characters discussing the assassination of Gandhi (January

1948) following India's independence and partition, much of the opening text seems superfluous, and not dissimilar in motivation to the terse, extra-terrestrial viewpoint used as a prologue for the August 1962 *Dr. Strangelove* script. As David King Dunaway has revealed, Huxley spent his last 25 years in and around Hollywood, where he actively worked on scripts from the late 1930s to early 1950s.[63] The *Ape and Essence* screen scenario is replete with atomic sexual innuendo, where 'essence' repeatedly rhymes with detumescence.[64] Sex and megadeath merge in Huxley's lavish and poetic literary fiction. The movie outline prefigures the 'preeversions' of *Strangelove*'s thanatological humour. The scenario of talking, post-nuclear mutant apes keeping nuclear scientists chained or on leashes, is the clear intellectual forerunner to the *Planet of the Apes* film series and its source novel by Pierre Boulle.

Similarly, Akira Kurosawa first considered his nuclear age fable *I Live in Fear* (aka *Record of a Living Being*, 1955) as a satire but ultimately felt overwhelmed by the difficulty of artistically sustaining such an approach.[65] Appalled by H-bomb tests near Japan and troubled by the despair and imminent death of his long-time musical collaborator, Fumio Hayasaka, Kurosawa decided to make a 'message' film drawing on humanist pleas for international cooperation to halt the anticipated march toward thermonuclear annihilation.[66] *I Live in Fear* depicts an elderly Japanese factory owner, Mr Nakajima, attempting to convince his family to flee to the southern hemisphere (Brazil) which he imagines to be a presumed safe-haven from an imminent nuclear fate. Kurosawa skilfully depicts the omnipresent paradox facing us all – recognition of the insanity that our species can virtually self-destruct at any given moment, and our collective denial that enables us to go on living a 'normal' life despite this circumstance.

Kubrick's third writing collaborator on *Strangelove*, satirist Terry Southern, had also crafted an atomic age parable – *Year of the Weasel*, an unproduced one-act stage play written in the mid-1950s. According to his son Nile, the play showcased his father's 'ardent pacifism'.[67] Nile describes the work as

> a Brechtian Cold War play about children being taught to survive a blast in personal nuclear fall-out shelters [including] a graphic description of the effects of the firestorm of Dresden on its people.[68]

David Tully regards the play as more 'absurdist' à la Ionesco.[69] The play was written around the time Southern began writing a children's book. The concept stemmed from observing a United Nations school in Geneva, where his wife was teaching at the time. Among the play's named characters are Smeller and Teller, a couple of vaudevillian 'bomb-shelter salesmen', with the latter satirical nomenclature clearly aimed at the notorious Manhattan Project and H-bomb physicist. At an elementary school children receive instructions from a 'government booklet on fallout protection'. Their teacher, Miss Smart, cheerily leads the children in a sing-along about Hiroshima, radiation and mutilation. The classroom becomes a grand, absurdist play space with the school group following a charismatic 'Director', who hands out grotesque masks. Every child dons a mask of mutilation and points at their neighbour, reciting in unison 'You're a funny sight', before descending into a fallout shelter constructed in the school's backyard.[70]

Kubrick also drew inspiration from the comic perspectives of children in one early script vignette dated 31 April 1962. He typed and then extensively annotated a fragment titled, 'BABES'. It described a documentary featuring the Pentagon's General Klapp quizzing elementary school kids about the effects of radiation and America's nuclear arsenal.[71] In a macabre schoolroom scene the children press buzzers in answer to the General's questions:

General Klapp:
How much [radiation] would a silly unprotected person receive within the first few hours fall-out after a nuclear device explodes? That's assuming he's still around. (He chuckles. They laugh.)
(A girl doesn't know and a boy presses buzzer.)

Buck Tooth 9 Year-old:
Between two thousand five hundred and five thousand roentgens.

General Klapp:
Good, 50 points to the boy. Would that be fatal?
(A small twitter of laughter.)

Buck Tooth:
(Smirking) It sure would, sir. The average guy dies from 750 roengtens, and some people can't even take that much. They die from as little [as] 160 roengtens.

General Klapp:
Does anyone know the symptoms of radiation sickness?

Curly Head – 7 Years:
First itching of the skin, then tiredness, vomiting and finally ... (starts to giggle) your hair falls out. (Several others giggle.)

General Klapp:
(Raises his hand for order.) Now – we know a kiloton is equal to 1000 tons of TNT. Does anyone know how big our stockpile of bombs is, in megatons?

Pretty Little Girl – 6 Years:
One hundred thousand mega — megatons...
(Various 'Wows' and 'Goshs'.)

General Klapp:
Do any of you boys know how many B-52s we've got?

Skinny Boy – 11 Years:
We've got six hundred B-52s and about one thousand B-47s which aren't as
good but which can still pack a whale of a punch.

Kubrick later revised this sequence to introduce popular American children's television host Art Linkletter as the interviewer and quiz-meister. In a further script development, the programme is screened before Doctor Strangelove and Pentagon personnel, along with a fallout shelter public service announcement showing an American nuclear family rejoicing at the sight of their new underground space. The wife beams and the boy and girl chirp in unison: 'Gee dad, thanks for thinking of us!' The only remnant of this script idea existing in the completed film is a civil defence poster that can be seen behind Mandrake when he tries to call the White House from a Burpelson Air Force base pay phone. On the corridor wall opposite Mandrake, the poster displays the children's catch phrase next to a cartoon-like drawing of the family and underground shelter.

One of the more intriguing deviations from the novel *Red Alert,* George's treatment, and Kubrick's *Delicate Balance of Terror* scripts of February and March, is the introduction and comic development of Dr. Otto Strangelove's character through April to late June 1962. Several script fragments involving Strangelove invoke sex and death, including a discussion at a Washington party about 'sperm banks', proposed presumably to ensure post-holocaust genetic viability.[72] Another tangent, hand-written by Kubrick, is an elaborate farce describing how Dr. Strangelove 'accidentally' rises to power when the entire American Cabinet is liquidated at a live weapons demonstration. Such displays of military might were commonplace during the Cold War and both Eisenhower and JFK regularly attended these events. In Kubrick's scenario, based on a parallel treatment by

Screen capture showing fictional 'Civil Defence is your business' poster on the wall behind Group Captain Lionel Mandrake (Peter Sellers) during the corridor phone booth confrontation with Col. Bat Guano.

President John F. Kennedy (center, wearing sunglasses) watches a 1962 manned weapons firepower demonstration at the Air Proving Ground Center, Eglin Air Force Base, Florida. With Vice President Lyndon B. Johnson (left) and Chief of Staff of the US Air Force, General Curtis E. LeMay. (Cecil Stoughton. White House Photographs. John F. Kennedy Presidential Library and Museum, Boston).

Peter George, a wayward missile comically obliterates the upper echelons of American government and military.[73]

The next in-line as Presidential successor is the innocuous US Postmaster General, Daniel E. Fapp, who appoints Strangelove as his chief nuclear and strategic adviser.[74] Earlier, Strangelove had been seduced by Fapp's photojournalist wife, Corrine, while on assignment. She is described as 'a very interesting and sexy woman in her early thirties' who interviews the doctor at his private Strangelove Institute.[75] Mrs. Fapp also meets Strangelove's research colleagues, including Dr. Lothar who is portrayed conducting post-nuclear human endurance experiments and is described as 'working on survival and patch up'.[76] In this late June script, Strangelove is introduced by the narrator as 'a still relatively unknown and unimportant scientists who headed up his own operations research study group, financed by government contracts'. While this narration corresponds with Herman Kahn's post-RAND Hudson Institute, there is little else that physically resembles Kahn in this fictional characterisation of Otto Strangelove (see chapter two). However, the Kahnian association is further amplified when Strangelove confesses to Mrs. Fapp that he 'seemed to have offended a lot of people' when his book, *The Facts on Nuclear War*, distinguished between ten and forty, or eighty and 180 million dead. The strategist also seems perplexed that his estimate of post-war national recovery in ten to twenty years was regarded as 'misleading'. Such qualified reservations mirror Kahn's own reflections in both *Thinking the Unthinkable* (1962) and the 1968 paperback edition of *On Thermonuclear War*.

In a sequence reminiscent of the brunette who is ruthlessly slapped by *Fail-Safe*'s nuclear strategist Groeteschele (Walter Matthau), abhorred by the woman's sexual arousal from his thanatological statistics of nuclear annihilation, Professor Strangelove is charmed by, but initially rebuffs, Corrine Fapp. Undeterred, Fapp – who has the ear of the new President – takes Strangelove under her wing and provides entrée to Washington society. Later, in a scene prefiguring the homo-eroticism of the disabled writer's domestic bodybuilder in *A Clockwork Orange* (1971), the newly installed President Fapp meets Strangelove in a massive White House gymnasium. Fapp is presented in a 'leopard skin male bikini' narcissistically pre-occupied with his work-out regime, continuing with his bar-bell sets, while offering Strangelove the plum job of Secretary of Defense, covering nuclear warfare and strategy.

This alternative story arc, titled *The Rise of Doctor Strangelove*, commences with a narrator explaining how the doctor became known as the 'White House Rasputin'.[77] Initially a modest and shy academic, he soon becomes publicly celebrated and popular, even rakish. To demonstrate the scientist's influence Kubrick proposed a montage showing Strangelove 'laughing with senior cabinet members' while advising the President that a giant survival bunker should be built 'looking very much like a plush hotel', with a high rotation of prostitutes available amongst the senior leadership to avoid boredom in the 'post-attack environment'. At the time these fictional scenarios were under script development in 1962 a secret government bunker had been recently built beneath a West Virginia resort hotel, the Greenbrier.[78] Burrowed over 700 feet into a hillside, the underground facility was designed to be self-sufficient and accommodate up to 1,100 people. It comprised meeting rooms for all Congressional members (Representatives and Senate) and contained a hospital with ICU, decontamination chambers, reservoirs, a power house, fuel storage, cafeteria, and radio and television studios.[79] Tourists can now visit this once top secret hideout, where the Greenbrier boasts, devoid of Strangelovean irony, that its bunker tour is 'wheelchair accessible'.[80]

By 23 July 1962 Kubrick returned to his original approach with George and hand-penciled a new draft titled, 'RED ALERT', including some typed material from the *D.B.O.T.* script version four months earlier.[81] Although closely adhering to George's novel, with character names mostly drawn from the book, there is still no discussion of a Doomsday Weapon. Why Kubrick renewed this approach remains a mystery. Perhaps he wanted to have a fallback proposal, further developed from the *D.B.O.T.* script for Seven Arts should the comic treatment fail to gain market attachment.

Throughout much of 1962 and early into the new year, Kubrick was still tussling with a number of comic plot devices, and varying his approach from scene to scene. Some

INT. WAR ROOM

The Electronic Display shows the tracks of the 843d Bomb Wing,
creeping steadily onward.

Four tracks are stopped with an X marker. They indicate planes the
Russians report destroyed.

> GENERAL RICHTER
> Mister President, Mister Ambassador,
> the air situation indicates twenty-eight
> aircraft of the 843d Bomb Wing moving
> steadily to their targets. Four aircraft
> have been destroyed by the Russians.
> There have been no reports that their bombs
> exploded.

> GENERAL RICHTER
> Our radar and surveillance net indicates
> Soviet bomber forces scrambling, but
> holding. Missile bases are apparently being
> brought to maximum readiness. There is
> a great deal of activity on the tactical fields
> facing NATO. Sixth Fleet reports being
> shadowed by a submarine pack.

> GENERAL RICHTER
> We believe that, though this activity is not
> unexpected under the circumstances, it could
> also indicate an all-out attack on the U.S.

Enter a Colonel who whispers something to General Franklyn.

> GENERAL FRANKLYN
> We've received word the base has surrendered.

7/23/62

late scripted sequences were rejected outright despite already being planned and with set construction budgeted. These include an elaborate introduction (Scene 28) showing President Muffley inside the Pentagon set within a 'Subterranean Corridor'. Without his security pass the President is denied access by over-zealous armed guards who recite chapter and verse of the military regulation forbidding entry.[82] With a knowing glance to his Secret Service agents, the guards are promptly disarmed and the President makes his exit on a 'hydraulic chair' entering the War Room through a trap door in the ceiling.[83] The proposed scene recalls elements of Ken Adam's *Dr. No* (1962) production design, and anticipated similar hydraulic entrances/exits in screen productions such as Gerry Anderson's ITV series *Thunderbirds* (1965). In a pencil draft, circa June 1962, Kubrick described the location as

PRESIDENTIAL UNDERGROUND COMMAND POST
*INT. HUGE 45FT HIGH CAVE ENTRANCE

The concept included 'Eight high speed elevators' for troops armed with light automatic weapons and two 'very wide staircases [that] serve as an emergency access and exit from the command post 200 feet below'. Kubrick accompanied this idea with his own design doodles in black ink on lined note cards.[84]

One consistent feature evident in many of these later scripts is that they remain incomplete. For the best part of a year Kubrick (and George) grappled with how to sensibly conclude their nightmarish comic thriller. Several months before Terry Southern's involvement, script pages from 20 August 1962 depict lengthy and comic Hot Line conversations, the War Room generals saying America might get its 'hair mussed' with only a few millions killed 'tops', and arguing over post-nuclear survival deep underground, warning the President of a potential US-Soviet 'mine-shaft-gap'.[85] The script concludes with the President on the phone to the Soviet Premier (Scene 74) who advises that the feared Doomsday Machine was not fully operational and has now been deactivated. However, if the American bomber succeeds in reaching its target inside Russia the Premier demands a city in return for the one destroyed. The script presents only a one-sided Hotline conversation from the President, solely from his perspective. His monologue peaks in a shrill and angry denunciation, bellowed down the line: 'No! It's too *symbolic*!' The script notes the President slams the phone down in a 'rabid fit of anger' and announces to the shocked War Room, 'that son-of-a-bitch wanted [to] take

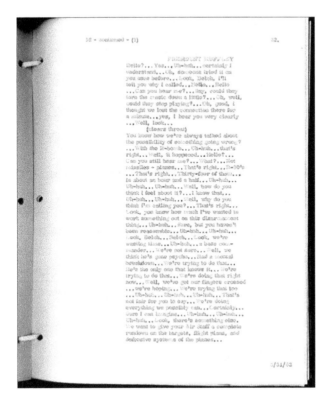

An early draft of the U.S. President's 'hotline' conversation with the Soviet Premier (named Belch in this version), from 31 August 1962. (Stanley Kubrick Archive)

out *Disneyland*!' This comic punch-line comes as a penultimate ending, immediately fol-lowed by the scripted direction 'FAST FADE' without any further notation.[86] At 140 pages, with a screen time of roughly over two hours and twenty minutes, the film would have already been considered too long, undoubtedly requiring substantial trimming. How the movie was to conclude remained a fluid and open option for the writer-director-producer until March 1963, nearly six weeks into principal photography.

Judging from the chronology of events and the materials held in the three co-writers' respective archives, it seems that the quantitative script contribution of Terry Southern has been over-estimated, much to the detriment of Peter George (and, to a lesser degree, James B. Harris). As with Peter Sellers and the common assumption that he ad-libbed nearly every line (see chapter two), much of the scholarly and popular literature on the film attributes to Southern – incorrectly – a range of comic ideas and flourishes that could not have been originally authored by him. Across the decades memories often become highly fallible. Even someone as close to the project's evolution as James B. Harris erroneously attributes the creation of the satirical title of the revised screenplay to Southern.[87] What is not in dispute, however, is Southern's crucial and critical role as a script doctor. His editorial advice and contributions greatly heighten *Dr. Strangelove*'s comedic impact through grotesque and absurdist nomenclature and dialogue, drawn from literary and essayistic skills that the writer had successfully honed in the decade prior.

Despite Kubrick's virtual 'invention' of the film in rough-cut and during post-produc-tion (see chapter five), trying to imagine *Dr. Strangelove* devoid of Terry Southern's input is like trying to imagine the film without Peter Sellers, and using instead the alternative actors Kubrick nominated for the individual roles.[88] At best, based on the extant scripts up until mid-November 1962, the final outcome may have been akin to Billy Wilder's Cold War satire *One, Two, Three* (1961) – a gratifying comedy but hardly memorable, and cer-tainly not a comic masterpiece that has entered the *zeitgeist* across generations.

Terry Southern first met Kubrick in mid-1962 during *Lolita*'s release, with the film a *cause célèbre* at the time. Southern was commissioned by *Esquire* magazine to interview the director. He had heard of Kubrick while living in New York in the early to mid-1950s and was slightly acquainted through mutual friends. Southern's wife, Carol, has recalled wryly that when she told Terry some guy named 'Stanley Kubrick' had given her his busi-ness card in a Greenwich Village bar, Southern was both bemused and impressed, having seen some of the independent director's films.[89] Kubrick encountered Southern's work when his novel *The Magic Christian* was handed out by Peter Sellers as a gift during the making of *Lolita* and the filmmaker responded to it with great enthusiasm.[90] However, the Southern-Kubrick *Esquire* interview was never published, deemed 'sedate' and large-ly humourless; odd, given Southern's normally adroit writing style.[91] Southern recalled that the pair 'got into a heavy rap – about death, infinity, and the origin of time'.[92] Instead, a follow-up interview was suggested, based on Kubrick's new project concerning 'nuclear war', a topic largely avoided during the conversation. However, Kubrick did reveal to Southern that his next film

> will star Peter Sellers and be a Kafkaesque satirical comedy about nuclear war. This seems to me to be the only honest way to deal with the thing.[93]

Six months later Kubrick contacted Southern and invited the writer to visit him in the UK for eight weeks during *Dr. Strangelove*'s pre-production.[94] He was paid $400 a week for his 'official' employment from 16 November to 28 December 1962.[95] However, correspondence with Kubrick's attorney suggests that Southern stayed on the books for another week. The director noted that he had 'personally employed Terry Southern … to do some polishing on the dialogue' through his production company Polaris and not through Columbia.[96] At the time Southern had a substantial and growing literary reputation with two cult novels and a string of influential works for notable magazines such as the *Paris Review*, *Harper's Bazar*, *The Nation*, *The Realist* and *Esquire*. As his biographer Lee Hill notes:

> If there was one thing Terry was master of, it was black comedy. [...] Southern understood that the most banal situations and statements could be charged with multiple meanings.[97]

It is an observation echoed in Kubrick's comment, 'Most of the humour in *Strangelove* arises from the depiction of everyday human behavior in a nightmarish situation'.[98] With James B. Harris, Kubrick had already skilfuly adapted *Lolita* and crafted visual and verbal sexual *double-entendres*. Combining Southern's deft revisions and Sellers' nuanced performance Kubrick perfectly balanced *eros* with *thanatos* in his darkly comic 'nuclear nightmare'. Perhaps the greatest distillation of Kubrick's relationship with Southern is summarised by his son Nile's observation that to 'get the best' out of his father Kubrick would often ask Terry: 'What's the most outrageous thing this character can say at this point and still be credible?'[99] Credibility and authenticity were similarly foregrounded by the writer as the core attributes that Kubrick retained from George's novel and guarded throughout his satirical approach. Southern noted:

> the entire complicated technology of nuclear deterrence in *Dr. Strangelove* was based on a bedrock of authenticity that gave the film what must have been its greatest strength: credibility.[100]

In various script fragments dated between 14 December 1962 and 1 January 1963 the dialogue becomes increasingly comic, but the narrative retains the suggestion from earlier drafts that the President might somehow be able to save the day. In Scene 61, Muffley says: 'I think I've got an idea of how to get the recall signal' to the sole remaining, damaged B-52 en route to H-bomb its ICBM target.[101] Yet these later scripts show little of what has been assumed as Terry Southen's input. For example, the script dated 1 January 1963 was certainly revised during Southern's tenure but there is no evidence of memorable lines such as Major Kong's 'Shoot, a fella could have a pretty good time in Dallas with all this stuff', which would suggest that this may have been an improvised ad-lib from Slim Pickens months later.[102] Several character names, even at this late date, remain unchanged such as General 'Buck' O'Connor, not yet renamed Turgidson. Southern's influence may, however, be inferred from multiple page inserts revising scenes, such as a new version of the phone conversation with the Soviet Premier (Scene 52) dated 14 January and a revision of dialogue concerning fluoridation (Scene 52) as of 27 January. The relatively late idea of framing General Ripper's dysfunctional sexual mania around the topical controversy of fluoridation, championed by right-wing groups such as the John Birch Society, was an inspired choice. The concept was developed in late December 1962 as 'notes on fluoridation'.[103]

As with the June draft's subterranean corridor scene, a new sequence (Scene 53) depicts the interior of an 'Air Command Communications Center' where 'a dozen Air Force language experts are communicating via radio'. While this scene was ultimately eliminated from the shooting, it is unclear whether an existing location was proposed or set construction was considered. By 14 January the lines concerning the Doomsday Machine (Scene 55) had been refined further and President Muffley's eleventh-hour idea (Scene 64) – still inexplicit and unarticulated – to signal the recall code to the plane remained in place. While these changes are outside the period of Southern's formal employment – by this time the writer had been joined in London by his wife and young son – Southern visited the set on occasion, particularly during rehearsals.

Further script revisions a week later (Scene 66) describe the Russians using ground based flashing lights, signaling the plane from below in Morse Code to spell out 'POE ... OPE'. The unexpected phenomenon creates division amongst the crew. A heated, racially charged exchange occurs between the southern-accented pilot T.J. (later renamed Major Kong) and 'negro' bombardier Jimmy (renamed Lt. Lothar Zogg, or 'Zoggy') which culminates in Jimmy being threatened with a court martial if he continues to question orders.[104] Throughout the sequence T.J. repeatedly demeans Jimmy, calling him 'boy', while steadfastly refuting the ground signal as anything but a Soviet ploy:

Jimmy:
You mean you think it's a trick?

T.J.:
Look, boy, don't tell me you're ready to yellow-dog-it home just because
a bunch of Commie searchlights say so.

Jimmy:
Yeah, but that's our code – the emergency base code.

T.J.:
You startin' to tell me which end is up, boy?

Jimmy continues to demur, querying T.J.'s logic by noting that the CRM-114 was 'smashed'. The pilot's reply insinuates insubordination and prefigures the racial vilification and invective used by Gunnery Sargent Hartman more than two decades later in *Full Metal Jacket* (1987):

T.J.:
You know, you almost talk like you want to see these Reds outsmart us,
watermelon.

Jimmy:
(flaring up) Don't call me watermelon, T.J. Just don't call me that.
I told you that before.

T.J.'s follow-up dialogue overlaps with Jimmy, threating him with a 'little trip to fist-city' before the other crew members intervene to de-escalate the confrontation. T.J. placates them by reciting his War College mantra 'never underestimate your enemy':

T.J.:
Now just suppose they got the code by knockin' down one of our planes and
torturin' holy hell out of one of the boys until they told it to 'em,
that's how they'd git it, and that's how they got it!

The crew quickly withdraws in assent. Shortly after, the damaged plane is further 'pummeled' by flack but continues to hurtle along towards its target at low altitude. With the co-pilot dead, the bomb bay doors jammed stuck, the plane unable to reach its designated safe zone and soon destined to run out of fuel, T.J. orders everyone to bail-out, but Jimmy seeks permission to refuse the order. Kubrick deliberately foregrounds the bathos of the scene, describing the pilot as being 'moved and wet-eyed' before promptly denying the request and again ordering for his subordinates to hit the silk. The crew remains motionless.

T.J.:

(almost ready to weep) What a bunch of crazy galoots. Did you ever see such
a scraggly collection of hair-brained, disobedient and stubborn airmen. Now
eject, damn it! Disobeying an order in combat is punishable by court martial.

The crew then bail-out, ad-libbing 'Geronimo!', 'God bless you King!', 'See you around ol'
buddy!' But only three chutes open. Suddenly Jimmy appears and asks his commander
'Mind if I sit next to you?' He moves into the adjacent co-pilot's seat. 'Hell, no', replies T.J.
and 'punches him affectionately in the arm'. The script self-consciously refers to T.J.'s
delivery as 'John Wayne-ish'.[105] Jimmy lights a cigarette for T.J. and puts it in between
the pilot's lips. The rapprochement is mutual and Jimmy is allowed to hold the steering
controls as they glide in towards the target.

In the script of 1 August the ethnic roles are different. In that earlier version the cha-
grined pilot apologises to his Latino (not African-American) bombardier for the 'crack I
made about your "Spik butt"', adding 'don't think I don't know that some of our best ball-
players and athletes are of Spanish decent'. The racial cliché is revised generically to
that 'of Negro descent' in the pages from mid-January. The latter script adds direction
and comically professes that, 'the two men are deeply touched by this Stanley Kramer-
ish moment of truth'. The scene ends with the bomber climbing rapidly to perform a
suicide-dive. The plane crashes into the target, its impact releasing a 'tremendous thermonuclear explosion caused by two 20-megaton H-bombs'.[106]

Apart from the length of the scene, it is not apparent why the sequence was ex-
cluded given that the production plans and shooting schedule lists dates for filming
and notes the prop requirements for a 'practical ejection seat' including parachute and
dummies.[107] Overall, this 'final' script, still incomplete, reads more like a transcript of
the dialogue from a rough cut, rather than a printed version. It is nevertheless full of
inconsistencies. The final scenes (74–9) of this late script briefly denote the pie fight,
described tersely (see chapter five) and followed by a 'moving shot pulling away from
earth with a roll up title about The Dead Worlds of Antiquity'.[108] Hence there is no final
script version, per se, a point acknowledged by Kubrick in correspondence with potential
publishers from March 1963 to January 1966. Much of the film was constructed in the
lead-up to final edit, as Kubrick's secretary, Anne Gravil, notes in a letter of 30 June: 'The
problem with publishing the script is that there is so little resemblance between even
the final script and the film itself.'[109]

Throughout these late script revisions, right up to the time of rehearsals and principal photography, it is evident that Kubrick had yet to decide on the montage of exploding
A- and H-bombs accompanied by Vera Lynn.[110] Nor was the narrative framing device of
bookending the production with an extraterrestrial introduction and coda removed. This

is confirmed by the costing for two animated sequences topping and tailing the production and their inclusion in the movie's weekly shooting schedule.[111] The stock footage of atomic and hydrogen bomb explosions was not ordered until March 1963 and the earliest evidence of Kubrick requesting Vera Lynn's recording of 'We'll Meet Again' is early April.[112]

Dr. Strangelove's script development subsequently proved controversial. A cable to Kubrick in early April 1963 from attorney Jack Swartzman informed the filmmaker that the Director's Guild had approved a waiver on end-tiles – which are absent from the film – but notes that Terry Southern must 'technically' be granted a 'co-screen play credit'.[113] Although Southern was not formally on the payroll in the new year, he continued to visit the set and offer advice, observing some rehearsals and helping Sellers with mastering a Texan accent for his proposed fourth role as Major Kong. The Southerns were also regular guests at the Kubrick home.[114] Hipster Southern, later acclaimed for inventing 'new journalism', was soon feted by the emerging 'swinging' London scene. New-found British friends such as Peter Sellers and Jonathan Miller spread the word about his comic gifts newly applied to cinema and the offers came in. Christiane Kubrick remembers Terry on set every now and then but that he was soon preoccupied with other film work.[115] The legal dispute over plagiarism against the *Fail-Safe* authors and producers dragged on over the first few months of 1963 (see chapter three) while Kubrick began concentrating on shooting and assembly editing.

Kubrick filming with hand-held Arriflex camera – a deleted scene featuring Peter Sellers in his uncompleted fourth role as Major Kong. Note the removable sectioning of the B-52 cockpit to enable tighter, documentary-style coverage. (Stanley Kubrick Archive)

Before the late January 1964 release of *Dr. Strangelove*, trouble emerged. Kubrick cabled associate producer Lee Minoff to 'correct impression Terry Southern wrote script' in an article by *Sunday Times* and *Queen* magazine scribe Francis Wyndham.[116] Southern increasingly found himself the subject of press profiles, such as for *Time* and *Life* magazines.[117] In August 1964 when pre-production publicity for Tony Richardson's adaption of Evelyn Waugh's *The Loved One* proclaimed Terry Southern the singular 'writer of *Dr. Strangelove*' Kubrick contacted the producers and threatened legal action.[118] He'd had enough and wanted to set the record straight:

> In the seven months since the premiere of 'Dr. Strangelove' I have refrained from commenting on the numerous magazine and newspaper articles and interviews with Terry Southern in which he is referred to as 'the writer' or 'the author' of 'Dr. Strangelove', though these references were plainly inaccurate and professionally damaging and embarrassing to Mr. Peter George and myself ... the screenplay credit given on the main-title of the film and on paid advertising reads' 'Screenplay by Stanley Kubrick, Peter George & Terry Southern, Based on the novel Red Alert by Peter George'.[119]

Sensing an opportunity to capitalise on the controversy, *Esquire* magazine's Harold Hayes cabled Kubrick and granted him space of 1,500 words for 'your version of who wrote *Dr. Strangelove*', adding that he had made the same offer to Southern.[120] However, the idea was not taken up. Instead, Peter George followed up *Life*'s profile on Southern with a letter to the Editor, stating that the magazine falsely implied 'Southern's intervention turned a serious script into an "original, irreverent" satirical film'. George countered with:

> The facts, however, are that when Mr. Southern first appeared at Shepperton studio, England, the script (a satirical adaptation of my novel *Red Alert*) was complete. Stanley Kubrick and I had been writing it for 10 months.[121]

George concluded by noting that Southern's six-week employment saw him 'fittingly receive a screenplay credit in *third place* behind Mr. Kubrick and myself'.[122] In actual fact, the Pablo Ferro screen credits clearly show Southern as second-named author, in between Kubrick and George. Despite this oversight, the correct listing appeared in advertising, and perhaps of most professional importance, the American Academy Award and British BAFTA nominations for Best Screenplay.

Southern's later perspective on the public spat pithily noted that what Kubrick 'neglected to say about his completed script is quite simple: it wasn't funny'. Yet the

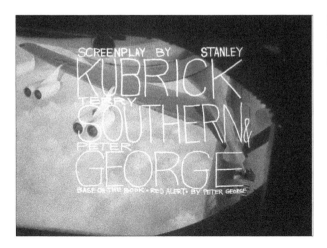

Frame capture of film credit sequence erroneously listing Terry Southern in second place.

existentialist author likely did not see what all the fuss was about. He was riding high with the re-release of *Candy* and script assignments for a string of Hollywood productions. Looking back in 1996, Southern's assessment of the conflict is nevertheless tinged with exaggeration:

> Having written this great best-seller, *Candy*, which was something like number one on *The New York Times* bestseller list for 21 weeks, my reputation eclipsed Stanley's, so I got total credit for all the *Strangelove* success in *Life*, *The New York Times* and other publications. The credit I was getting was just so overwhelming and one sided credit that naturally he was freaking out. He took out full page ads in every paper in America saying Terry Southern has nothing to do with it. He felt that and rightly so and lashed out, but it was like an overnight thing. I wrote a letter to *The New York Times* explaining that there was no mystery involved and that I was brought in to just help with the screenplay.[123]

Despite the occasional creative rancor erupting, such as the later dispute over credit for creating *Blue Movie*, Kubrick and Southern remained on friendly terms and occasionally collaborated.[124] Christiane Kubrick recalls that her husband felt Southern 'was somebody who was really a master of comedy'. After reading *The Magic Christian* Stanley 'realized this was his man'. When Stanley came to the conclusion that 'it could only be done as a really unbelievable *black* comedy', he discussed the idea with Southern. According to Christiane, Stanley saw that Terry 'got it' immediately. She recalls the pair working in their Kensington flat, 'doing great little sidelines on what else could happen ... and shame we can't put that in, and getting themselves totally hysterical' about the dangers of living in the era of the Bomb.[125]

Recent access to the various writers' archives now demonstrate that Terry Southern's overall contribution to *Dr. Strangelove* has been quantitatively overestimated. There is now ample evidence to show that Southern's brilliant and anarchic discursive contributions – ones that elegantly and economically finesse the Kubrick-George screenplay – are fewer than first suspected, and nothing like the major attribution given by writers such as Hill, LoBrutto and Baxter. This is not to discount the power of Southern's touché satirical interventions, nor to undermine the comic value of those offerings but, rather, to further recognise that the writer did little at the time, or subsequently, to dispel the growing public perception that he was indeed the 'author' or the principal creative force behind *Dr. Strangelove*. Hence, the dubious and erroneous claim by writers like Paul Duncan that 'only the initial premise of George's novel was used in *Dr. Strangelove* – the rest is all Southern and Kubrick' mostly circulate unchallenged.[126]

NOTES

1 Harris-Kubrick also employed *Paths of Glory* co-writer Calder Willigham, a friend of Nabokov who gave the producers a copy of the book, to develop a screenplay of *Lolita*.

2 Harris, 1999, interview transcript, 'Inside Dr. Strangelove', (2000).

3 Department of State, 'U-2 Overflights and the Capture of Francis Gary Powers, 1960', *Office of the Historian*; https://history.state.gov/milestones/1953–1960/u2-incident.

4 National Security Archive, 'The Berlin Crisis 1958–1961'; http://nsarchive.gwu.edu/nsa/publications/berlin_crisis/berlin.html.

5 'The Berlin Wall, Fifty Years Ago', (2011); http://nsarchive.gwu.edu/NSAEBB/NSAEBB354/.

6 Kubrick letter to Mr Scanbury, 14 August 1961, SKPC.

7 Kubrick letter to Blau, 22 August 1961, SKPC.

8 Kubrick letter to Blau and Jack Schwarztman, 5 September 1961, SKPC.

9 Kubrick letter to Mr Leslie, 3 October 1961, SKPC.

10 John McKeller White letter to Kubrick, 3 October 1961, SKPC.

11 Peter D. Smith, *Doomsday Men: The Real Dr. Strangelove and the Dream of the Superweapon* (London: Penguin, 2007), 403–4.

12 Cocks, *The Wolf at the Door: Stanley Kubrick, History, and the Holocaust*, 115.

13 Harris-Kubrick letter to Burdick and Wheeler, 19 January 1962, SKPC.

14 It is curious that this letter and its enclosures were not sent until nearly a month later (by registered mail on 19 January 1962), more than three weeks after Burdick and Wheeler made this offer. Also curious is that in the proposed Harris-Kubrick film adaptation of *Red Alert*, they retain the principal plot devices of the novel but reverse the nuclear first-strike from American to Soviet forces.

15 John McKeller White letter to Kubrick, 17 October 1961, SKPC.

16 Kubrick, quoted in James Howard, *Stanely Kubrick Companion* (London: B.T. Batsford, 1999), 91.

17 Kubrick letter to George, 4 November 1961, PGA.

18 Kubrick letter to George, 24 November 1961, PGA.

19 George letter to Kubrick, 4 December 1961, PGA.

20 Shore letter to Meredith, 13 December 1961, SKPC.

21 Meredith letter to Shore, 22 December 1961, SKPC

22 Burdick letter to Kubrick, 26 December 1961, SKPC.

23 George letter to Louis Blau, 12 March 1963, 1, PGA and George quoted in copy pages for *The Daily Worker*, circa February-March 1964, 5, PGA

24 George, *The Daily Worker*, circa February-March 1964, 1, PGA.

25 Peter George to Blau, 12 March 1963, 1, PGA.

26 George, ibid.

27 George, ibid., 2.

28 George, *The Daily Worker*, 4, ibid.

29 Sara George, interview with the author, May 2016, and see George, *The Daily Worker*, 5, ibid.

30 These claims are made by Lobrutto, Baxter and Duncan, amongst others. According to Sara George, her father described how he was interrogated by a couple of 'American security officers' in 1961, personnel she says that Peter assumed were from the CIA. After dismissing the base commander, the two Americans 'grilled him for a couple of hours' about *Red Alert*, his idea of a 'hotline' and the location in Russia of the Soviet stockpile of doomsday weapons. At the time Sara recalls her father pouring over a huge map of Russia trying to figure out where such locations might be, deciding on the Urals. Presumably this struck a nerve for US intelligence, even though the manuscript was previously checked by the UK Air Ministry and cleared for publication in 1958. Certainly the ICBM targeted by the B-52's, near Kotlass [sic], became a location of interest for CIA spy flights, including the U-2 piloted by Francis Gary Powers, which was destined to overfly the Russian town, but was shot down just prior. Satisfied that author Peter George had not obtained information illegally the operatives ended their interrogation saying: 'By the way, the President has read your book, and enjoyed it very much.' Sara George, interview with the author, May 2016. It is well known that JFK was a 'voracious reader' from childhood, and he loved espionage thrillers, especially Ian Fleming's 007 novels; see http://www.csmonitor.com/USA/Politics/Decoder/2013/1123/John-F.-Kennedy-Why-books-were-a-big-part-of-his-life-video.

31 Sara George, ibid.

32 Peter George quoted in *The Daily Worker*, ibid.

33 Sara George, ibid.

34 For example, see Lee Hill, *A Grand Guy: The Art and Life of Terry Southern* (New York: Harper, 2001), 125.

35 Christiane Kubrick, ibid.

36 Ibid.

37 Peter George to Stanley Kubrick, letter dated 7 August 1962, PGA. George's letter responds to Kubrick's queries of 5 and 26 May regarding back-pay or monies owing the author and George confirms they had been settled.

38 Peter George, Treatment, scenes 1–104, 15–25 January 1962, SKPC.

39 Kubrick letter to W. E. Kricker, 30 January 1962, SKPC.

40 Leslie Colitt, 'Berlin Crisis: The Standoff at Checkpoint Charlie', *The Guardian* (2011); https://www.theguardian.com/world/2011/oct/24/berlin-crisis-standoff-checkpoint-charlie.

41 Script fragment, 12 February 1962, SKPC

42 Ibid.

43 Big John in this context could specifically refer to actor John Wayne (as are later scripted dialogue deliveries in the manner of 'John Wayne', or the Big John could refer to a toilet (john), a perennial thematic concern in Kubrick's oeuvre, or a prostitute's client, a 'john'. Also of relevance is the film version depiction of 'Dear John' painted on one of the H-bombs, the humiliating opening cliché that came to be recognised as a lover's letter terminating a relationship.

44 Ibid.

45 Script, 21 February 1962, SK/11/1/10.

46 Ibid.

47 Ibid.

48 History Channel, 'Hotline Established between Washington and Moscow'; http://www.history.com/this-day-in-history/hotline-established-between-washington-and-moscow.

49 Ibid.

50 Tom Clavin, 'There Never Was Such a Thing as a Red Phone in the White House', *Smithonian Mag* (2013); http://www.smithsonianmag.com/history/there-never-was-such-a-thing-as-a-red-phone-in-the-white-house-1129598/?no-ist.

51 Thomas E. Stimson, 'Is Our Atomic Stockpile Dangerous?', *Popular Mechanics*, no. Annual Auto Issue (1961): 278.

52 Peter Krämer, *Dr. Strangelove* (London: British Film Institute, 2014).

53 Ibid., loc 1362.

54 PreProduction files, box 1 of 3, SK/11/2.

55 Kubrick note in pen, 2 pages, SK/11/1/21.

56 SKA

57 Kubrick Interviewed by Gene D. Phillips, 1973, 148.

58 Harris, 2005, interviewed by the author, Los Angeles.

59 Harris, 2000, interview transcript, *Inside Dr. Strangelove*.

60 John Wranovics, *Chaplin and Agee: The Untold Story of the Tramp, the Writer, and the Lost Screenplay* (New York: Palgrave McMillan, 2005).

61 Matt Anderson, 'Chaplin and Agee', *Movie Habit* (2005); http://www.moviehabit.com/essay.php?story=chaplin_agee.

62 See Sanford E. Marovitz, 'Aldous Huxley and the Nuclear Age: 'Ape and Essence' in Context', *Journal of Modern Literature* 18, no. 1 (1992): 115–25.

63 David King Dunaway, *Huxley in Hollywood* (New York: Harper & Row, 1989). Huxley's major credits comprise *Women's Vengence* for Universal in 1948, as sole author, and as co-author on *Pride and Prejudice* (MGM 1940) and *Jane Eyre* (Fox 1940). His uncredited script treatment for *Madame Curie* (MGM 1943) formed the basis for that production, and he was not credited for co-authoring *Alice in Wonderland* (RKO 1951).

64 Aldous Huxley, *Ape and Essence* (Chicago: Elephant Paperback, 1992), 36.

65 Mick Broderick, ed. *Hibakusha Cinema: Hiroshima, Nagasaki and the Nuclear Image in Japanese Film* (London: Kegan Paul International, 1996), 14.

66 James Goodwin, 'Akira Kurosawa and the Atomic Age', in *Hibakusha Cinema: Hiroshima, Nagasaki, and the Nuclear Image in Japanese Film*, ed. Mick Broderick (London: Kegan Paul International, 1996), 184.

67 David Tully suggests that there may have been a planned second act but there is no manuscript, even in draft form. See David Tully, *Terry Southern and the American Grotesque* (Jefferson NC: McFarland, 2010), 50.

68 Mel Gusso, 'Terry Southern Literary Archives Go to New York Public Library', *The New York Times* (2003); http://www.nytimes.com/2003/04/03/books/03SOUT.html?pagewanted=all.

69 Tully, *Terry Southern and the American Grotesque*, 51.

70 Ibid.

71 Script fragments 'SK – 4–31-62 BABES -3', April 31 1962, SK/11/1/16.

72 Script fragments, June 18 1962, SK/11/1/?.

73 David George has recently restored his father's (Peter George) scenario for Kubrick in the expanded edition of the film novelization of *Dr. Strangelove*. The 2015 Candy Jar Press edition includes the 'lost' 8,000 word back story, 'Some Notes on the Character of Strangelove including "Strangelove's Theory"'.

74 Screen scenarios concerning Presidential succession in times of emergency include *Battlestar Gallactica*, (2004) and *Designated Survivor* (2016): https://www.youtube.com/watch?v=N_f1vONx5Sw&feature=youtu.be

75 A margin note by Kubrick alongside this description adds: 'She is also well known for a book of female nudes. A scene later on in her studio??!!'

76 Script pages (on pink) June 26 1962, SK/11/1/15.

77 Ibid.

78 An excellent repository on the Greenbrier history can be found at the exemplary Cold War site, Conelrad.com featuring a range of items on the secret underground complex: http://www.conelrad.com/groundzero/greenbrier.html

79 'The Greenbrier's Bunker History'; http://www.greenbrier.com/Activities/The-Bunker/Bunker-History.

80 http://www.greenbrier.com/Activities/Bunker-Tours.

81 'Serious version', RED ALERT, SK/11/1/2.

82 Such a guarded, underground passageway is shown in the January 1961 issue of *Popular Mechanics* (125) where the author questions: 'Yet there are other hazards besides accidental ones. What if a person who has access to a bomb goes crazy and explodes it on purpose? Military personnel and scientific technicians have been known suddenly to go insane.'

83 White script pages, December 19 1962, SK/11/1/8.

84 Script notes, SK/11/1/?.

85 Script pages (pink), August 20 1962, SK/11/1/15 and SK/11/1/11.

86 The gag invokes reprisal over the unhappy diplomatic incident in 1959 when Soviet Premier Nikita Khrushchev was barred from visiting Disneyland on his national tour of America. After a hostile reception hosted by 20th Century Fox's President, Spyros Skouras, when told he could not visit Disneyland, the Premier fumed: "And I say, 'I would very much like to go and see Disneyland.' But then, we cannot guarantee your security, they say. Then what must I do? Commit suicide? What is it? Is there an epidemic of cholera there or something? Or have gangsters taken hold of the place that can destroy me?" See Andrew Glass, 'Nikita Khrushchev barred from Disneyland, Sept. 19, 1959', Pilitico.com, 19 September 21012; http://www.politico.com/story/2012/09/

this-day-in-politics-081359#ixzz4JNFq5hpC. See also Peter Carlson, Nikita Khrushchev Goes to Hollywood", *Smithsonian Magazine,* July 2009; http://www.smithsonianmag.com/ist/?next=/history/nikita-khrushchev-goes-to-hollywood-30668979/

87 James B. Harris quoted in Hill, *A Grand Guy: The Art and Life of Terry Southern*, 113.

88 Amongst the proposed actors, as early as February-March 1962 Kubrick notes that Paul Newman was 'ready' and 'available' in August for the film version of *D.B.O.T.* (SK/11/3/5 Production Notes). Other actors considered for the serious script versions, and the early comic treatments, include: Orson Wells as the Soviet Ambassador and Burt Lancaster as a general (SK/11/1/7). Other lists mention Richard Basehart and Dane Clark (SK/11/1/10). Just prior to *Strangelove*'s production, sensing potential trouble with Scott, Kubrick sought the availability of Lee J. Cobb for the role of Turgidson. Similarly, Noel Coward was first offered the role of the Russian Ambassador (as was comic improviser Ted Flicker), so brilliantly played by Peter Bull (see SK/11/2/1). Gene Kelly was also offered the Role of General Ripper before Sterling Hayden. Imagine, for example, a sultry Barbara Feldon (*Get Smart*'s "Agent 99") playing Miss Foreign Affairs instead of Tracy Reed? (SK/11/2/1).

89 Carol Southern, interview with the author, New York 2005.

90 Southern, interviewed by Lee Server, *Now Dig This: The Unspeakable Writings of Terry Southern, 1950–1995* (New York: Grove Press, 2002), 7.

91 Hill, *A Grand Guy: The Art and Life of Terry Southern*, 107.

92 Ibid., 113.

93 Nile Southern, 'Strange Loves', *Written By*, 16 January 2016, 49.

94 Kubrick Telegram to Southern, Hill, *A Grand Guy: The Art and Life of Terry Southern*, 108.

95 Ibid., 114; Southern, 'Strange Loves', 51.

96 Kubrick letter to Michael Flint, 14 January 1963, SKPC.

97 Hill, *A Grand Guy: The Art and Life of Terry Southern*, 114.

98 Kubrick, interviewed by Joe Gelmis, in Gene D. Phillips, *Stanley Kubrick: Interviews* (Jackson, Miss.: University Press of Mississippi, 2001), 97.

99 Southern, 'Strange Loves', 52.

100 Terry Southern, 'Notes from the War Room', *Reprinted from Grand Street*, no. 49 (1996); http://www.visual-memory.co.uk/amk/doc/0081.html.

101 Script pages (pink), 14 December 1962 and script pages (white), January 1 1963, SK/11/1/8.

102 Several continuity reports detail Pickens' improvising dialogue across takes and several days of shooting the scene, on 17 April (scene 22BB slate 284), 26 April (26BB/323) 'retake of slate 284', and 2 May 63 (scene 26BB slate 338).

103 'Notes on Fluoridation', December 1962, SK 11/1/5.

104 Script, scene 66d, 1 January 1963. SKPC.

105 Preceding Private Joker's mocking incantation in *Full Metal Jacket* of the Duke's familiar western drawl, several drafts of *Dr. Strangelove* not only refer to John Wayne-like vocal delivery but also name the B-52 bomber 'Big John'. It is quite possible that the oft repeated – and entirely unsubstantiated – claim that John Wayne was first offered the part of Major Kong stems from these scripted editorial asides. Terry Southern has said 'Wayne was approached, and dismissed it immediately', however there is no correspondence corroborating the claim. See Southern interviewed by Lee Hill, in Patrick McGilligan, *Backstory 3:*

Interviews with Screenwriters of the 60s (Berkeley: University of California Press, 1997), 378.

106 Script page 109, Scene 69g, SK/11/1/22. Apart from the generic reference to Kramer's oeuvre, it likely refers specifically to *The Defiant Ones* (1958) starring Tony Curtis and Sydney Poitier.

107 See shooting schedules, SK/11/2/2 and props, SK/11/2/8.

108 The extraterrestrial narrative perspective is later reprised by Kubrick in both *2001* and *A.I.,* from both a post-human and alien perspective.

109 Gravil letter to Ernst Rossman, 30 June 1964, SKPC.

110 It was reportedly Sellers' co-Goon collaborator, Spike Milligan, who suggested to Kubrick to use Vera Lynn's song with the nuclear montage; see Roger Lewis, 'Some Sunny Day – My Autobiography: Dame Vera Lynn', *The Daily Express* (2009); http://www.express.co.uk/entertainment/books/121730/Some-Sunny-Day-My-Autobiography-Dame-Vera-Lynn; George Case, *Calling Dr. Strangelove: The Anatomy and Influence of the Kubrick Masterpiece* (Jefferson N.C.: MacFarland, 2014), 108.

111 Letter dated 4 February 1963 regarding the animation of 'space' and 'weird animal', SK/11/2/8.

112 See notes in Props and Miscellaneous orders, SK/11/2/8.

113 Schwartzman cable to Kubrick, 3 April 1963, SKPC.

114 Carol Southern, ibid., SKPC.

115 Christiane Kubrick, ibid., SKPC.

116 Kubrick cable to Minoff, 9 January 1964, SKPC.

117 'Southern Exposure', *Time*, 12 June 1964; Jane Howard, 'A Creative Capacity to Astonish', *Life*, 12 August 1964, 39–42.

118 Stanley Kubrick press release, Columbia Pictures, New York, 9 August 1964.

119 Ibid.

120 Hayes cable to Kubrick, 11 August 1964, SKPC.

121 Peter George, letter to the Editor, 18 September 1964, *Life*, 32.

122 Ibid.

123 Southern interviewed by Hill, *A Grand Guy: The Art and Life of Terry Southern*. http://www.altx.com/int2/terry.southern.html

124 The intellectual ownership of the *Blue Movie* idea led to a dispute between the parties. Following a May 1964 interview with Southern in *The Realist,* Kubrick threatened to sue Southern and publishers Random House for plagiarism if they proceeded. Kubrick letter to Legal Department, Random House, 21 August 1964, SKPC. Nevertheless, the pair stayed on good terms with Southern contributing (unused) dialogue fragments in the early 1980s for Kubrick's adaptation of Arthur Schnitzler's *Traumnovelle* for *Eyes Wide Shut* (1999).

125 Christiane Kubrick, ibid.

126 Duncan, *Stanley Kubrick: Visual Poet 1928–1999*, 51.

CHAPTER TWO

Doctors Strangelove

O ver the years a number of characters have purportedly been the inspiration for the eponymous 'Doctor Strangelove' (*Merkwürdigichliebe*), the ex-Nazi 'director of weapons research and development'. Since the film's original release and critical reception these real-life personalities, either identified individually or collectively, have been consistently nominated as primary influences. So, how accurate are these speculations? Given the nature of the screenplay contributions by individual co-writers Kubrick, George, Southern and their varying approaches to the multiple treatments and character nomenclature, it is abundantly clear that Doctor Strangelove is the embodiment of no single public identity.

Rather, several sources of 'inspiration' inform this fictitious composite persona. These include the well-known and lesser-known authors of the large body of strategic and scientific nuclear scholarship that Kubrick exhaustively consulted during development of the project. The scriptwriters also drew from contemporary and historical screen representations of strange loves, militarists, evil scientists, martinets and psychopaths. Other influences stem from the collaborative liaison Kubrick and George adopted in their respective treatments, scripts, character vignettes and the additional, sharpened dialogue from Terry Southern. Importantly, the performative and gestural incarnation of Strangelove by Peter Sellers owes much to the comic (and often opportunistic) inspiration the actor found in rehearsal and otherwise while on set (the black glove, Arthur Fellig/Weegee's voice, the rebellious arm etc.), as well as Sellers' own extensive back-catalogue of characters from the Goons 'atomic caper film', *Down Among the Z Men* (1952), to *The Mouse that Roared* and *Lolita*.

Hence, the candidates of influence vary from real-life mathematician-physicists and scientists (John von Neumann, Edward Teller and Wernher von Braun) and nuclear

Crazed scientist Rotwang with (mechanical?) gloved right hand gesticulates menacingly before wealthy industrialist, Frederson, in *Metropolis* (1927).

strategists (Bernard Brodie, Henry Kissinger, Herman Kahn, Oscar Morgenstern and Albert Wohlstetter) to fictional screen villains (Rudolf Klein-Rogge as Rotwang in *Metropolis* (1927), Peter Lorre as Dr. Gogol in *Mad Love* (1935) and Joseph Wiseman as the eponymous *Dr. No*).

NOMENCLATURE

It has been frequently assumed that the name and concept of 'Strangelove' originated with hipster satirist Terry Southern.[1] However, as far back as May 1962, long before Southern became involved with the project, the idea and character name was literally being doodled by Kubrick on office pads and incorporated into multiple drafts and script fragments. While Peter George was certainly not considered a satirist, and comedy, let alone black comedy, was clearly not his preferred métier, working alongside Kubrick, the pair successfully developed a feature-length comic script, sufficient to gain the backing of Columbia Pictures. Much of this original version remains recorded on film, and well before Terry Southern's engagement to edit and enhance the existing dialogue and character names. Kubrick biographer John Baxter, repeats the assertion that Southern

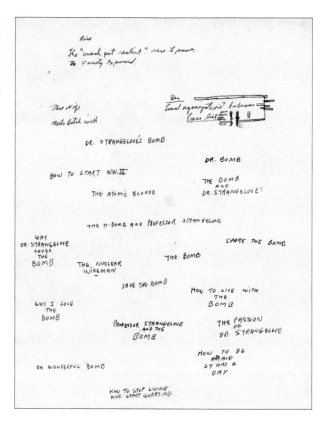

invented the name 'Strangelove' and the film's extended title, as well as perpetuating the unfounded claim that George 'was an active member of the Campaign for Nuclear Disarmament'.[2] (Baxter's section on *Strangelove* is muddled with multiple errors and an incorrect chronology of events, from development to post-production and release.)[3]

As shown in the previous chapter, the journey from the taut, suspenseful novel *Red Alert* to *Dr. Strangelove*'s nightmare comedy was a complex and sometimes contested one. For example, there is no such character as the ex-Nazi scientist in George's underlying literary work. As Peter Krämer has demonstrated, Kubrick's initial concept of a Strangelovean persona was for a 'nuclear wiseman' – possibly riffing on American slang for a 'wise-guy', 'wise acre' or 'smart ass'.[4] In New York parlance, a 'wise guy' also connoted a mobster, or someone who worked for the mafia. It was a criminal allusion that appears across several drafts of the *Strangelove* screenplay. Kubrick returned over and over to his rhetorical charge (ultimately excised from the final cut, see chapter five), made by the President to the Soviet Ambassador in the War Room, that the 'great nations have always acted like gangsters and the little ones like prostitutes'.[5] The wise man figuration also connotes shamanistic attributes, of being venerated by a community for profound knowledge, akin to the Biblical magi, further enhancing the association with a nuclear 'priesthood'.[6]

In early script notes, handwritten by Kubrick, the genesis of Strangelove emerges under a different name – 'Professor A.B.C. Ice'. As Krämer has suggested, the initials most likely conform to the acronym used in military and civil defence parlance to describe 'Atomic, Biological and Chemical' defence.[7] Kubrick's brief character vignette, scribbled on notepaper, describes him thus:

> Crackpot realist. Horny and relatively celibate. Vain. Ambitious. Glib. Persuasive. Amoral. Quick eyes and movements. Frank forthright attitude. Speaks quickly. Sexually shy and unused to having women throw themselves at him but quickly adapts. Loves gadgets. Hi Fi. Cameras. Luxurious living.[8]

'Crackpot' realism is at the heart of *Dr. Strangelove*'s nightmare comedy and remained the core vision that Kubrick undergirds aesthetically and intellectually throughout the film. Halfway through production Kubrick told a *Newsweek* interviewer: 'Suddenly, after talking casually about overkill and megadeaths you find that everything you say, you say with a laugh. It's a sort of crackpot realism, but both sides have to pretend they're willing to fight a nuclear war. Personally, I doubt if either side really is.'[9] Kubrick next sketched out a scenario set in a university classroom where the junior 'Assist Professor Ice' is correcting the proofs of his new book *Man into Numbers*. This satirical title perfectly embodies the mindset that Kubrick constantly encountered during his exhaustive study of nuclear strategy and conversations with strategists who equated human beings with numerical agglomerations. Reflecting on this odious mentality Kubrick commented to Terry Southern:

> What has struck me is their cautious sterility of ideas, the reverence of obsolete national goals, the breeziness of crackpot realism, the paradox of nuclear threats-manship, the desperately utopian wish fantasies about [an enemy nation's] intentions, and the terrifying logic of paranoiac fears and suspicions.[10]

Kubrick's scene describes the wife of the US Foreign Minister, Mrs. Edith Angelwhite, 'a sexy bitch in her middle forties', who meanders away from a speech given by her husband in a nearby university hall and wanders into Professor Ice's classroom. Ice lets her read his work and she 'becomes visibly excited as he reads her some of the more shocking statistics in the book' and the pair make love on a library table. Later that same night, in a hotel suite where Professor Ice attends a cocktail party, Kubrick describes the cuckolded Cabinet Minister:

Paul Angelwhite is an unconvincing, unattractive liberal. He says all the right thing [sic] but without persuasiveness, vitality or charm. Shelly [sic] Berman would be perfect for the type. He is plagued by heartburn and fear of halitosis. He is also nervous about his wife and makes a number of self-effacing, snorting jokes, kidding on.

In these early, broad outlines we can find the overriding theme ubiquitous throughout what would become *Dr. Strangelove* – a satirical preoccupation with sex and death in the nuclear age. The character vignettes also demonstrate Kubrick already imagining potential actors for such roles. Shelley Berman, in this instance, was a Jewish-American stand-up comic famous for lengthy telephone monologues, something Kubrick would hilariously craft for the President of the United States, in what the director-producer-principal writer carefully promoted in cartoon versions of the advertising campaign, as a 'Hot-line Comedy'.

Other script variations assign Strangelovean text and characterisation to 'von Klutz', who has several pages of dialogue, heavily annotated by Kubrick, describing survival in mine shafts and the participant selection process.[11] Similarly, in a script dated 1 January 1963 much of the scientific Doomsday Machine dialogue is attributed to 'Ambassador De Sade', not the Strangelovean von Klutz. Indeed, in this version (Scene 57), 'Dr. Strangelove' is only mentioned in passing at the very end, as referenced by *The New York Times*.[12]

It is important to understand the evolution of Kubrick's thinking regards the awful abstraction of nuclear strategy and the presumed inability of audiences to maintain interest or comprehend the ramifications of such paradoxical logic. As Kubrick explained to Jeremy Bernstein, it was the building of the Berlin Wall that intensified the filmmaker's existing interest in nuclear weapons and nuclear war.[13] After reading widely for a couple of years Kubrick felt that he had effectively covered the topic and was no longer learning anything new: 'When you start reading the analyses of nuclear strategy, they seem so thoughtful that you slip into a temporary sense of reassurance', Kubrick explained. 'But as you go deeper into it, and become more involved, you begin to realize that every one of these lines of thought leads to a paradox.'[14] It was this constant element of paradox in nuclear stratagems, and in the ambivalent public attitudes toward them, that Kubrick embraced as the principal logic driving the creative approach to *Dr. Strangelove*.

As Bernstein observed, up until *Strangelove* Kubrick had adapted existing novels – something he initiated with Peter George for this project but abandoned in order to craft a narrative drawn exclusively from an 'intellectual notion', namely 'the inevitable paradox posed by following any of the nuclear strategies to their extreme limits'. Kubrick explained the folly of such antimony:

By now, the bomb has almost no reality and has become a complete abstraction, represented by a few newsreel shots of mushroom clouds ... people react primarily to direct experience and not to abstractions; it is very rare to find anyone who can become emotionally involved with an abstraction. The longer the bomb is around without anything happening, the better the job that people do in psychologically denying its existence. It has become as abstract as the fact that we are all going to die some day, which we usually do an excellent job of denying. For this reason, most people have very little interest in nuclear war ... and the longer a nuclear event is postponed, the greater becomes the illusion that we are constantly building up security, like interest at the bank. As time goes on, the danger increases, I believe, because the thing becomes more and more remote in people's minds.[15]

This conceptual impasse and the associated hubris was fundamental to Kubrick's vision of a nightmare comedy, precipitated by a realistic scenario, though highly stylised, where a psychotic general unleashes his nuclear bombers to attack the Soviets, not by accident, but by 'exceeding his authority' and usurping chain of command – a flaw inherent to the Top Secret Presidential predelegation orders in circulation at the time (see chapter four). As Kubrick surmised:

A lot of effort has gone into trying to imagine possible nuclear accidents and protect against them. But whether the human imagination is really capable of encompassing all the subtle permutations and psychological variants of these possibilities, I doubt. The nuclear strategists who make up all those war scenarios are never as inventive as reality, and political and military leaders are never as sophisticated as they think they are.[16]

NUCLEAR STRATEGISTS, OR A CANTICLE FOR CLAUSEWITZ

As noted in chapter one, in early November 1961 Kubrick wrote to author Peter George modestly placing his filmmaking credentials and knowledge of nuclear strategy before the author:

I read 'Red Alert' some weeks ago and enjoyed it immensely. I've been wrapped up in Brodie, Kissinger, Kahn, Morgenstern for quite some time and found your book to be the only nuclear fiction I'd come across that smacked of knowledge. [...] Have you written any other stories dealing with nuclear subject matter? I should be most interested to read them if they exist.[17]

Hence it is worthwhile contextualising these defence intellectuals and their respective contributions to the evolving genre of nuclear strategy. Kubrick had amassed a substantial library of nuclear texts, including subscriptions to major journals and magazines, and acquired key works on the subject. Records of his research holdings from his Childwickbury home and those on deposit at the Stanley Kubrick Archive, show he owned a wide range of primary research materials and remained interested in nuclear affairs well after *Dr. Strangelove* was completed and released. Amongst his nuclear books are: *Strategy in the Missile Age* (Brodie), *The Legacy of Hiroshima* (Teller and Brown), *Strategy of Conflict* (Schelling), *World Peace Through World Law* (Clark and Sohn), *The Future of Mankind* (Jaspers), *Soviet Military Strategy* (Sokolovski), *Preventing World War Three* (Wright), *The Voice of Dolphins* (Szilard), *The Limits of Defense* (Weskow), *On Thermonuclear War* (Kahn), *Thinking about the Unthinkable* (Kahn), *May Man Prevail* (Fromm), *100 Million Lives: Maximum Survival in a Nuclear War* (Fryklund), *Man's Means to his End* (Watson-Watt), *War and Peace in the Space Age* (Gavin), *Deterrent or Defense* (Hart), *The Anatomy of Peace* (Reves), *How to Survive the H-Bomb* (Frank), *Now it Can Be Told* (Groves), *Brighter than a Thousand Suns* (Jungk), *The Effects of Nuclear Weapons* (AEC), *An Alternative to War or Surrender* (Osgood), *Power* (Bertrand Russell), *The Question of National Defense* (Morgenstern), *American Strategy for the Nuclear Age* (Hahn), *God and the H Bomb* (Keyes), *The Peace Race* (Melman), *Arms and Arms Control* (Lefever), *Strategy of Peace* (Kennedy [Hamilton]), *Civil Defense 1961*, *Strategy in Arms Control* (Schelling), *Has Man a Future* (Russell), *No More War* (Pauling), *The Cause of World War Three* (Wright Mills), *America Too Young to Die* (Seversky), and *Arms and Influence* (Schelling), through to more recent titles such as *Dr. Strangelove, I Presume* (Foot), *The Logic of Accidental Nuclear War* (Blair), *Command and Control of Nuclear Forces* (Bracken), *Third World War: A Future History* (Hackett), *War in 2080: the Future of Military Technology* (Langford) and *Unless Peace Comes: A Scientific Forecast of New Weapons* (Calder).

The first strategist that Kubrick mentions in his late 1961 letter to *Red Alert* novelist Peter George is Bernard Brodie. A Chicago-born Jewish-American, Brodie studied at the University of Chicago and later taught at Dartmouth College before serving in the Office of the Chief of Naval Operations during World War II. Brodie taught at Yale before becoming a strategic theorist at the RAND Corporation from 1951 to 1966. RAND (short for 'Research and Development') was established originally as an internal department within the Hughes Aircraft Corporation during the war but separated in 1948 to form an independent entity, initially servicing the US Air Force as its sole client in order to 'connect military planning with research and development decisions'.[18] At RAND Brodie soon became known as 'the American Clausewitz', a reference to the Prussian general Carl von Clausewitz and his influential tome on military strategy, *On War* (1832). Brodie was one of the earliest intellectuals to grasp the problem of formulating a strategy for the use of atomic weapons, and became one of the most articulate proponents of *deterrence*. He was the first scholar of strategic studies to convey the revolutionary impact of nuclear weapons on warfare, signaling a revision of the concepts, language and theories of modern war fighting.

Brodie wrote the seminal booklet on nuclear strategy in 1945, *The Atomic Bomb and American Security*. A year later, in *The Absolute Weapon: Atomic Power and World Order*, Brodie anticipated the development of the doctrine of 'massive retaliation', which became central to US nuclear strategy in the 1950s. The June 1947 issue of *The Bulletin of the Atomic Scientists* carried his important commentary 'War Department Thinking on the Atomic Bomb'. After joining RAND in Santa Monica he worked on defence and nuclear strategy until 1966. In 1959, Brodie published the influential *Strategy in the Missile Age*, followed by *From Cross Bow to H-Bomb* in 1962 and *Escalation and the Nuclear Option* in 1966, partly as a rejoinder to Herman Kahn's *On Escalation* (1965).

Biographer Barry Zellen believes Brodie cultivated a clearly defined, Janus-like, public and private face. His unclassified publications projected a sensitivity 'attuned to the underlying psychological issues' of nuclear warfare but were, according to Zellen, 'perhaps a tad squeamish when it came to the hard, military realities'.[19] Many commentators imply Brodie was much less strident in approach and discourse than his fellow RAND colleagues, such as Herman Kahn, yet he peppered his work with psychoanalytical and sexual terms. However, in his privately commissioned and secret consultancies, such as his internal 1951 RAND working paper 'Must We Shoot from the Hip?', Brodie's essay seems to Zellen 'particularly Kahnian, or perhaps one might say, Strangelovian' when extrapolating on human casualties from nuclear conflict. For Zellen, the RAND strategist was 'no less willing to think about the unthinkable' than contemporaries such as Kahn, and

> no less willing to embrace the notion that the collateral slaughter of millions of people could in fact be construed to be a strategic advantage to the attacker, a *bonus* of sorts in addition to the strictly material effects of strategic bombardment. [20] [emphasis added]

Although Brodie did not employ the term 'megadeath', he clearly appreciated the concept. For example, in 'Must We Shoot from the Hip?' Brodie writes:

> For the purpose of the present discussion we are not concerned with moral considerations per se. Agreed that no one wants to kill people *uselessly*, and that the war we are talking about would be one in which the stake is nothing less than sheer survival,

the question [is] whether we should maximize, minimize, or disregard human casualties in our strategic bombing campaign ... where the sole criterion is whether we
thereby help or hinder our program towards victory and the achievement of our
national objectives.[21] [emphasis added]

The idea that strategists and militarists would countenance killing people 'useless-
ly' is particularly chilling. In a description that today echoes, but actually precedes,
Strangelove's rhetoric, Brodie says 'a corpse presents no problems other than dispos-
al. All his anxieties are liquidated as are those of his family concerning him. Liquidated
too are all his potential hostilities to the regime which governs him. A corpse makes
no demand for food or shelter.'[22] This resonates strongly with the (Kahnian) tenor of
Strangelove's War Room dialogue. Responding to President Muffley's concern that survivors would 'envy the dead', a direct reference to Kahn's *On Thermonuclear War*, the
Doctor explains with enthusiasm when detailing the post-holocaust environment (his
right arm Nazi-saluting uncontrollably):

> when zey go down into zee mine everyone vould still be alive. Zere vould be no
> shocking memories, and zee prevailing emotion vill be one of *nostalgia* for those left
> behind, combined with a spirit of *bold curiosity* for zee adventure ahead!

Nevertheless, Brodie concludes his article by observing that great benefit will come
from making an effort to spare civilian populations from 'indiscriminate' nuclear annihilation, although still couched in the rhetoric of equivocation: 'If we do not know that it is
a bad thing to kill Russians indiscriminately, that is not the same as saying that we know
it to be a good thing.' Brodie adds that 'it might be a very important factor in helping us
to decide such problems as whether the centers of cities or industrial concentrations
within cities' should be targeted for attack. Writing three years before the first testing of
the more powerful hydrogen bomb, Brodie concludes indifferently that post-war Russia
appears as a 'perfect setup' for an attack 'which exploits psychological weapons', adding
that 'the atomic bomb looks like the perfect weapon for psychological exploitation. Why
not bring these two things together?'

Kubrick's second-named strategist, Henry Kissinger (1923–) is best known for
his role as National Security Advisor, and his consecutive appointments as Secretary
of State to Presidents Richard Nixon and Gerald Ford, from 1969–1977. During this
period, he oversaw foreign relation interventions such as the secret bombing of Laos
and Cambodia, détente with the Soviets and rapprochement with the Chinese, the Paris
peace accord, the overthrow of Allende government in Chile and the Yom Kippur War.

Born in Bavaria to Jewish parents he fled to London with his family in 1938 before quickly relocating to New York. He became a US citizen in 1943, was drafted into the Army, and posted to military intelligence due to fluency in his native German language. Kissinger saw combat at the Battle of the Bulge and by war's end was involved in denazification programmes as a counter intelligence officer. He returned to the US and completed his undergraduate degree at Harvard University in 1950, followed by his Masters and PhD in 1951 and 1954. While at Harvard, Kissinger published and lectured on foreign affairs and nuclear strategy and co-founded the Center for International Affairs. From 1954 he acted as a consultant to numerous think tanks and government agencies such as the Operations Research Office, the National Security Council, the Council on Foreign Relations, the Arms Control and Disarmament Agency, the Department of State and the RAND Corporation.

According to Christiane Kubrick the writings of Henry Kissinger were quite familiar to her husband: 'Stanley read a lot of the stuff that Kissinger wrote', she confirmed.[23] Nevertheless, most Kubrick scholars dismiss any real likelihood of Kissinger having much influence on, let alone being a role model for Strangelove due to the assumed marginality and relative obscurity of the professor. However, the filmmaker *explicitly* names Kissinger amongst the handful of strategists he foregrounds in his first letter to Peter George. By the time of that November 1961 missive, Kissinger was already on John F. Kennedy's staff, publicly announced as a special advisor (on foreign affairs).[24]

Kissinger's 1957 book *Nuclear Weapons and Foreign Policy* created a storm upon its release, especially his advocacy of the concept of 'limited' nuclear war. The young Harvard associate professor made several appearances on national television profiles, interviewed for CBS's *Face the Nation* in 1957 and *The Mike Wallace Interview* on ABC the next year discussing the limitations of the doctrine of massive retaliation. He was hardly invisible to Americans interested in current affairs, or like Kubrick, those New Yorkers increasingly concerned with life in the thermonuclear age.

In a media release dated 27 February 1961 the Kennedy administration announced Kissinger's appointment as 'a part-time consultant' to the President, noting the Harvard professor would 'work in the area of national security problems on specific questions on which the White House asks for his views'. His contract designated him as a consultant to the National Security Council and enabled him to retain his academic role at Harvard University while working for government.[25] Overseen by Kennedy's National Security Advisor, McGeorge Bundy, Kissinger's appointment led to a number of projects for the Administration. Given his wartime intelligence work Kissinger was especially useful in providing advice on Germany and the Four Powers stalemate in post-war Berlin. And it was the Berlin Crisis that served as the catalyst for Kubrick's final motivation to make a film on the nuclear episteme.

Two reports written by Kissinger for JFK broach the issue of nuclear war and Berlin, but Kissinger resigned from his role just prior to the Cuban Missile Crisis, so was not a part of the Administration's deliberations in the matter. In the years and decades following the release of *Dr. Strangelove* the public stature and notoriety of Kissinger grew larger and more problematic, with some commentators such as Christopher Hitchens calling for the former Secretary of State to be tried as a war criminal.[26] In a classic case of life imitating art, Tony Frewin recalls that Kubrick felt, in retrospect, 'the person that *Dr. Strangelove* presaged ... was Henry Kissinger, right down to Henry's mannerisms and speech'.[27]

Nevertheless, Kissinger does make the briefest and most tangential appearance in the film. The *Playboy* centerfold that Major Kong ogles inside the B-52 depicts 'Miss Foreign Affairs' (Tracy Reed), the very same 'secretary' that Buck Turgidson entertains in a Washington hotel room and who fields the General's incoming calls. In the *Playboy* spread a copy of *Foreign Affairs* magazine is strategically draped across her buttocks, leaving her otherwise naked. The cover of this January 1963 edition, used as a cheesecake prop, featured a major article, 'Strains on the Alliance' by Kissinger, concerning the difficulties facing the trans-Atlantic partnership and NATO, and mistrust by European allies in American negotiations over the Berlin Crisis.[28] This *Foreign Affairs* centrefold image also became central to several iterations of the studio's international marketing campaign, on posters and lobby cards, ironically in 'allied' territories such as Germany and Italy.

However, the third strategist named by Kubrick, and the one most commonly identified with the fictitious persona of Dr. Strangelove, is Herman Kahn.[29] Born a generation later than most of his strategist and scientist peers, Kahn was raised in the Bronx, like Kubrick, and came from a Jewish, East European immigrant heritage. Kahn majored in physics at UCLA, eventually gaining a B.Sc and then a M.Sc after the war, where he was stationed as an Army linesman in Burma monitoring transmissions on the Chunking wire. It was his physicist friend and subsequent inventor of the neutron bomb, Sam Cohen, who invited Kahn to join RAND Corp. He later worked with Edward Teller, John von Neumann and Albert Wohlstetter on thermonuclear weapons development before concentrating on military and nuclear strategy, chiefly advising the US Air Force.

As Fred Kaplan notes, Kahn was an imposing presence, partly because of his huge physical bulk, and nothing like the lean and shriveled, wheelchair-bound Strangelove. At his numerous military seminars Kahn would loom before a podium, with

> briefing stands at either side of him, flipping one chart over another, talking at a maddeningly fast pace, interjecting jokes, chuckling, pointing to charts, tables, graphs comparing the number of fatalities under various wartime conditions, illustrated under such captions as 'Will the Survivors Envy the Dead?' and 'Tragic but

Distinguishable Postwar States'.[30]

From these late 1950s lectures Kahn distilled his infamous and influential work *On Thermonuclear War*. The discourse Kahn deploys throughout the work is deliberate, precise and profoundly amoral. As Kaplan observes, some of the dialogue in *Strangelove* seems 'virtually lifted' from the pages of Kahn's nuclear age treatise, and several military and strategic studies 'insiders' felt the film's eponymous character was a clear 'parody' of Kahn.[31]

Kahn was well known to Peter George and Stanley Kubrick for some time before their collaboration commenced on what became *Dr. Strangelove*. Both men had independently followed Kahn's work, although George's fiction drew him to Kahn's attention prior to Kubrick's cautious solicitation of the British author in November 1961. As we have seen, Kubrick's initial three-page letter to George added a brief postscript:

> I suppose you know that Herman Kahn mentions you and 'Red Alert' in his book 'On Thermonuclear War'.

Indeed, Kahn had written to George in 1960, expressing his enthusiasm for *Red Alert* telling the British author that 'virtually every American strategist I know has read your book ... and most of us hand out copies to people'. Kahn's endorsement and note about the book's wide circulation was later deployed as evidence in the statement George made when issuing plagiarism proceedings against *Fail-Safe* authors Burdick and Wheeler and their American and British publishers (see chapter three).

Although Kahn had been in touch with Peter George, Kubrick's wife Christiane recalls that it was actor Paul Newman who introduced Kahn to Stanley after Newman had read *On Thermonuclear War*. Christiane affirms that her husband had several meetings with Herman Kahn during the development of the project, with Kahn expounding to Stanley in '*gory* detail'.[32]

> Herman Kahn was *the* most terrifying person because he had abstracted all his theories, which were so mathematical and so on the button. And he had so many theories, so many numbers, and scenarios, to throw at you. And he would always have a whole palette of 'what ifs' that were interwoven into 'this could happen' that way or that way or that way, and there were always fifty varieties of how it would definitely happen. And with his very fast speech and his tremendous logic and memory for numbers ... we understood everything for – or I should speak for myself – I could grasp onto some of his theories maybe for twenty seconds and then my brain would collapse!

According to Sharon Ghamari-Tabrizi in her comprehensive and compelling *The Worlds of*

Herman Kahn, the strategist liked Kubrick and George's film and found it amusing, but seemingly chided the producer-director-co-writer for royalties, given the free use of his intellectual property. Kubrick flatly refused and reportedly told Kahn: 'It doesn't work that way.'[33] Kahn wrote to George from the Hudson Institute in March 1964, a week after he had seen *Dr. Strangelove* with his wife Jane, where the pair joined Kubrick for dinner after the show:

> To our surprise we both liked the picture enormously though I personally felt that the character of Dr. Strangelove was too surrealistic and in a way too obvious. I would have probably been much more aggravated but I think the picture would have been improved if you had the Strangelove part played by a distinguished looking grey-haired scientist who jarred the audience with his cold-blooded analycity and his obvious detachment, rather than an ex-Nazi obviously at war with himself. My net reaction to the picture as a social document as opposed to a movie is that it is basically anti-American, anti-Russian, and in some sense, anti-human; that is, it portrays human beings as they may probably be, but one cannot take great pleasure in it. I am thinking particularly of the actions in the last scene including the Soviet ambassadors photographing of the war room.[34]

Despite expressing these caveats, Kahn 'found it an enormously moving and entertaining picture and was in every way impressed'.[35]

During development and production the Kubricks met with Kahn in his hotel rooms or in restaurants. He never visited the Kubricks at home, something that was mutually agreeable to Christiane and Stanley. 'I think he was not a man who particularly wanted small children', she recalled, 'and we often didn't want our children to be there, listening to what he had to say.' The conversations would be gruelling. 'First of all he's a man who spoke easily ten times faster than most people. So you'd be totally riveted to what he would say, between bites, as it were. And we would go home shattered from meetings with him.' Her memories of the encounters with Kahn are still lucid and those memories remain sobering:

> You know that state when you wake up from a bad nightmare and you can't quite shake the feeling of it? Talking to him, you would walk away very depressed. Very convinced – like you are of a dream – we're going to *fry* any minute. And slowly the fog would lift and you would go back to your happy head-in-the-sand state. And I remember each meeting had that affect.[36]

The other vivid impression that Kahn left on the Kubricks was his physique: 'I remember observing this very strange man – being so self-destructive, you know, to be so enormous. The very peculiar combination of somebody so intelligent … he died very young – obviously that comes from weighing 600 pounds. But, yeah, what a "phenomenon".'

Their encounters with Kahn were both enriching and intellectually intimidating:

> I thought this man's brain has obviously run away from him a long time ago. He could think so fast. And he must have been so isolated from the rest of the world. Can you imagine being that much more intelligent than everybody else? Which he was. And at first it struck me a little bit like *Rain Man*, you know. A savant. [...] He just was that much more intelligent than other people. He could think that much faster than other people because he could speak that much faster than other people, and had this all round total recall of absolutely everything – a memory, I mean, just a much bigger computer. And we would sit there astonished. How boring it must be for him, sitting with two golden retrievers and trying to explain mathematical truths to them! That's what we both felt like, you know … in fact I think he slowed down considerably for us just so he had company. But that's what we felt. Sort of sitting up and trying to understand *desperately*.[37]

Despite the appalling context and content of Kahn and other nuclear strategists' projection of monstrous casualties and fatalities from global thermonuclear war, Kubrick embraced the subject matter. Yet, as Christiane relates, often the works of scientists, alongside Kahn and other strategists, were baffling, dense and sometimes impenetrable. She recognised that despite Kubrick's personal prowess in maths and physics, he would 'very often sit and think: "I've read this ten times and I still haven't understood it".' The experience was a challenging one but the subject matter impelled Kubrick towards deeper comprehension in order to translate the complex and abstract concepts for a general audience. According to Christiane, Stanley asked Kahn and other specialists to

> translate it into idiot language for him, and then had a huge grasp on it. And then he'd try to explain it to other people, and he said, 'often while I'm explaining it to other people I realise I *still* don't understand!' He wasn't at all arrogant, he really *tried* to understand how it all hangs together. And he said 'if I find it *that* difficult, how *impossible* it is going to be [...] How would anybody understand? If I brood over one chapter all night and still don't get it, how can you *popularise* it, how can you explain it to the people?' You cannot, it's too complex. And that's terrifying.[38]

Nevertheless, such sustained textual and discursive encounters with 'megadeaths' and 'overkill' led to unexpected outcomes. After a meeting with Kahn, for example, the

Kubricks would find themselves drifting into uncontrollable gallows humour, which no doubt served to reinforce the director's later creative decision to embrace black comedy as the natural medium for engaging with the apocalyptic paradox of the nuclear age. In the car on the way home Stanley and Christiane would pause and check each other. Barely suppressing giggles they would enquire: 'Isn't that what he said?' 'No, no, he said a different number...' 'I think he said that...' and become increasingly terrified. Christiane relates, 'it was nervous laughter' and the more Stanley read he would say:

> 'I know it's not funny. [laughing]. It really isn't funny', and laugh his head off! And he said that's what people do when ... it's too overwhelming, you get the giggles, if you're lucky. And this is never true of direct physical danger, you don't laugh a bit.[39]

Tony Frewin, Stanley Kubrick's personal assistant from 1965–68 and 1979–99, recalls that, post-*Strangelove*, the filmmaker mentioned Kahn and *On Thermonuclear War* 'a few times', suggesting that they sent the occasional cordial note to one another: 'It disturbed [Stanley] that one could talk "rationally" about acceptable deaths, megadeaths, and so on.' Nevertheless, Kahn was always considered 'very much on the side-lines of American politics'.[40]

Ultimately, as Fred Kaplan observes in *The Wizards of Armageddon*, 'Kahn's specialty was to express the RAND conventional wisdom in the most provocative and outrageous fashion imaginable'. This witty, irreverent, 'rolly-polly' strategist, dubbed a 'thermonuclear Zero Mostel', also adopted Bernard Brodie's internal RAND memo comparing US war plans with sex. Brodie had described a SAC plan to withhold bombing urban-industrial sites as equating to *coitus interruptus,* or withdrawal before ejaculation, just as General Ripper would describe denying women his 'life essence'. Brodie further considered the overwhelming and monolithic SAC war plan (LeMay's 'Sunday punch') as 'like going all the way' with a corresponding 'quick and messy climax' (Zellen 2009).[41] Adapting Brodie's sentiment, Kahn had the audacity to tell SAC officers contemplating their massive nuclear strike in the late 1950s, 'Gentlemen, you don't have a war plan, you have a war orgasm', or *wargasm*, as the anecdote has become popularly known.[42] While simultaneously fascinating and appalling, such thanatological expositions met their logical and artistic match in the scenario conceived by Kubrick and George – and in particular, Terry Southern's outré dialogue and Sellers' grotesque improvisations, discourse that the director encouraged his collaborators to contribute and push to its conceivable limits.

Kubrick's last-named nuclear strategist is Oskar Morgenstern, born in Germany in 1902 and raised in Vienna, where he attended university and gained a PhD in political science. After winning a three-year Rockefeller Foundation fellowship he became a professor of economics at the University of Vienna and was greatly influenced by the mathematical modeling of John von Neumann and its potential application to economic theory. After visiting Princeton University in 1938 Morgenstern chose to remain in the US as fascism spread throughout Europe. Increasing his collaboration with von Neumann at the Institute for Advanced Studies in Princeton, the pair pioneered economic game theory and co-authored *The Theory of Games and Economic Behavior* in 1944. He became an American citizen that same year.

Like von Neumann, Morgenstern was employed as a consultant to RAND Corp. throughout the 1950s. An abiding career interest, most pronounced throughout the Cold War, was his striving to develop scientific theories of economics whereby government and industry could rationally plan for sustained outputs in pre- and post-nuclear war environments. In 1959, he espoused the establishment of an American 'sub economy', one literally *sub*-terranean. After World War II the US government had sequestered into a National Stockpile billions of dollars worth of metals and other resources in case of future war or national disaster. Once the Soviets acquired the atom bomb and then matched the US with hydrogen weapons and delivery technologies, many strategists and scientists advocated for medical and emergency supplies to be warehoused in the event of nuclear war.[43] By 1956, for example, Edward Teller offered the ludicrously optimistic and implausible estimate that by sheltering people deep underground, along with power plants and machinery, a significant percentage of the US economy could be 'rebuilt within a year'.[44] Even Doctor Strangelove had to pause momentarily in order to estimate that the libidinous mineshaft survivors would take 'twenty years' to re-establish the then current gross domestic product.

In 1959, Morgenstern published his influential, though pessimistic, *A Question of National Defense*, suggesting the chance of thermonuclear war occurring was greater than fifty percent. Given this prognosis Morgenstern proposed, as would Strangelove, that a 'portion of American industry, including machine-tool plants, nuclear power facilities, and pharmaceutical industries, as well as hospitals and refineries' should be 'installed permanently underground'.[45]

The Princeton economist was also a strong public advocate of a national fallout shelter programme, something championed by the Kennedy Administration only a short time later. However, in *A Question of National Defense* the RAND consultant candidly observed of senior defense officials – in contradistinction to how General Ripper quotes Clausewitz to deride 'politicians' in *Dr. Strangelove* – 'Military matters have become so complex and involved that the ordinary experience and training of generals and admirals [are] no longer sufficient to master the problems.'[46] In essence, according to Morgenstern, in the nuclear age, war should be left to the strategists.

One other, major Cold War nuclear strategist is worth considering as a primary influence on *Dr. Strangelove*. Although unnamed by Kubrick in his letter to George, Albert

Wohlstetter (1913–??) is an important figure, and as yet unrecognized in the Strangelove literature. Wohlstetter was a mathematician, logician and senior staff member at RAND in the 1950s and 1960s. He became one of America's leading post-war security strategists and his work developed the key concepts of 'second-strike' and 'fail-safe', ideas that greatly informed Cold War debates about nuclear deterrence and efforts to reduce the probability of accidental war.

Most germane to *Dr. Strangelove* was Wohlstetter's 1958 RAND report *The Delicate Balance of Terror*. This was the title that formed the basis of the earliest treatment and script, initially outlined by Kubrick and James B. Harris in October 1961, and then written with Peter George from early January 1962.[47] In his report, later reprinted in the January 1959 issue of *Foreign Affairs*, Wohlstetter warns how accidents, miscalculation or – importantly and euphemistically – 'aberrations of individuals, perhaps, quite low in the echelon of command' could lead to global nuclear war. Combined with the (then new) safeguarded 'fail-safe' process for nuclear armed B-52 bombers on constant airborne alert, Wohlstetter foregrounded the vital necessity of any deterrence posture to both minimise accidents and limit susceptibly to a Soviet first strike:

> One of the principles of selecting a [deterrence] strategy should be to reduce the chance of accident, wherever we can, without a corresponding increase in vulnerability to a rational surprise attack. [...] This is the significance of the recently adopted 'fail-safe' procedures for launching SAC. [...] Such a procedure requires that bombers, flushed by some serious yet not unambiguous warning, return to base unless they are specifically directed to continue forward ... in case of a false alarm and a failure in communications, the single bomber or handful of bombers that did not receive the message to return to base might, as a result of this mistake, go forward by themselves to start the war.[48]

This scenario is precisely what constitutes the plot of *Dr. Strangelove* and the unauthorised command from General Ripper for his B-52 wing to attack targets inside Russia. As Wohlstetter drolly understates, 'of all the many poor ways to start a war, this would be perhaps the worst'.[49] What the RAND strategist understood fully well at the time was that such a deterrence mechanism could, at best, only provide an aggressor nation additional time:

> While 'fail-safe' or, as it is now less descriptively called, 'positive control' is of great importance, it by no means eliminates the possibility of accident. While it can reduce the chance of miscalculation by governments somewhat by extending the period of final commitment, this possibility nonetheless remains.[50]

In Wohlstetter's calculation such a pause becomes an *inevitable* course of action, leading to 'final commitment'. For General Jack D. Ripper, it is not 'accident' or 'miscalculation' that sends his wing past their fail-safe points but the paranoiac Air Force General's *deliberate* breach of Presidential chain of command, initiating what Ripper believes will be an *irrevocable* course of action, requiring 'total commitment' from SAC in order to avoid an annihilating 'red retaliation'.

While an analyst at RAND, Wohlstetter wielded a powerful influence on US foreign policy throughout the Cold War. Biographer Craig Unger suggests that by the mid-1960s he was known as a 'mad genius', 'collecting and molding young minds to follow in his footsteps'.[51] Hence, Unger maintains, Wohlstetter was one of several analysts who became 'a model' for Kubrick, given he introduced dramatic phrases (such as 'fail-safe' and 'second strike') into the US nuclear lexicon, while he lobbied constantly to increase American military spending. According to Unger to be onside with Wohlstetter, 'one had to embrace unquestioningly his worldviews, which eschewed old-fashioned intelligence as a basis for assessing the enemy's intentions and military capabilities in favor of elaborate statistical models, probabilities, reasoning, systems analysis, and game theory developed at RAND'.

Post-*Strangelove*, while a professor at the University of Chicago, Wohlstetter gathered a firebrand of young, right-wing intellectuals around him, such as Richard Perle and Paul Wolfowitz, and he helped establish a generation on neo-conservatives still influential today. Many of these acolytes adopted the same, aggressive strategic ideology of pre-emption, common to John von Neumann, Edward Teller and Wohlstetter during the Cold War. As one contemporary Wohlstetter disciple more recently pronounced, echoing the earlier generation of RAND strategists: 'If you look down the road and see a war with, say, China, twenty years off, go to war now.'[52]

'KNOWING SIN' – THE NUCLEAR SCIENTISTS

While Kubrick does not specifically mention scientists in his letter to George, the works by these notable public figures were amongst his extensive research library of nuclear related books, journals and magazines. The shock revelation of the atom bombing of Japan suddenly and collectively thrust the secret work of physicists, mathematicians, chemists and engineers into the public spotlight in a manner hitherto unknown. Promoted by an eager international press hungry for compelling stories of Allied victory, almost overnight these backroom scientists (predominantly men) became heroes around the world. And yet, their sudden elevation into the pantheon of wartime champions was tinged with centuries-old suspicions of the amoral pursuit by scientists of knowledge above all else. These cross-cultural narratives ranged from the classical

German legend of necromancer Dr. Faustus selling his soul to the devil (reworked by Marlow, Goethe, Mann and Murnau), to the later, demented or duplicitous scientists toying with mortality and the fabric of the universe, such as Dr. Frankenstein, Dr. Moreau, Dr. Jekyll, Dr. Caligari and Dr. Cyclops.[53]

Amid the adulation for the Manhattan Project scientists, after the war also came reproach, some of it self-inflicted. Reflecting on his Promethean accomplishment, J. Robert J. Oppenheimer said unambiguously that the atom bomb 'was shit' and that the physicists had 'known sin', perhaps as a corollary to his original thought at witnessing the Trinity detonation – of Vishnu becoming 'the destroyer of worlds'. Freeman Dyson further qualified Oppenheimer's assertion:

> The sin of the physicists ... did not lie in their having built a lethal weapon, they did not just build the bomb. They enjoyed building it. They had the best time of their lives building it. That, I believe, is what Oppenheimer had in mind when he said that they had sinned.[54]

Other scientists, many paradoxically conflicted by sheer joy at their success and the immediate apocalyptic ramifications of their work, were more damning. The director of the Trinity project, Kenneth Bainbridge, said at the time: 'Now we are all sons of bitches.'[55] Bainbridge later explained to Oppenheimer that his statement expressed the concern that posterity would judge the Bomb scientists harshly: 'as the creation of an unspeakable weapon by unfeeling people'. Bainbridge added 'that the weapon was terrible and those who contributed to its development must share in any condemnation of it'.[56] Upon seeing photographs and film of the destruction of Hiroshima and Nagasaki, many of the scientists were mortified. As Joel Shurkin has noted, a large quantity of the key scientists working on the bomb project were

> Jewish refugees from Hitler, and while they saw Japan as the enemy of their adopted country, they did not have the same moral outrage against Japan as they did against Nazi Germany. Some also worried about the morality of dropping the atomic bomb on a civilian target without warning.[57]

Leo Szilard, who had convinced Einstein in August 1939 to sign a letter to warn President Roosevelt of German nuclear developments, quickly drafted and circulated a petition on 3 July 1945 opposing the impending atomic strike on Japan. The letter to President Truman, created two weeks before the Trinity test in New Mexico and a full month prior to the A-bombings, was eventually signed by 69 scientists 'working in the field of atomic power'. It requested that Truman exercise his 'power as Commander-in-Chief to rule that the United States shall not, in the present phase of the war, resort to the use of atomic bombs'.[58]

However, not all important Manhattan Project team members showed such scruples. Among the primary candidates of scientists considered influential in the development of the Dr. Strangelove persona is John von Neumann, a brilliant mathematician, polymath and pioneering computer scientist who was wheelchair-bound later in life. Born in Hungary in 1903 von Neumann, or 'Johnny' as he was commonly called, was the son of a successful Budapest banker. As a child he was celebrated for his photographic memory, a capacity that would serve him well in life both as a mathematician and reciter of an innumerable jokes. After graduating from high school, von Neumann studied in Berlin and Zurich and undertook a PhD in mathematics at the University of Budapest. In 1929, he accepted an invitation to attend Princeton University and in 1933 became one of the first, and youngest, professors in the newly-founded Institute for Advanced Study. In 1937 he became a United States citizen.

A lover of games and toys, von Neumann began to develop ideas and principles that would lead to his pioneering studies in Game Theory in collaboration with Oskar Morgenstern. The card game of poker fascinated von Neumann but he understood that probability alone could not be the sole defining characteristic of such game play, so he attempted to define the concept and processes of 'bluffing' as a strategy of deception to fool opponents and leverage advantage.

In 1943, von Neumann was invited to work on the Manhattan Project where he produced crucial calculations on the implosion design for the atomic bomb, allowing for a more efficient and powerful weapon. Von Neumann's mathematical models were applied to Air Force bombing runs to minimise their attrition rates. He also helped select the top secret locations in Japan to bomb, including potential targets for the A-bomb. As a member of the Target Committee von Neumann appreciated the psychological implications of the new bomb, as well as its physical characteristics, overseeing computations for the anticipated bomb yield and blast effects, the expected death tolls, and calculating precisely the altitude above ground that the detonation should occur in order to maximise and compound its effect.[59]

Based on *Kriegspiel*, a chess-like game he played as a child, von Neumann extended the application of Game Theory beyond economics towards governmental, political and military simulations. He created new methodologies to trial Cold War action/reaction between the superpowers, modelled as adversaries in a zero-sum game. In 1948, von Neumann was appointed a consultant to the Air Force and RAND Corp. to game the possibilities of nuclear war and detail strategies to initiate, respond to, or prevent it. According to William Poundstone, von Neumann's major contribution in the post-war years was his development of the digital computer.[60] Building on his successful upgrading of the

US Army's Electronic Numerical Integrator and Computer (ENIAC) during the war, von Neumann improved the computer's logic design, helping the US Navy and other sources to more accurately predict weather patterns.

He subsequently produced a set of calculations fundamental for the successful testing of the hydrogen bomb after co-designing the appropriately named MANIAC (Mathematical Analyzer Numerical Integrator and Computer). Von Neumann subsequently helped design the multi-billion dollar Semi-Automatic Ground Environment (SAGE) computer system, programmed to detect a Soviet nuclear attack, which became the backbone of SAC and the North American Air Defense Command (NORAD)'s automated defense systems from the 1950s to the 1980s. From 1951, von Neumann was a regular consultant to government, including the recently established Central Intelligence Agency, until the time of his premature death in 1957 at age 53. In 1955 Dwight Eisenhower appointed him an Atomic Energy Commissioner around the same time damning testimony from Edward Teller contributed to Robert J. Oppenheimer losing his security clearance and AEC appointment. In 1955, von Neumann contracted bone cancer, quite possibly as a result from fallout exposure as a scientific observer at the Bikini Atoll atomic tests in July 1946.[61]

Several commentators have noted that von Neumann had his quirks, including bouts of heavy drinking. He was also 'an aggressive and reckless driver, supposedly totaling a car every year or so'.[62] Johnny became so notorious as a motorist that one Princeton intersection was nicknamed 'von Neumann corner' due to his multiple accidents there. More bizarrely, colleagues were alarmed at von Neumann's habit of visually appraising any new office secretary by bending 'way, way over, more or less trying to look up' their dresses.[63] Some female employees were so bothered by von Neumann's intrusive behaviour that they put cardboard partitions at the front of their desks to block his view.

Von Neumann was no shrinking violet when it came to concepts of pre-emptive nuclear attack, which made him even more popular amongst senior Air Force officials. He publicly described himself as 'violently anti-communist' noting that he was a 'good deal more militant' than most.[64] During the first decade of the Cold War von Neumann became an unfailing advocate of 'preventive war'. Unlike many of his contemporaries in the defence establishment throughout World War II he believed that Soviet espionage agents would *inevitably* discover key elements of the Allied bomb design and ultimately rival America as a competing nuclear power. He deduced that if the Soviet Union were permitted to build a nuclear arsenal, then an atomic war would be unpreventable. Hence, von Neumann was a strident and consistent exponent in recommending a *pre-emptive* nuclear strike on Russia in order to eliminate the nascent threat of post-war global communism and to prevent a calamitous future war should the Soviets acquire nuclear parity with America. According to Janet Chen *et al.*, one of von Neumann's famous quotes, spoken with a noticeable Hungarian accent, was:

> With the Russians it is not a question of whether but of when. [...] If you say why not bomb them tomorrow, I say, why not today? If you say today at five o'clock, I say why not one o'clock?[65]

Dale Carter has demonstrated how the increasing strategic reliance on thermonuclear weapons and their sophisticated systems of delivery shifted funding away from air superiority toward ballistic missiles.[66] Within a mere five years (1952–57) a vast acceleration of American industrial development produced Boeing's B-52 for the Strategic Air Command alongside the first supersonic fighter plane, the F-100. The US Navy launched the atomic-powered *Nautilus* submarine and DuPont built hydrogen bombs for the newly-merged, inter-service Defense Department, which exploded them at the Pacific testing grounds. At the same time, the US Air Force long-range rocket study group, led by von Neumann, concluded that ballistic missiles were 'not only feasible but unstoppable, apocalyptic, and therefore essential'. This posture reoriented American investment in rocketry to colossal heights, far outstripping procurements of new jet bombers and fighter aircraft.[67] President Eisenhower approved the highest national priority for ICBM and IRBM missiles and submarine launched missiles (SLBMs).

Biographer Stephen Wolfram suggests von Neumann was deeply flattered to be constantly called upon by the military and White House to undertake nuclear and defense consulting:

> He certainly treated the government with considerably more respect than many other scientists of his day. [...] Nevertheless, von Neumann's military consulting involvements left some factions quite negative about him. It's sometimes said, for example, that von Neumann might have been the model for the sinister Dr. Strangelove character in Stanley Kubrick's movie of that name.[68]

Indeed, as Wolfram points out, amplifying the allusion to Strangelove, von Neumann was in a wheelchair during the last year of his life. Yet despite his terminal illness, von Neumann continued to advise the Eisenhower administration and military officials, being shuttled about Washington DC and elsewhere in limousines. One colleague described how, despite suffering from cancer, he continued his gruelling appointment schedule with the Air Force and Pentagon staff, arranging meetings and then being 'propelled' into venues in his wheelchair, pushed from behind by a 'military aide'.[69] Another factor resonating with Strangelove was von Neumann's prominent Hungarian accent – a notable feature of 'otherness' that served to stereotype many pre-war scientific émi-grés, such as Albert Einstein. In his study of five major Hungarian scientists (nicknamed 'the Martians') who immigrated to America, Istvan Hargittai argues that World War II 'transformed the relationship between scientists and the elected leaders of the United States' for the better:

> People who were often timid foreigners or recently admitted new citizens before the war now emerged as esteemed advisors for the most powerful decision-makers ... what a change it was compared with their experiences in Hungary and Germany. Even in the United States some of them had been considered at times to be unruly foreigners with crazy ideas and impossible accents. After the war, foreign accents became respectable when scientists had them'.[70]

While some observers recall that von Neumann's Hungarian accent was 'charming' others suggest he 'carefully preserved certain mispronunciations' – artificially – as deliberate affectations to play on expectations.[71] As with Sellers' performances, von Neumann consciously acted the part and he played to an audience, including politicians and the military, just as he was fondly regarded as the 'life of the party' around Princeton.

While mostly working in think tanks and government agencies, von Neumann's last year was a highly visible one given that he was the recipient of three publicly announced awards. Firstly, he received the prestigious 1956 Albert Einstein Commemorative Award, followed by the $50,000 Enrico Fermi Award for his 'contributions to the design and construction of computing machines used in nuclear research and development'. The third accolade was perhaps his most treasured, the US Medal of Freedom, awarded 'for exceptional meritorious service in promoting the scientific progress of this country's armament program'.[72] Press photos of the time showed President Eisenhower bending down to present the medal to the wheelchair-bound scientist. Eisenhower paid tribute to von Neumann's 'rare and great gifts of mind' which he applied to 'the defense of his adopted land and the cause of freedom'.[73]

However, within a few months John von Neumann had slipped into a physical and mental state that greatly disturbed his friends and associates. Ensconced in a secure wing of the Walter Reed Hospital in Washington DC, von Neumann continued to liaise with Pentagon, Atomic Energy Commission and Defense Department officials from his sickbed. Former Los Alamos colleague, Edward Teller, was particularly distressed at the sight of his old friend crippled by cognitive impairment and rambling erratically in his final days.[74] According to one von Neumann biographer, the scientist underwent a complete psychological breakdown with panic attacks, and screaming in uncontrollable terror every night.[75] Teller later recalled, 'I think that von Neumann suffered more when

John von Neumann, in his wheelchair, receiving the 1956 US Medal of Freedom from President Dwight Eisenhower. (US National Archives)

his mind would no longer function, than I have ever seen any human being suffer'. In his dying days von Neumann's brother, Michael, read passages of Goethe's *Faust* to the barely conscious scientist. So concerned was the military that von Neumann might babble top secret national security information in his heavily medicated delirium that the Air Force posted a 24-hour guard at his door.[76]

The scientist most prominent in the public eye and who remains mostly closely associated with Dr. Strangelove is Edward Teller. Born into a wealthy Jewish family in Budapest, Teller completed school in Hungary before undertaking studies in chemical engineering in Germany and later earning his PhD in physical chemistry. Teller specialised in atomic physics and studied under Niels Bohr in Copenhagen before marrying and emigrating to the USA in 1935, where he taught at George Washington University. Teller became a US citizen in 1941 and soon joined Enrico Fermi's group at the University of Chicago working on the first atomic pile to create a sustainable nuclear chain reaction. He was subsequently invited by Robert J. Oppenheimer to join the Manhattan Project's theoretical planning group in Berkeley before travelling to New Mexico and the secret Los Alamos laboratory in 1943.

According to Manhattan Project physicist Robert Serber, Teller's office in Los Alamos had a large blackboard that listed ideas for all kinds of nuclear weapons, with the largest device designated 'Backyard', named thus since the bomb would 'probably kill every-one on earth, there was no use carting it elsewhere'.[77] This theoretical wartime chalk drawing ultimately evolved into a serious proposal by Teller in 1950 to build a thousand-megaton hydrogen bomb, or gigaton bomb. At the time — only a year after the Soviets exploded their first atomic bomb, and six years after Trinity, Hiroshima and Nagasaki — a controversial debate raged internationally concerning American moves to develop an H-bomb, vastly more powerful than the existing atomic weapons. As the chief proponent and advocate, Teller ultimately convinced Congress to fund the development and testing of the 'Super' weapon, or 'Hell-bomb' as it was popularly described by the media.

Teller's interests in pushing the science of nuclear weapons to their extremes occa-sionally aligned with former Nazi rocket scientist Wernher von Braun's fantasies of space travel. For instance, once the Americans developed an ICBM of sufficient thrust, in order to catch up with Sputnik, Teller thought it would be nice to aim one at the moon and explode a nuclear bomb on its pristine surface. Teller argued that this would clearly demonstrate US technological prowess while providing some atomic pyrotechnics for half the planet (especially the Soviets) to observe, creating an American propaganda coup.[78] Although the Air Force rejected the idea it approved Teller's proposed series of nuclear detonations in near space a few years later. One test, designated Starfish Prime, was conducted on 9 July 1962, just as Kubrick and George were wrapping up their comic version of the *Strangelove* script. After blasting off from the Johnston Atoll, the Thor mis-sile's 1.4 megaton warhead was detonated 400km above the Pacific generating a huge, artificial atomic aurora glowing red from the massive radioactive discharge.[79] The explo-sion also created an electromagnetic pulse (EMP) of unexpected strength that blew out hundreds of street lamps, caused telephone outages and disrupted the electronics of planes in flight and radio communication hundreds of kilometres away in Hawaii.[80]

Such schemes cemented in the public's view Teller's idiosyncratic, if not idiotic, nuclear zeal, where he never met a thermonuclear device he didn't like nor missed an opportunity to rail against nuclear arms control. In the time leading up to and during the Manhattan Project, Teller was mostly regarded as an affable if sometimes intellectually combative colleague. He was also a key and sometimes big player in major historical events. An example of both was Teller driving fellow Hungarian scientist Leo Szilard to meet Albert Einstein on Long Island in July 1939 in order for Einstein to sign Szilard's draft letter to President Roosevelt, the document initiating America's ultra-secret A-bomb project.[81] With the defeat of the Nazis in Germany, and the end of war in Europe, Teller became (self-)identified as amongst those scientists expressing qualms at the proposed atomic attack on Japan, especially without warning. However, Teller's Stanford University colleague, historian Barton Bernstein, has debunked this myth by revealing that Teller refused to 'protest' the bombing, and in a letter to Szilard the day before the petition was drafted, Teller wrote that use of the atomic bomb in combat 'might even be the best thing', arguing that it 'might help to convince everybody that the next war would be fatal'.[82]

After the war Teller became increasingly identified as shamelessly self-assured; a bully and self-promoter. Yet his bluster inevitably won the ear of successive US Presidents from Harry Truman to Ronald Reagan. Teller was, however, permanently bruised by his rabid pursuit of the 'Super' hydrogen bomb, and his subsequent testimony that helped revoke the security clearance of his former boss, Robert J. Oppenheimer.

Physically there is little to suggest Peter Sellers' characterisation of the blonde ex-Nazi resembled this nuclear physicist at all. As with Henry Kissinger, Teller retained strong traces of his European origins throughout his life, evident in his deep rumbling baritone, one that was heavily inflected with a Hungarian accent. He certainly had a palpable presence and charisma. Like Strangelove in the War Room, when Teller spoke, people listened. As biographer Istvan Hargittai says, 'Teller did everything with a zealot's conviction, as if he were on a mission.'[83] Being spiteful and holding grudges contrasted curiously with Teller's paradoxical sense of uncertainty, and his 'desire to please others, or at least to correspond to their expectation of him'. This is precisely the way I felt when I interviewed him at his Stanford University home in 1999. At the end of our videotaped conversation, he was keen to ensure that he had come across well and that he hadn't missed, or messed, anything important. Seated in a deep leather sofa, holding his ever-present handle-less cane, Teller was dressed impeccably, instantly commanding yet disarming, grumbling loudly in his best Hungarian guttural: 'I am partly blind and going deaf. Other than zis, I am fine!'

While this exchange was nothing like Seller's explosive realisation, 'Mein Führrer, I can valk!', Teller did demonstrate throughout his life a forceful public and private certainty of opinion. He was a man who suffered fools little. When asked about his Livermore Laboratory Plowshare programme (1959–73) plans to detonate 'clean' hydrogen weapons for large civil engineering projects, he erupted derisively with 'Clean! Vot is "clean"?' – a question that seemed to instantly undermine his decades-long campaign to fight opponents of nuclear testing on the basis of fallout and contamination. Such interjections were entirely reminiscent of Sellers' Teutonic outburst to the Soviet Ambassador, upon learning of the Doomsday Device: 'Vy didn't you tell ze vorld, 'eh?!'

Despite Teller's propensity for such intemperate exclamations, one physical trait that resonates with Seller's embodiment of Doctor Strangelove is that Teller was also disabled. Although never wheelchair-bound like von Neumann in later life, Edward Teller could no more lose his accent than he could the prosthetic foot that made him limp throughout his life. As a student in Munich his foot was severed in a trolly-car accident, an injury many believe toughened his character and his often stubborn resolve in overcoming adversaries later in life.

Nevertheless, Edward Teller was highly susceptible to criticism and constantly bristled at the mere mention of 'Strangelove'. Unlike Herman Kahn and other RAND consultants, Teller found little to be amused about in any perceived association with the film's ex-Nazi scientist. Teller was similarly interviewed in 1999 by Gary Stix for *Scientific American* but he did not appreciate any Strangelovian aspersions. Frail and in his eighties he railed at the interviewer:

> My name is not Strangelove. I don't know about Strangelove. I'm not interested in Strangelove. What else can I say? ... Look. Say it three times more and I throw you out of this office.[84]

But the association had long stuck in the zeitgeist no matter how hard Teller tried to impugn its lineage over the years. The stridency of Teller's further championing of Peaceful Nuclear Explosives (PNEs), defending nuclear power after Three Mile Island and Chernobyl, supporting the Strategic Defense Initiative (popularly known as 'Star Wars') and his advocacy of nuclear *hormesis* (the theory that radiation exposure in low doses is beneficial to human development and species evolution) drew the ire of public health scientists and environmentalists worldwide.

The other prominent scientist frequently considered influential on the characterisation of Dr. Strangelove is Wernher von Braun. Born in rural eastern Germany (now Poland) in 1912, von Braun moved with his family to Berlin where he attended boarding schools and developed a passion for astronomy and space travel. In his teens he began to master calculus and trigonometry in order to apply this to the physics of rocketry. He joined the German rocket society, *Verein für Raumschiffarht* (VfR) in 1929 and within three years graduated from the Berlin technical college gaining a diploma in mechanical engineering. He went to work for the German army under the Weimar Republic developing ballistic missiles while completing his PhD in physics. By November 1937 von Braun had joined the Nazi party and in 1940 he became a member of the SS (*Schutzstaffel*) and by 1943 promoted to the rank of major (*Sturmbannführer*) by Heinrich Himmler.[85]

With the blessing and resourcing from the highest levels of Nazi Germany (from Albert Speer to Adolf Hitler) von Braun oversaw scientists and engineers working at Peenemünde, perfecting terror or 'vengeance' weapons (*Vergeltungswaffens*), such as the V-1 pilotless pulse-jet bomb and the V-2 liquid-fueled ballistic missile. Nazi wartime industry frequently drew from slave labour at nearby concentration camps.[86] For rocket scientists like von Braun, who had benign pre-war dreams of interplanetary travel, military production pressures led him to the death camp at Buchenwald where 'he personally picked labor slaves' to work (and die) at his rocket assembly factories.[87]

Paul Grigorieff has studied the Mittelbau complex near Nordhausen in central Germany and its associated factories, storage depots, facilities and prisoner camps, used to manufacture and test V-2s.[88] Grigorieff estimates the number of prisoners used by von Braun for V-2 production at Mittelbau surpassed 60,000. Over 25,000 of these (mostly foreigners) were killed between August 1943 and April 1945 by beatings, execution, starvation and/or sickness. Prefiguring Strangelove's industrial mineshaft survival plan (via Teller, Morgenstern and Kahn), much of the sensitive V-2 work was conducted underground in vast tunnels and mines. The central Mittelbau plants were located in the southern Harz Mountains, inside a cavernous gypsum mine that was 'large enough to house extensive facilities in secrecy'.[89]

Fearing capture by the advancing Russians, in the spring of 1945 von Braun led five hundred engineers and scientists away from the missile facility in order to surrender to the nearby Americans. After commandeering a train using forged papers the group escaped from the pursuing SS who had been ordered to kill von Braun and his Peenemünde technical corps and destroy their records. However, the engineers managed to evade the troops and hide their documents in a mineshaft (later recovered by US engineers). Realising the importance of von Braun's group, the US military rushed to Peenemünde and seized the remaining V-2s before destroying the work sites with explosives. In a famous series of photographs, the youthful von Braun is shown after his surrender to the Americans with

Von Braun after capture by OSS agents in 1945. (US National Archives)

one arm raised to shoulder height by a plaster cast and support splint. Ironically, the SS scientist appears to be frozen in a permanent state of Nazi salute.

Von Braun and his colleagues were repatriated by the secret Operation Paperclip taskforce, organised by the Office of Strategic Services (OSS), which transported to America over 1,500 Nazi scientists and technicians (many deemed security risks or war criminals), to prevent their capture by the Soviets or British.[90] After debriefing, von Braun was quickly issued a security clearance and sent to the White Sands Proving Ground in New Mexico to reconstruct and test the captured V-2s.

In 1950, von Braun and his team were transferred to Huntsville, Alabama, which became his home for the next two decades. Between 1950 and 1956, von Braun led the US Army's rocket development team, creating the Redstone ballistic missile, and later witnessed its first live firing of a nuclear warhead and its explosion. In 1955 von Braun became a US citizen and worked part-time on a range of educational projects conceptualising and popularising space travel for imaginatively illustrated books and magazines such as *Collier's* and television programmes for Walt Disney. Many featured nuclear-powered rockets or orbital weapons platforms that could be used to wage atomic war from space. As Director of the Development Operations Division of the Army Ballistic Missile Agency (ABMA), von Braun and his team next developed the Jupiter-C, a modified Redstone rocket that was used to successfully launch America's first satellite four months after the shock news of Sputnik.

Despite these public successes community opprobrium of von Braun and his Nazi peers became increasingly evident in the late 1950s. Before he embarked on a new civilian role with NASA a number of public relations exercises designed to extinguish or mitigate his wartime activities often only served to highlight the incongruous nature of his work. The 1960 Hollywood bio-pic *I Aim at the Stars,* featuring Curd Jürgens as von Braun (an actor Kubrick had penciled in as a potential player in *Strangelove*), was gleefully scorned with an apocryphal subtitle 'but sometimes I hit London', a line often ascribed to one of Kubrick's favourite satirists, Mort Sahl.[91] Sahl also mercilessly ridiculed Herman Kahn in one of his skits: 'He is a fascist ... a genocide who goes home at night and plays with his kids and asks them, "What are you going to be *if* you grow up?"'[92]

Von Braun's notoriety continued into the 1960s and by the year after *Strangelove*'s release, singer-songwriter Tom Lehrer famously lampooned the scientist in his 1965 performance 'Wernher von Braun' on NBC's *That Was the Week that Was*:

> Gather round while I sing you of Wernher von Braun,
> A man whose allegiance
> Is ruled by expedience.
> Call him a Nazi, he won't even frown.

'Ha – Nazi schmatzi', says Wernher von Braun.

Don't say that he's hypocritical,

Say, rather, that he's a-political.

'Vunce zee rockets are up, who cares vere zey come down?

Zat's not my department', says Wernher von Braun.

Some have harsh words for this man of renown,

But some think our attitude

Should be one of gratitude,

Like the widows and cripples in old London town

Who owe their large pensions to Wernher von Braun…

Von Braun was not the only Nazi war criminal to avoid prosecution and be recuperated by the Allies in order to work on their post-World War II advanced arsenals. Nazi physician Dr. Hubertus Strughold was chief of Aeronautical Research for the Luftwaffe, and similarly repatriated by the American OSS under Operation Paperclip. After the war Strughold became the first professor appointed to the US Air Force's School of Aviation Medicine and Chief Scientist of NASA's Aerospace Medical Division. He worked on the physiology of high-altitude flight, pressure effects and the vacuum of space.[93] Strughold was a major scientist overseeing several human biosystems for the Mercury, Gemini and Apollo space programmes. It was revealed late in his career that Strughold had experimented on children and concentration camp prisoners during his time with the Luftwaffe. Under the Nazi decree, Action T-4, epileptic children housed at the Brandenburg Euthanasia Centre were made available for his experimentation in vacuum chambers. Later, Strughold was implicated in war crimes conducted at Dachau including experiments on Jews and gypsies which 'involved freezing people to near death and re-warming them, measuring how quickly they might recover, or not … nearly 200 people were either tortured to death by freezing, or subsequently murdered if they survived as part of these experiments'.[94] Several of Strughold's aeronautical medical colleagues (including his research assistant) were found guilty of crimes against humanity at the Nuremberg Trials, some of whom he supported via sworn affidavit.[95]

Despite his extraction and expedient shielding by US authorities, Strughold faced multiple inquiries into his wartime conduct. Unlike von Braun, neither Walt Disney nor Hollywood came to Strughold's aid to produce a sympathetic bio-pic for the American public.[96] As these revelations grew, Strughold's prestigious reputation dwindled, and his civil and scientific honours and commemorative building names were removed across America. Ironically, one of Strughold's experimental subjects at NASA, Mercury astronaut and later US Senator John Glenn, became a national hero and a fierce opponent of secret human biomedical research.[97]

CINEMATIC STRANGE LOVES

It is clear from documents in the Stanley Kubrick archive that the invention of the name 'strangelove' emanates solely from the director-producer.[98] However, the term and nomenclature were not born in a cultural or cinematic vacuum. While Kubrick worked as a *Look* apprentice photographer the magazine ran a full-page advertisement for *The Strange Love of Martha Ivers* on 20 August 1946, followed a month later by a favorable review for its 17 September edition. Featuring Barbara Stanwyck and debuting Kirk Douglas, Kubrick's future star-collaborator (*Paths of Glory*, *Spartacus*), Martha Ivers' 'strange love' is revealed to be one fuelled by murder and obsessive, though unrequited, desire. Based on John Patrick's Academy Award-nominated original story 'Love Lies Bleeding', and directed by Hollywood veteran Lewis Milestone, the film conforms to the narrative and stylistic standards of mid-1940s film noir. Irrespective of the subject matter, it is almost inconceivable that the seventeen-year-old Stanley, an obsessive cinema-goer at this point, would not have read these editions nor seen the film some-time after its July 1946 theatrical release. Indeed during the months of August and September 1946 when *Look* showcased the full-page advertisement and movie review, Kubrick was shooting and filing a range of photographic assignments, including the banal and perfunctorily titled 'Meet the People ... Men Who Use Cologne'.[99]

While this enigmatic film title may have settled into the recesses of Kubrick's consciousness his frequent searching for, and exposure to, both commercial and high-brow cinema during his late teens (and throughout the rest of his life) acquainted him with a broad spectrum of American and international film. Kubrick was known to be a lover of Ophuls and Bresson, and Bergman's Swedish dramas. As Kubrick's personal assistant Tony Frewin has stated, the director was a life-long aficionado of science fiction literature and film, including childhood reverie in pulps such as *Amazing Stories*.[100] Early in life Kubrick had seen several German art film classics, including Fritz Lang's silent masterpiece, *Metropolis*. The film's mad scientist Rotwang, played by Rudolf Klein-Rogge, is an alchemist and necromancer (echoing Faust), who seeks revenge against the city's patriarch, Fredersen, by creating a robot in female form. Rotwang's mania derives from his rivalry with Fredersen, still jealous after losing his object of desire to the city's wealthiest man. According to Alexander Walker, *Metropolis* not only informs the characterisation and performance of Sellers' Strangelove, but the cavernous War Room set design.[101]

Following on from the evil scientist Rotwang, it was Peter Lorre's role as the love-sick and demented Doctor Gogol in Karl Freund's *Mad Love* (1933) that graphically depicted the horrors of man/machine symbiosis, a disturbing incarnation destined for trauma and mental instability. With stunning black and white photography by Greg Toland,

Freund's direction of the increasingly manic and sexually perverse Dr. Gogol reaches
an unsettling but bizarrely comic climax when Lorre appears at his unrequited lover
Yvonne's apartment. Dressed in disguise, wearing black and with dark sunglasses, Gogol
pretends to be the reanimated corpse of an executed murder, Rollo, whose hands were
transplanted by Gogol to replace those of Yvonne's concert pianist husband, Stephen
Orlac, severed in a train crash.

Mad Love reworks the earlier Austrian silent film *The Hands of Orlac* (1924), directed by Robert Wiene and starring Conrad Veidt. Based on the novel *Les Mains d'Orlac* by
Maurice Renard, the plot is essentially a murder mystery that follows the recipient of a
double hand transplant (the pianist Orlac) who feels uncontrollably impelled to act on
the previous owner's homicidal resolve. *Mad Love* varies the approach while utilising the
same basic plot. With his distinctly high-pitched German accent, frozen sardonic grin
and wild mechanical hand and arm gestures, Dr. Gogol (as Rollo) uncannily prefigures
Sellers' Strangelove. Coupled with themes of psychotic violence and sexual repression,
Mad Love provides a tantalising forerunner to the ex-Nazi scientist in Kubrick's film.
Coincidentally, Peter Lorre was one of Peter Sellers' earliest and most cherished voices
to impersonate.[102]

Similarly, there are clear synergies between the first screen adaptation of 007
James Bond and his initial nemesis that offer interesting antecedents. Directed by

Terence Young and shot widescreen in Technicolor, *Dr. No* was filmed on location in Jamaica and at Pinewood Studios. The production showcased the talents of production designer Ken Adam who was soon to work with Kubrick on *Dr. Strangelove* (and later *Barry Lyndon* (1976)). Much closer to the Cold War context of Kubrick's film, *Dr. No* showcased aspects of a privatised military-industrial complex gone mad (the criminal organisation SPECTRE). The character of Dr. No, played by Joseph Wiseman, is presented as a Eurasian nuclear scientist operating a clandestine, paramilitary base on a Caribbean island down-range from the US missile facility at Cape Canaveral.[103] Powered by Dr. No's subterranean atomic reactor, the island complex beams powerful radio transmissions that intercept and destroy American missiles and space probes after their launch from Florida.[104]

Working with the CIA, British intelligence agent James Bond (Sean Connery) is sent to Jamaica to discover and halt the source of the sabotage. Dr. No is first introduced to Bond seated at an ornate table, smoking. He clutches his cigarette holder with a black-gloved (and seemingly mechanical) hand, revealed by his adversary to have been damaged from working with radiation. Hence *Dr. No* presents another accented evil scientist working with technologies of mass destruction. His replacement hands are lethal metallic weapons, covered in black insulating rubber, shown capable of effortlessly crushing objects and impervious to electricity. At the film's penultimate conclusion, Bond battles with Dr. No perilously above a cluster of nuclear fuel rods sunk within the scientist's atomic reactor coolant. Wearing an inflatable 'clean suit' with transparent plastic head cover to protect from inhaling radioactive particles, Dr. No struggles to grip a partly submerged metal elevator, his only mode of escape from the atomic pile after he plunges into the cooling pond. Bond releases the fuel rods causing the reactor to go critical and overheat. Dr. No perishes in the boiling radioactive liquid, his artificial hands, covered with black rubber, incapable of holding on to the elevator's slippery framework.

The finale reveals Bond and his 'accidental' helper, Honey Ryder (Ursula Andress) escaping from the island by boat, as various henchmen and sundry nuclear personnel dive into the sea before the island explodes in a giant nuclear conflagration, an allegorical atomic apocalypse in microcosm.

SELLERS' STRANGELOVE

Peter Sellers' formal involvement in *Dr. Strangelove* came relatively late, around the time of the early pre-production process, his participation seemingly dictated by Columbia Pictures. Publicly, Kubrick professed that Sellers was the 'best' person for the role(s) while privately the director was reported to rail at the decree from head office, that Sellers be attached to the project. According to Terry Southern an infuriated Kubrick told him 'What we are dealing with is film by fiat, film by frenzy!'[105] Nevertheless, just at the point where Kubrick was contemplating Sellers for the multiples roles, the actor's earlier (and inspired) collaboration with the director became visible to audiences with the international release of *Lolita* in June 1962.

The hybrid and unconventional nature of *Lolita*'s screenplay is worth revisiting, given Sellers' elevated contribution to the production. Originally assigned to Calder Willingham, the script was comprehensively re-written by Harris and Kubrick after novelist Vladimir Nabokov initially produced a draft of hundreds of pages that would have run for several hours of screen time. In undertaking a major rewrite Harris and Kubrick reoriented both plot and structure to include, as an introduction and coda, a murder mystery, related in flashback, to reveal the motivations behind Professor Humbert Humbert (James Mason) shooting dead television writer Clare Quilty (Peter Sellers).

The character of Quilty is expanded substantially in the revised script. In the novel, the shadowy nemesis of Quilty is mentioned towards the end of the narrative and he mostly remains a phantom, like Sherlock Holmes' adversary Moriarty (coincidentally, an unscrupulous criminal character played by Sellers on radio in *The Goons*). In the film adaptation Quilty is omnipresent, though chameleon-like. He punctuates the narrative with unexpected appearances and assumed sightings. Indeed, the character of Clare Quilty afforded Peter Sellers an opportunity to excel in displaying his range of stunning mimicry and comic impressions. From Quilty's post-orgy, hung-over torpor in the opening scene, where he hilariously channels western-genre sidekicks (Walter Brennan and Gaby Hayes) as he reads Humbert's letter, through to impulsively and perniciously impersonating an inquisitive and increasingly impertinent state policeman to impugn Humbert's 'normal' relationship with his 'lovely, little' teenage step-daughter, Lolita.

However, the principal performance of relevance to the personae of Dr. Strangelove is manifest in Sellers' depiction of Clarie Quilty wearing a disguise, sitting silently in the dark, pretending to be Lolita's school psychologist, Dr. Zemph. Sellers' surprise appearances are sometimes spectral and frequently bizarre (especially when in the company of his Vampira-esque companion, Vivian Darkbloom). Quilty is first seen in *Lolita* emerging from behind a shrouded lounge chair, ghost-like, before wrapping the sheet around his shoulder, toga-style, and intertextually conjuring *Spartacus*. Bleary-eyed and unsteady, he disdainfully challenges the revolver-wielding Humbert to a 'lovely little game of Roman ping-pong'. As Humbert stands at the other end of the table tennis table, donning gloves, Quilty queries this move, before distractedly playing with a bat, self-reflexively adopting an unorthodox grip, commenting distractedly: 'I remember one guy, he didn't have a hand. He had a bat instead of a hand.' Like a stand-up comedian slowly dying before his audience, an increasingly desperate Quilty strives for any comic inspiration that might provide a brief diversion in order to flee and forestall his execution. Kubrick's repeated visual motif of the hand (evident from the opening title sequence) and Sellers' hyperactive performance leads Quilty to put on boxing gloves and seek satisfaction à la Marquess of Queensberry rules. Growing tired of the inane gamesmanship an impatient and agitated Humbert shoots at Quilty point blank, the bullet passing through his left boxing glove narrowly missing his fingers.

Long after this introductory sequence, when Humbert has absconded with Lolita to live together in the mid-west, the literature professor returns from work one night and casually enters his house, pushing open a door to the dining room. As light from the hallway enters the room it illuminates a mysterious, and seemingly disembodied pair of hands, reminiscent of the mise-en-scène of *Mad Love* where a heavily disguised Dr. Gogol also sits at a table, menacingly pretending to be a reanimated murderer, his metallic hands glistening. Caught unawares, Humbert switches on the dining room light to reveal a man in a dark suit with a moustache and slick back hair, wearing Coke-bottle glasses and speaking in a strong German accent. He identifies himself as 'Dr. Zempf', the psychologist from Lolita's high school and proceeds to repeatedly mispronounce Humbert's name as 'Doctor Hombardz'.

Zempf fidgets and squirms in his seat, as will Sellers as Strangelove, jerking awk-wardly in his wheelchair. Zempf promptly reaches into his right breast pocket to pull out some note cards, an action mirrored by Strangelove's comic fumbling for his bomb effects and fallout calculator. When Zempf vehemently strikes the table repeatedly with his right hand, emphasising points about Lolita 'zuffering from acute repression of zee libido' and of 'zee natural inztincts', the sequence anticipates Dr. Strangelove describing his rationale for choosing women 'of a highly stimulating nature' for sexual service in the post-holocaust mineshafts. The irony of Quilty as Zempf addressing a fellow European émigré, Dr. Humbert, as 'Vee Americans, vee are progrezzively modern' echoes the swathe of pre-war refugee scientists and post-war Operation Paperclip Nazis brought to the USA by the Office of Stratgeic Services, later embodied in the hybridised character of Strangelove.

As with the first sighting of Sellers as Quilty in Lolita, the actor makes a similar appearance in *Dr. Strangelove* as Group Captain Lionel Mandrake, stepping out from behind a huge print-out of continuous computer paper, one that entirely obscures his presence. As Zempf, Seller's performance also prefigures his role of Dr. Strangelove, who similarly lurks in the dark. As General Turgidson summons everyone to prayer, he speaks of delivery from the 'wings of the angel of death' and the 'forces of evil' and Kubrick cuts to a silent Strangelove sitting in the dark of the War Room. Other Sellers' actions in *Lolita* resonate with *Dr. Strangelove*. When Humbert shoots Quilty in the leg as he tries to escape atop a staircase, the TV writer cannot stand and drags his motionless legs along the landing behind a framed oil painting. The action is similar to an excised scene in the

War Room where Strangelove pulls himself along the floor desperately trying to reseat himself in his wheelchair (see chapter five).

Speaking with an exaggerated and clichéd German accent, Quilty similarly channels any number of cinematic Nazi foes in his increasingly menacing performance as Dr. Zempf. At one point, after offering Humbert a smoke ('Zigarrette?'), he follows up with 'Keep zee pack...', a line of dialogue stereotypically familiar to movie and television audiences, often associated with a 'good cop' during interrogation.[106] Hence, Sellers' performance of Quilty – performing Dr. Zempf – is metatextual as he assumes for Humbert the role of an ally by offering to forestall an external panel of school experts from entering the home, in order to prevent them from 'meddling': 'I feel zat you and I should do all in our power to stop zat old Dr. Cutler and his quartet of zychologists from fiddling around in zee home situation.'

Well before *Lolita*, Peter Sellers had developed a range of characters and voices that informed his Strangelove persona. Appearing on radio with fellow Goons, as Major Dennis Bloodnok, Sellers mercilessly lampooned military commanders. As one online fan site describes him, Bloodnok was a 'corrupt military cad, pervert and idiot ... who suffers terrible flatulence'.[107] The farcical antics of the Goons, drawn from World War II cabaret and stand-up comedy, became increasingly anarchic later in the 1950s. However, Sellers, as part of the Goons, never quite made the transition from radio to film with any real impact. An early attempt at this new medium was the limp and tepid feature *Down Among the Z Men*. Shot on a very low budget the plot nevertheless has some thematic resonance with *Strangelove*. Ostensibly a comic caper involving an atomic scientist, Professor Osrick Purehart (Michael Bentine) at the Warwell Atomic Research Camp, chased by gangsters for his secrets, the Goons adopt the military roles familiar to their radio fans. Inexplicably, Bloodnok (Sellers) is cast as a bumbling though good-natured colonel. As Col. Bloodnok, a plump looking Sellers is made up with greying hair and moustache; his military poise has only the slightest resemblance to RAF Major Mandrake. However, the film does provide Bloodnok/Sellers with the opportunity to lampoon American service personnel. In a perfunctory scene, the Goons perform in a military service review, where Col. Bloodnok alternately portrays a US Army officer and a lowly soldier, adopting broad, but different, American accents for both. The skit is meant to mimic a scene from an American war film that Bloodnok had recently viewed, but his impersonations fall dismally flat, and the heavy stage curtain closes in on him mid-sentence.

Sellers' friend Graham Stark appeared as a petty crook opposite Sellers in *Down Amongst the Z Men* and both were excited and naïve enough to suggest to their harried director their respective character's 'motivations' and idiosyncrasies. Sellers muttered something about 'undercurrents of repression' and a 'noticeable twitch'. Surveying the cheap and tiny set the director blankly explained to Stark and Sellers the industrial-economic facts of life: 'I've got eight minutes' screen time a day to shoot. Do it quickly.'[108] Sellers would later reflect that *The Goon Show* had its 'drawbacks' since 'many filmmakers tend to think of you as a funny voice man instead of being a serious actor'.[109]

Yet it was Sellers' multiple roles in the modest nuclear age comedy *The Mouse that Roared* that truly earned him Hollywood's attention. Based on Leonard Wibberley's six-part serialisation for the *Saturday Evening Post*, the novel was adapted by Wibberley and directed by 1950s science fiction maestro Jack Arnold for Columbia Pictures. The satire broached Cold War politics and the superpower arms race as it parodied American international aid directed at European nation rebuilding after World War II. When the miniscule (and fictitious) duchy of Grand Fenwick has its sole export, a popular vintage pinot, undermined by American competition, Grand Fenwick declares war on the USA in the hope of a swift settlement to be followed by generous US State Department foreign aid to prop up the ailing economy. However, the plan is thwarted when a small ragtag band of Fenwick's agrestic 'volunteers', wearing medieval chain mail and carrying bows and arrows are dispatched to New York to invade the USA. However, they arrive in Manhattan during a massive national civil defence exercise, where the entire metropolis is evacuated and citizens forced to take shelter underground. The drill is motivated by the prototype development of eccentric scientist Dr. Kokintz's football shaped and toaster sized 'Q-bomb', several magnitudes more powerful than the H-bomb, and capable of obliterating an area of two million square miles. As with the Soviet Ambassador's nonchalant reply in *Dr. Strangelove* when quizzed about the secrecy of the unannounced Doomsday Machine, when Dr. Kokintz is questioned why he experiments with the Q-bomb in his New York office laboratory instead of working with other scientists at Oak Ridge, his daughter Helen comically replies that he 'likes to work alone'. Quizzed further, the physicist reveals that the Q-bomb is 'based on quodium, which is a hundred times more powerful than hydrogen'. Helen adds nonchalantly: 'He uses an H-bomb just to trigger this one. It could blow up North America.'

Kokintz looks uncannily like Dr. Thorkel (Albert Dekker) from *Dr. Cyclops* (1940) and both speak with pronounced mid-European accents. Although Kokintz's receding hair is short and grey, unlike the bald Dr. Cyclops (perhaps as an effect of exposure to radiation), their moustaches and circular, Coke-bottle glasses are identical, as are their stooped postures. During his experiments in radioactivity Dr. Cyclops wears a protective helmet, gown and gloves similar in shape and design to the transparent suit donned by Dr. No.

Grand Fenwick's bumpkin army locate the scientist and commandeer the nuclear device, along with a pompous US Army general and a few New York cops, held as hostages, before returning to the European duchy, seemingly victorious. Horrified at the turnaround, the duchy's parliament is nevertheless soon solicited by American, Soviet and British representatives, all suing for peace and monopolistic possession of the devastating Q-bomb. Grand Fenwick agrees to American terms and generous economic settlement but refuses to surrender the bomb insisting, rather, that it remains in the possession of the 'little countries of the world' until the nuclear powers disarm.

In *The Mouse that Roared* Peter Sellers starred as the unassuming heroic rube Tully Buscome, and two other roles, both of which involved substantial make-up: Prime Minister (and Count) Mountjoy and the elderly and portly Grand Duchess Gloriana. None of the roles provide Sellers with much space to shine artistically and are more reminiscent of Alec Guinness in *Kind Hearts and Coronets* (1949) or George C. Scott *et al* disguised in *The List of Adrian Messenger* (1963), rather than the 'comic ecstasy' of the *Strangelove* characterisations.

Director Jack Arnold remarked: 'Peter was a marvellous improvisational actor, brilliant if you got him on the first take. The second take would be good, but after the third take he could be really awful. If he had to repeat the same words too many times they became meaningless.'[110] Starring opposite Jean Seaberg, who constantly forgot her lines while concentrating on her Method Acting approach, Sellers tried to keep up, but 'by take 25 Peter didn't know what he was saying either. He was just spouting gibberish. I could see he was really getting crazy.'[111] The same multi-take process occurred on *Lolita* opposite the ill-prepared Shelley Winters.

Yet the film was not without its charms and of relevance to nuclear fears. It also has some interesting, though limited, parallels with Kubrick's nuclear comedy. In a comically subtle Brechtian intervention, mid-scene, a wide screen Technicolor shot depicts an atomic explosion and broiling mushroom cloud that disrupts the plot while the unseen narrator intones insouciantly:

> This is not the end of our film. But something like this could happen at any moment.
> We want to prepare you and put you in the mood. Thank you. Now back to our story.

This Atomic Energy Commission stock footage is immediately followed by four international diplomats sitting at a table playing a board game 'Diplomacy' resembling Monopoly. The Soviet representative rolls the dice and declares 'I bomb Philadelphia! You owe me 500 heavy bombers', while the American's dice throw leads to exile in a salt mine. *The Mouse that Roared* also depicts a War Room where military planners chart the progress of the east coast Air Raid exercise on a series of big boards. Unlike the multiscreen projections in *Dr. Strangelove*'s War Room, the information in *The Mouse that Roared* is physically moved and drawn by soldiers clambering on ladders, similar to the SAC headquarters in the mid-1950s.

SAC's underground command post display and closed circuit television relay, 1961. (US National Archives)

The final sequence, in which the US Secretary of State negotiates a peace treaty with Grand Fenwick, has Tully dictating that his tiny duchy will retain the bomb along with Dr. Kokintz in order to break through the international impasse of nuclear disarmament. The exchange deploys a similar logic and rhetoric to that drafted by Kubrick for his President to espouse at the end of *Dr. Strangelove*, describing the actions of smaller nations, the lack of trust between superpowers, the inevitability of nuclear war and the deterrent threat of a nightmare weapon:

Secretary of State:
What about the Bomb?

Tully:
The bomb stays here. And Dr. Kokintz too.

Secretary of State
But surely you realise you can't keep the Bomb indefinitely.

Tully:
We'd like your President to persuade the United Nations to let the little countries look after the Bomb. We want disarmament with the little nations in charge of the inspection.

Secretary of State:
I see, I think. But everybody's cried for disarmament for years and
nothing happened. What do you offer the big nations?

Tully:
We offer trust. They can't agree because they all suspect each other.
We all hoped things would be better after the last war.
They're worse with all these bombs.

Secretary of State:
You believe big nations will trust small nations to set up a disarmament
policy for them?

Tully:
I hope so. Because if they don't, we'll just have to explode the Bomb.

Secretary of State:
You'd be blown up too!

Grand Duchess:
Mr Secretary... If there were an atomic war, Fenwick would be destroyed.
Aren't we just prolonging the agony?

Secretary of State:
I see what you mean. America wants nothing more than peace.
I'll do my very best.

Hence, *The Mouse that Roared* inverts the logic of Strangelove's megadeath and Kahn's doomsday devices by secretly suppressing the knowledge that their tiny nation's ultimate nuclear deterrent is a ploy, one that will ensure world peace. The geopolitical tables are turned – it becomes the little countries that behave like gangsters and the big nations like prostitutes – inverting one of Kubrick's favourite, though later discarded, script lines (see chapter five).

At the film's conclusion Tully, Dr. Kokintz and Helen check on the bomb. After accidentally dropping it, the device is declared by Kokintz to be 'a dud'. Tully shrewdly puts his finger to his lips, gesturing silence, and smiles. 'Only we know', he says with a wink. Yet a brief coda suggests the Q-bomb remains operative when a small white mouse exits the contraption and sets off the visible and audible trigger mechanism, followed by a superimposed title reads 'THE END', followed by 'We hope...'.

The film was produced in late 1958 for a mid-1959 release. During this time New York and the rest of the USA has undergone a series of annual civil defence drills authorised by President Eisenhower, designated Operation Alert. These exercises became increasingly debated and publicly contested. By 1960, hundreds of women and children refused to participate and marched in protest. The civil disobedience actions by the Catholic

Worker's Dorothy Day and others initially drew small numbers but within a few years had expanded to thousands of supporters, including celebrities such as Norman Mailer.[112]

Other influences on the evolution of *Dr. Strangelove* can be traced through Peter Sellers' playful appropriation and improvised approach to characterisation and performance. Kubrick remarked that Sellers

> was the only actor I knew who could really improvise. Improvisation is something useful in rehearsal, to explore a role. But most actors, when they improvise, stray into a sort of repetitive hodge-podge which leads them down a dead end, while Sellers, by contrast – even when he wasn't on form – after a time fell into the spirit of the character and just took off. It was miraculous.[113]

During the *Lolita* rehearsals, Kubrick is reported to have told the cast to forget the lines they had previously learned by heart – except for Sellers, whom the director instructed to entirely disregard his scripted dialogue and 'make things up on the spur of the moment'.[114] In his autobiography co-star James Mason later reflected that Sellers 'was the only one allowed, or rather encouraged, to improvise his entire performance. The rest of us improvised only during rehearsals, then incorporated any departures from the original script that it seemed particularly effective.' Mason noted, somewhat ironically, that Peter told the *Lolita* cast that 'he did not enjoy improvising' and having 'to think on his feet when giving a live performance', observing that he approached his screen role with great diligence ('he was painstaking and meticulous in preparation').[115]

The importance of improvisation in Kubrick's early career can be further understood by the director's response to Nabokov's late-1965 proposal to produce a printed version of his original screenplay. Nearly two years after the release of *Dr. Strangelove* and well into production on *2001: A Space Odyssey* (1968), Kubrick was concerned about Nabokov's 'artistic post-mortem'. He sought the writer's understanding for the necessity of improvised dialogue from actors. He carefully outlined why he and Harris altered the *Lolita* script, explaining:

> It is the nature of making films that screenplays never are shot the way they are written. The improvisation of the moment and the need to ... optimize on the actors' strengths and weaknesses must be taken into account in order to produce the best result.[116]

DR. STRANGE GLOVE'S NUCLEAR ARMS

While Kubrick gave Sellers free reign to perform with great spontaneity in *Lolita*, turning what was originally planned to be a brief appearance into a far lengthier, multifaceted

and menacing role of great complexity, in *Dr. Strangelove*, the comic script also bene-
fitted from the audacious élan of Terry Southern's dialogue. Hence, Sellers' verbal and
performative improvisations are truly inspired, but discursively, they add only nuance
to the existing text. Where Sellers truly came into his own was his acute comic timing
and skilled personifications. As the wheelchair bound (ex-)Nazi Doctor, Sellers created a
magical transformation of character, one that drew from Kubrick's intuitive suggestion
and instantly blossomed into one of the most celebrated and iconic performances of his
generation of actors. During one take with Sellers playing Strangelove, without warning,
his arm was thrust out in front of him and the actor shouted 'Heil Hitler!' Sellers recalled
the experience:

> One day Stanley suggested that I should wear a black glove, which would look rather
> sinister on a man in a wheelchair. 'Maybe he had some injury in a nuclear experi-
> ment of some sort', Kubrick said. So I put on the black glove and look at the arm and
> I suddenly thought, 'Hey, that's a storm trooper's arm'. So instead of leaving it there
> looking malignant I gave the arm a life of its own. That arm hated the rest of the body
> for having made a compromise. That arm was a Nazi.[117]

Critic Alexander Walker, who visited Shepperton studios on a number of occasions during production, confirmed the sequence of events, noting that Kubrick often wore black

Kubrick giving direction, possibly during rehearsal. The image captures the director in a pose similar
to Dr. Strangelove who battles with his rebellious, Nazi saluting arm. (Stanley Kubrick Archive)

gloves while adjusting the lights on set.[118] In early 1964, while in North America, a smiling Sellers told television interviewer Steve Allen that, of the three roles, he 'enjoyed playing Dr. Strangelove the most'. Allen reproduced the Strangelovean action of his hand gripping his own throat and asked Sellers about his contribution to the role, as opposed to what was scripted:

> As it happens, it was sort of fifty-fifty ... Stanley's idea was that he would have a black glove, so that his hand was injured in some kind of nuclear experiment, and then I got it further by thinking that the hand was a Nazi while the rest of him had made the compromise, which was to live in America, but this hand here, you see [his right arm thrusts in a Nazi salute, which is suppressed and returned to order by his other hand, as the audience and host laugh]. And then it got him here [strangling himself] and then it went, it went 'ape' as they say [more audience laughs].[119]

So Sellers' inspiration came not only from Kubrick's allusion to *Dr. No* and other stereotyped mad scientists on screen, but a psychopathology embodied in the character's physical being – a kind of Freudian return of the repressed meets Tourette's syndrome. Indeed, while the spasms, tics and gross motor jerks afflicting Tourette sufferers was well-known in medical circles prior to *Dr. Strangelove*, Sellers' performance has become legend amongst neuropsychologists. Almost single-handedly, Sellers' character has become synonymous with a phenomenon variously named since the 1970s as 'Alien Hand', 'Anarchic Hand' or 'Autonomous Hand' syndrome.[120] Two forms of Alien/Anarchic Hand have been subsequently diagnosed as emanating from either cerebral callosal lesion or mesiofrontal damage. Both forms manifest as triggering an involuntary movement, such as 'forced grasping' and/or the 'spontaneous elevations of an arm'.

Symptoms associated specifically with 'frontal' alien hand syndrome include 'reflexive grasping' and 'groping', something Sellers' comic antics reveal and Kubrick's camera relishes.[121] Throughout the film Strangelove's non-dominant hand battles with his anarchic right arm as it salutes and refuses to release objects, such as his cigarette and the circular Bomb Effects Calculator. When the scientist describes the 'highly sexual' nature of the female cohort required for mineshaft reproductive duties, his rebellious hand gropes about his groin, below the frame and off-camera, while in mid-close up Sellers squirms uncomfortably at the unseen but implied activity, and his other hand battles to wrest control.

As Heilman and Valenstein argue, following Della Sala, only patients with callosal lesion consider their hand 'alien' and controlled by someone or something else, like a controlling 'other mind'.[122] This manifestation is the rarer form of the syndrome, one that is explicitly linked to a patient's 'lack of recognition of one's own hand'.[123] The misrecognition is described as one of most intriguing phenomenon in neurology today, with the extant clinical interpretation still open for debate. When redefining the symptomology of 'alien' towards 'anarchic' hand, Marchetti and Della Salla[124] describe Anarchic Hand 'as a phenomenon so bizarre that is verges on the comic'. It comprises:

> Movements of an upper limb which are clearly goal-directed and well executed but unintended. [...] The unwanted movements cannot be voluntarily interrupted and might interfere with the desired actions carried out by the other (healthy) hand. Patients are aware of the bizarre and potentially hazardous behavior of their hand but cannot inhibit it. They often refer to the feeling that one of their hands behaves as if it has a will of its own, but never deny that this capricious hand is part of their own body. The bewilderment comes from the surprising and unwanted actions, not from a sensation of lack of belonging of the hand.[125]

This pathology replicates Peter Sellers' description of his own rationalisation for the Nazi hand, unreconciled with its owner's accommodation and embrace of life in America. The idea is confirmed in a letter to Peter George from Kubrick's secretary, updating the writer for his novelisation, with new information from the recently altered script, revised

Letter to Peter George from Kubrick's secretary Pat Ivens noting changes to the script, for incorporation into the novelisation.
(Peter George Archive)

character names and performances, where she relates that 'Dr. Strangelove is suffering from a psychosomatic reflex of the right arm – the right arm is rebelling against the treachery of the rest of his body'.[126] Interestingly, this written account, undoubtedly dictated by Kubrick, is one that favours the perspective of the rebellious arm, not that of the rest of the body, which seeks to control and suppress the 'uncompromised' appendage.

Indeed, Sellers' performance became so iconographic it attained instant cult status amongst neurologists and non-experts alike. According to Marchetti and Della Salla, 'The similarity between Sellers' performance and the phenomenology observed in some patients is overwhelming. So much so that "Dr. Strangelove syndrome" has been proposed, albeit unsuccessfully (probably because of a non-cinephile reviewer) as a descriptive label for alien hand syndrome.'[127] Before the pathology was (mis)named, it continued to be misdiagnosed, even by the likes of Dr. Oliver Sacks,[128] despite popular culture being replete with narratives and imagery of such aberrant behaviour.[129]

Alien/anarchic/autonomous hand syndrome is a condition that truly invokes the *unheimliche,* especially Freud's concept of the uncanny association provoked by the liminal space between the dead and the undead.[130] For Freud, 'dismembered limbs, a severed head, a hand cut off at the wrist ... all these have something peculiarly uncanny about them, especially when ... they prove able to move of themselves in addition. As we already know, this kind of uncanniness springs from its association with the castration-complex.'[131] The reanimated and stitched corpse hands of Mary Shelley's conglomerate *Frankenstein* monster, for example, provided generations of movie-goers with imagery of such dexterous appendages, something the 1931 film and its sequel emphasise throughout.[132] In the literary and cinematic versions of *The Hands of Orlac*, the severed hands of a murderer are experimentally grafted onto a gifted pianist. As noted earlier, the scenario also informs the expressionist version, *Mad Love*, where Peter Lorre's Dr. Gogol presents as a reanimated corpse with gleaming metallic hands. The Freudian association with sexual impairment, whether castration anxiety or impotence, is intrinsic to these literary and screen tropes, just as they are with the sexual psychoses and dysfunction inhabiting the characters of *Dr. Strangelove*.

Hence, the opportunistic appropriation of Kubrick's utilitarian black glove, resonant with cultural references, encouraged Sellers to extend the suggestion of a hand damaged from a radiation accident to one possessed by an anarchic desire to rebel against its owner's alien ideology. Given Sellers' own antipathy to America, one might speculate that the hand was also a more primordial response to his own distaste at trying to reconcile American commercialism and Hollywood. Sellers' son Michael recalled the actor really detested Hollywood and much of American culture. He loathed the 'California jet set' and phony showbiz types and vowed to avoid filming in the USA in future.[133]

One final, though tenuous and unlikely, influence may have been author Peter George, who visited the *Strangelove* set a number of times while he was further employed during production as a 'technical advisor', despite having completed the script work and the novelisation draft. George's son David has related how his father 'pranged' a plane during flight training in Canada in 1943 and damaged his right hand and wrist.[134] This was not a good look for an RAF pilot or navigator and an event that likely caused some professional embarrassment. While the injury was not enough to prevent him from further flying or undertaking other aeronautical duties, his fine motor skills were somewhat impaired and he struggled to write using his right hand for the rest of his life. George's written annotations, corrections of treatments and his signatures display a decidedly laboured and shaky style, with a pronounced left-leaning cursive script.

NOTES

1   Several commentators such as John Baxter (177) have made this claim, one speculatively supported by Southern's son Nile and ex-wife Carol. See their interviews in *Inside Dr. Strangelove*.
2   John Baxter, *Stanley Kubrick: A Biography* (Cambridge MA: Da Capo Press, 1997), 170.
3   Amongst the factual errors and omissions in Baxter's section on *Strangelove* are the following: (i) he completely neglects to credit Harris in the scriptwriting/development conducted in New York in early 1962 (172); (ii) that Kubrick and George continued to work on 'Two Hours to Doom' in autumn of 1962 (they had advanced to the comedy by then with the new satirical title); (iii) that Kubrick initiated dissolution of the partnership with Harris (173); (iv) John Wayne was offered the role of B-52 pilot and refused immediately (173); (v) that shooting commenced at Shepperton in October 1962 (175); (vi) Southern was responsible for re-titling the film to 'Dr. Strangelove' (177); (vii) considers it likely that Kubrick and Southern 'borrowed' *Fail-Safe*'s Groteschele 'as the basis of Strangelove' (179); (viii) asserts Peter George 'detested the film's facetiousness' (180); (ix) claims Ken Adam 'found all he needed in technical magazines like *Flight*' for the B-52 design (182); (x) that Kubrick shot a scene with President Muffley 'consulting a computer – actually an IBM 7090', stating the 'scene was cut' (186–87); (xi) claims Kubrick, not Sellers, created the 'black-gloved artificial arm' (187); (xii) and claims that principle photography concluded on 23 April 1963 (191).
4   The association between *Dr No*, played by Joseph Wiseman, and Kubrick's announcement in a *New York Times* article that his film would feature 'an American college professor who rises to power in sex and politics by becoming a nuclear Wise Man', is according to Grant B. Stillman, a 'clincher' or a 'tongue-in-cheek giveaway' that Frederick 'Wise-man' as *Dr No* was a primary inspiration.
5   PGA, script 14/1/63
6   On the 'nuclear priesthood' see Karl Grossman, 'The Nuclear Cult', *Counterpunch* (2012); http://www.counterpunch.org/2012/06/18/the-nuclear-cult/.
7   Krämer, *Dr. Strangelove*, loc 1345.

8   SK11/1/7.

9   Anon, 'Coming: The End of the World', *Newsweek*, 3 April 1963, 60.

10 Kubrick quoted in Southern, 'Strange Loves', 52–53.

11 Script fragments on white pages, SK/11/1/21.

12 Script pages on white, 1 January 1963, SK/11/1/22.

13 Jeremy Bernstein, 'How About a Little Game?', *The New Yorker*, 12 November 1966.

14 Ibid., 28.

15 Ibid., 29.

16 Ibid.

17 Kubrick letter to George, 4 November 1961, PGA.

18 RAND Corporation, 'History and Mission'; http://www.rand.org/about/history.html.

19 Barry Zellen, 'Bernard Brodie and the Bomb: At the Birth of the Bipolar World' (2015), 148.

20 Ibid., 147.

21 Bernard Brodie, 'Must We Shoot from the Hip?', in *working paper* (RAND Corporation, 1951), 25.

22 Ibid., 27.

23 Christiane Kubrick, interview with the author, Childwickbury, April 2005.

24 While clearly not the same role, being 'special advisor' is indeed what the eponymous movie doctor describes himself as in the film. Much play is made of Tracy Reed as 'Miss Foreign Affairs', and Kissinger was notorious for his sexual appetite and in pursuing and dating glamorous women, something the aborted Otto Strangelove character demonstrates as the 'White House Rasputin'.

25 http://www.jfklibrary.org/About-Us/News-and-Press/Press-Releases/Henry-Kissingers-Kennedy-Administration-Files-Opened.aspx.

26 Christopher Hitchens, *The Trial of Henry Kissinger* (London: Verso, 2002).

27 Anthony Frewin, email to author November 18, 2015.

28 Kissinger's article can be viewed here: Henry Kissinger, 'Strains on the Alliance', *Foreign Affairs* (1963); https://www.foreignaffairs.com/articles/cuba/1963–01-01/strains-alliance.

29 For example, see Boyer, *Fallout: An Historian Reflects on America's Half-Century Encounter with Nuclear Weapons*; Smith, *Doomsday Men: The Real Dr. Strangelove and the Dream of the Superweapon*. Sharon Ghamari-Tabrizi also details multiple references at the time to Kahn as the 'real' Dr. Strangelove, including in 'The Think-Tank Man', *Life*, 6 December 1968. See Kissinger, 'Strains on the Alliance'.

30 Fred Kaplan, *The Wizards of Armageddon* (Stanford, CA: Stanford University Press (ebook), 1991), 226, Loc 3868.

31 Ibid., 230, Loc 3947.

32 Christiane Kubrick, interview with the author, Childwickbury, April 2005.

33 Sharon Ghamari-Tabrizi, *The Worlds of Herman Khan: The Intuitive Science of Thermo-Nuclear War* (Cambridge, MA: Harvard University Press, 2005), 41–42.

34 Herman Kahn letter to Peter George, 27 March 1964, PGA.

35 Ibid.

36 Christiane Kubrick, ibid.

37 Ibid.

38 Ibid.

39 Ibid.

40 Anthony Frewin, email to author, 18 November 2015.

41 Barry Zellen, 'Bernard Brodie: A Clausewitz for the Nuclear Age', *Strategic Thinkers* (2009); http://securityinnovator.com/index.php?articleID=15954&sectionID=43.

42 194 Kaplan, Fred, 1991, *The Wizards of Armageddon*, Stanford University Press (ebook), 222, Loc 3794.

43 Kenneth D. Rose, *One Nation Underground: The Fallout Shelter in American Culture* (New York: New York University Press, 2001), 117.

44 Teller quoted in ibid.

45 Ibid.

46 Morgenstern quoted in Sylvia Nasar, *A Beautiful Mind* (New York: Faber & Faber, 2012), 41.

47 Albert Wohlstetter, 'The Delicate Balance of Terror', *P-1472* (1958); http://www.rand.org/about/history/wohlstetter/P1472/P1472.html, also printed in a truncated form as 'The Delicate Balance of Terror', *Foreign Affairs* 37, no. 2 (1959): 211–34.

48 Ibid.

49 Ibid.

50 Albert Wohlstetter and Henry Rowen, 'Objectives of the United States Military Posture', *RM-2373* (1959); http://www.rand.org/about/history/wohlstetter/P1472/P1472.html.

51 Craig Unger, *The Fall of the House of Bush* (New York: Scribner, 2007), 42–46.

52 Ibid.

53 See Roslynn D. Haynes, *From Faust to Strangelove: Representations of the Scientists in Western* Literature (Baltimore: John Hopkins University Press, 1994).

54 Dyson quoted by Mark Freuanfelder in BoingBoing, October 11, 2011, http://boingboing.net/2006/10/11/george-dyson-on-nucl.html.

55 Quoted in Alex Wellerstein, 'Trinity at 70: "Now We Are All Sons of Bitches"', *Nuclear Secrecy* (2015); http://blog.nuclearsecrecy.com/2015/07/17/now-we-are-all-sons-of-bitches/.

56 Ibid.

57 Joel Shurkin, 'Edward Teller, "Father of the Hydrogen Bomb", Is Dead at 95'; http://news.stanford.edu/news/2003/september24/tellerobit-924.html.

58 See the full text of the petition here: http://www.dannen.com/decision/45-07-03.html.

59 John von Neumann; http://www.atomicheritage.org/profile/john-von-neumann.

60 William Poundstone, *The Prisoner's Dilemma* (Anchor, 2011), 76.

61 In *The Prisoner's Dilemma* Poundstone implies that the cancer resulted from the radiation Von Neumann received while observing the atomic tests at Bikini: 'A number of physicists associated with the bomb succumbed to cancer at relatively early ages', 189.

62 Janet Chen, Su-I Lu, and Dan Vekhter, 'Von Neumann and the Development of Game Theory'; https://cs.stanford.edu/people/eroberts/courses/soco/projects/1998–99/game-theory/neumann.html.

63 Ibid.

64 Smith, *Doomsday Men: The Real Dr. Strangelove and the Dream of the Superweapon*, 362.

65 Janet Chen, Su-I Lu, and Dan Vekhter, Ibid.

66 See Dale Carter, *The Final Frontier: The Rise and Fall of the American Rocket State* (London: Verso, 1988).

67   Ibid.

68   Stephen Wolfram, 28 December, 2003; http://blog.stephenwolfram.com/2003/12/john-von-neumanns-100th-birthday/

69   Norman MacRae, *John Von Neumann: The Scientific Genius Who Pioneered the Modern Computer, Game Theory, Nuclear Deterrence, and Much More* (American Mathematical Society, 1999), 376–77. In a scene deleted from the final cut of Strangelove, as part of the Pie Fight sequence, General Turgidson happily pushes Strangelove around the War Room, after the inter-service melee.

70   Istvan Hargittai, *The Martians of Science: Five Physicists Who Changed the Twentieth Century* (Oxford: Oxford University Press, 2006), 132.

71   Ibid., 228.

72   Alexander Leitch, *A Princeton Companion* (Princeton University Press, 1978).

73   http://etcweb.princeton.edu/CampusWWW/Companion/von_neumann_john.html

74   Heims, *John Von Neumann and Norbert Wiener: From Mathematics to the Technologies of Life and Death*.

75   Ibid.

76   MacRae, *John Von Neumann: The Scientific Genius Who Pioneered the Modern Computer, Game Theory, Nuclear Deterrence, and Much More*, 380.

77   Smith, *Doomsday Men: The Real Dr. Strangelove and the Dream of the Superweapon*, 364.

78   Alex Wellerstein, 'Edward Teller's 'Moon Shot'', *Nuclear Secrecy* (2011); http://blog.nuclearsecrecy.com/2011/12/12/edward-tellers-moon-shot/

79   This event was eerily anticipated a year before in Irwin Allen's nuclear age fable, *Voyage to the Bottom of the Sea* (1961), where, conversely, a nuclear missile is used to extinguish the burning Van Allen radiation belts circling the globe.

80   Phil Plait, 'The 50th Anniversary of the Starfish Prime: The Nuke That Shook the World', *Discover Magazine* (2012); http://blogs.discovermagazine.com/badastronomy/2012/07/09/the-50th-anniversary-of-starfish-prime-the-nuke-that-shook-the-world/#.VOfsuauG_FI.

81   'The Einstein Letter – 1939', Atomic Heritage Foundation; http://www.atomicheritage.org/history/einstein-letter-1939.

82   Shurkin, 'Edward Teller, "Father of the Hydrogen Bomb", Is Dead at 95'.

83   Hargittai, *The Martians of Science: Five Physicists Who Changed the Twentieth Century*.

84   Gary Stix, 'Infamy and Honor at the Atomic Café: Edward Teller Has No Regrets About His Contentious Career', *Scientific American* (1999): 42–43.

85   See 'Werner Von Braun'; http://www.newworldencyclopedia.org/entry/Wernher_von_Braun.

86   'Slave Labor Built V-Weapons'; http://www.nationalmuseum.af.mil/factsheets/factsheet.asp?id=8093.

87   'Werner Von Braun', *Operation Paperclip*; http://www.operationpaperclip.info/wernher-von-braun.php.

88   Paul Grigorieff, 'The Mittelwerk/Mittelbau/Camp Dora'; http://www.v2rocket.com/start/chapters/mittel.html.

89   Andrew Dunar and Stephen Waring, 'Power to Explore', (1999); http://history.msfc.nasa.gov/vonbraun/excerpts.html.

90   See 'Joint Intelligence Objectives Agency. Foreign Scientist Case Files 1945–1958', *US National Archives and Records Administration*; http://www.archives.gov/iwg/

declassified-records/rg-330-defense-secretary/.

91 Actually the phrase is heard spoken in the film itself by an acerbic American journalist.

92 Louis Menand, 'Fat Man: Herman Khan and the Nuclear Age', *The New Yorker* (2005); http://www.newyorker.com/magazine/2005/06/27/fat-man

93 On Strughold, see http://www.gwu.edu/ffnsarchiv/radiation/dir/mstreet/commeet/meet13/brief13/tab_f/br13f3.txt

94 'Scientist with Nazi Past Removed from Nm Space History Museum Hall of Fame', *Anti-Defamation League* (2006); http://archive.adl.org/NR/exeres/2D6AAE8C-3DE8-4E5E-9A51-B530031786D0,0B1623CA-D5A4-465D-A369-DF6E8679CD9E,frameless.htm.

95 On Strughold's affidavits, see Harvard Nuremberg Trials Project; http://nuremberg.law.harvard.edu/php/search.php?DI=1&FieldFlag=1&PAuthors=596

96 On Disney, see Mike Wright, 'The Disney-Von Braun Collaboration and Its Influence on Space Exploration', *Marshall Space Flight Center History Office*; http://history.msfc.nasa.gov/vonbraun/disney_article.html. On the 1960 bio-pic, *I Aim at the Stars* (J. Lee Thompson), see http://www.tcm.com/tcmdb/title/27789/I-Aim-at-the-Stars/

97 Michael Ross, 'Glenn Urges Probe for Toxic Experiments: Health: Senator Says US Should Disclose If Any Patients Were Unwittingly Exposed to Any Hazardous Substance in Tests Like Those for Radiation', *Los Angeles Times*, 7 January 1994.http://articles.latimes.com/1994–01-07/news/mn-9354_1_radiation-testing.

98 See Kubrick's doodles of the title variations, SK-11–1-16–001.

99 Mather, *Stanley Kubrick at Look Magazine: Authorship and Genre in Photojournalism and Film*, 274–75.

100 Tony Frewin phone interview with the author, May 2016.

101 Alexander Walker, *Stanley Kubrick, Director: A Visual Analysis* (London: Widenfeld & Nicolson, 1999), 129.

102 See Sellers, 1974, interview by Michael Parkinson; https://www.youtube.com/watch?v=1mbUdsQfSqO .

103 Coincidentally, Wiseman preceded his role in *Dr. No* as an atomic energy SPECTRE operative, with a starring role in Rod Serling's *The Twilight Zone*. In 'One More Pallbearer' Wiseman plays a megalomaniac industrialist, Paul Radin, who builds a fallout shelter three hundred feet under the New York skyscraper that he owns. He invites and then entraps a trio of former acquaintances, fooling them with an elaborate hoax, using rumbling sound effects and fake civil defense warnings, that a nuclear attack is imminent. Radin offers the group salvation in his shelter if they apologise for the past wrongs that he perceives were directed against him. Each refuses and leaves, contemptuous or pitying, preferring the uncertainty of an apocalyptic war rather than surrendering to his psychotic control. With his revenge thwarted, Radin becomes manic, imagining the holocaust is real, trapped in a nightmare of his own making.

104 For an interesting reading of *Dr. No's* influences see Ross Stillman's etymology of the Strangelove name is interesting but ultimately mired in coincidental stretches, such as those conflating D. H. Lawrence and Ian Fleming's 'Strangeways' characters.

105 Kubrick, quoted in Southern, 'Notes from the War Room'.

106 When Quilty/Zempf extracts a softpack of cigarettes the brand is 'Drome', the same smokes Quilty endorses on the magazine pin-up page beside Lolita's bed.

107 'Characters from The Goon Show' at http://www.thegoonshow.net/characters.asp

108 Graham Stark, *Remembering Peter Sellers* (London: Robson Books, 1990), 29.

109 Derek Sylvester, *Peter Sellers* (London: Proteas Press, 1981), 24.

110 Ed Sikov, *Mr. Strangelove: A Biography of Peter Sellers* (New York: Hyperion, 2002), 120.

111 Ibid., 121.

112 PBS, 'Operation Alert, Race for the Superbomb', *The American Experience*; http://www.pbs.org/wgbh/amex/bomb/peopleevents/pandeAMEX64.html.

113 Sikov, *Mr. Strangelove: A Biography of Peter Sellers*, 161–62.

114 Ibid., 160.

115 Ibid., 160–61.

116 Kubrick letter to Nabokov, 15 December 1965, SK/10/8/2.

117 Sikov, *Mr. Strangelove: A Biography of Peter Sellers*, 195.

118 Walker interview in 'Inside Dr. Strangelove'.

119 Peter Sellers, interview by Steve Allen, 1964. https://www.youtube.com/watch?v=OyWn_8SUWtg

120 See Sergio Della Sala, 'The Anarchic Hand', *The Psychologist* 18, no. 10 (2005): 506–601; Celia Marchetti and Sergio Della Sala, 'Disentangling the Alien and Anarchic Hand', *Cognitive Neuropsychiatry* 3, no. 3 (1998): 191–207; Kenneth M. Heilman and Edward Valenstein, eds., *The Alien Hand: Terminology and Pathogenesis*, 4th ed., Clinical Neuropsychology (Oxford: Oxford University Press, 2003), 358–60.

121 Jose Biller and Alberto J. Espay, 'Alien Hand Syndrome', in *Practical Neurology Visual Review* (Baltimore, MD: Lippinott Williams & Wikins, 2013), 54–55.

122 Heilman and Valenstein, *The Alien Hand: Terminology and Pathogenesis*, 359.

123 Marchetti and Della Sala, 'Disentangling the Alien and Anarchic Hand', 200.

124 Ibid., 196.

125 Ibid., 106.

126 Pat Ivens to Peter George, 8 April 1963. Also in this letter, Kubrick informs George that Captain 'Ace' Owens 'does get wounded and eventually dies', and 'Major Kong goes down to the bomb bay to mend a structurally faulty part and falls from the bay – presumably to his death. We see no more of the crew or the plane after this.'

127 Marchetti and Della Sala, 'Disentangling the Alien and Anarchic Hand', 196.

128 Heilman and Valenstein, *The Alien Hand: Terminology and Pathogenesis*, 358.

129 Marchetti and Della Sala, 'Disentangling the Alien and Anarchic Hand', 191.

130 Freud's concept also informs the robotics theory of the 'uncanny valley' where corpses, zombies and prosthetic hands are emblematic of the uncanny frisson.

131 Sigmund Freud, 'The Uncanny', (1919); http://web.mit.edu/allanmc/www/freud1.pdf , 14.

132 Robert Horton, *Frankenstein* (New York: Columbia University Press, 2014), 49.

133 Michael Sellers, *P.S. I Love You* (London: Collins, 1981), 90.

134 David George, interview by the author, Hastings 2005.

CHAPTER THREE

'Gentlemen, you can't fight in here...': Brinksmanship Amongst the Authors and Producers of *Dr. Strangelove* and *Fail-Safe*

As *Dr. Strangelove* was Stanley Kubrick's first studio film as producer-director-(co-) writer, it marked a significant professional development and advancement for the emerging auteur as he attempted to secure complete artistic control over his increasingly complex and innovative productions.[1] The controversy over the alleged antagonisms between Kubrick's movie and the competing Columbia Studio feature, *Fail-Safe*, has been recounted only marginally in film scholarship to date.[2] Never before has access to primary materials enabled a comprehensive analysis of Kubrick's pre- and post-production processes, technical engagements, artistic methodologies, collaborative practices and legal pursuits.[3]

Less than a year after Kubrick's death, Harvey Wheeler, co-author with Eugene Burdick of the novel *Fail-Safe*, wrote a piece for *The Idler* reflecting on the origins of *Fail-Safe* and its then current geopolitical context.[4] Wheeler's article appeared in late May 2000 and coincided with the screening on CBS of George Clooney's made-for-TV remake of the 1964 Sydney Lumet film. What is curious about Wheeler's commentary is its historical revisionism. In essence, Wheeler was re-writing history at a time when the key principals associated with these events had since passed away. He wrote:

In 1963 Columbia Pictures and Stanley Kubrick sued the authors, publishers and movie producers of *Fail-Safe* for infringement of copyright. Everybody involved was thrown into shock – McGraw Hill, the publisher, Curtis Brown, the agent, Martin Gang, the lawyer, and especially Max E. Youngstein the movie producer. Not me. How that suit was blown away traces back to the beginnings of the *Fail-Safe* plot.[5]

This opening salvo is clearly meant to suggest that the Columbia-Kubrick suit was demolished in favour of Wheeler's team. It ignores the fact that author Peter George instigated the proceedings and had advised the *Fail-Safe* authors and publishers a full year prior to the legal suit of his concerns.[6] That correspondence was ignored.

Wheeler recalls a meeting with McGraw-Hill fiction editor, Ed Kuhn:

Ed was in the grand tradition of the 'creative editor' of olden times. He was practically our co-author. [...] Once as an aside he asked, 'you fellas ever heard of a British novel with a similar plot?' Neither of us had. 'No matter', he said, 'I've seen it. Not very good. Back to work.' It later turned out he meant Peter (Bryant) George's *Red Alert*.[7]

This is a curious admission, given the events that would follow. It suggests that even if authors Burdick and Wheeler claimed not to have heard of *Red Alert*, then their 'creative editor' and 'practically co-author' Ed Kuhn had read George's novel. Further into detailing the history of the *Fail-Safe* book project, and despite the reported 'shock' of the action, Wheeler recounts his assured confidence. After Max E. Youngstein agreed to make the film (reportedly paying $500,000 to the authors), the suit for plagiarism was meant to be unforeseen and a surprise:

Then came the infringement of copyright suit by Columbia Pictures and Kubrick. Panic struck. Except for me...

Wheeler relates that his calmness was based on an ace-in-the-hole revelation. He had written a short story titled 'Abraham '59 – a Nuclear Fantasy' published in *Dissent* magazine in January 1959, under the pen name F. B. Aiken long before he and Eugene Burdick began their collaboration on the novel *Fail-Safe*. The dire attitude of Burdick's lawyer, Frank Wells (assigned by his principal Martin Gang), immediately changed upon learning of the *Dissent* short-story:

A big grin spread across his face. He picked up the magazine and ran through the offices waving it and yelling 'We won! ... We won!' And we did, handsomely.

With these words, Wheeler closes his revisionist article. However, his overall story slant and its strongly implied victory is pure fabrication. The suit was not blown away, nor did the publisher, agent, lawyer or film producer win – handsomely, or otherwise. It was quite the contrary.

Hence, to unravel the myth and opposing narratives concerning the dispute, this chapter draws from a range of primary documents from the Peter George archive (PGA), the Stanley Kubrick papers at Childwickbury (SKPC) and their subsequent deposit at the University of the Arts archives in London (SKA), interviews with creative personnel on both *Dr. Strangelove* and *Fail Safe*, and Stanley Kubrick's (and Peter George's) attorney, Louis Blau. The lawsuit by George *et al.* against authors Burdick and Wheeler, the publishers/producers of *Fail-Safe*, and its final settlement terms, have remained disputed historical events, with claim and counter-claim regarding the litigation and its outcome still circulating in the extant scholarship.[8]

Nevertheless, Wheeler's millennial missive conveniently glosses over one of the strangest episodes in the history of Hollywood legal proceedings. In the early 1960s, under the stewardship of Mike Frankovich, Columbia Pictures agreed to produce and distribute two competing narrative dramas with startlingly similar themes – the unauthorised and accidental use of American nuclear weapons against the Soviet Union. Two screenplays were developed into feature-length productions based on underlying literary works. The first of these books was *Two Hours to Doom* by Peter George using the pseudonym 'Peter Bryant' (and published as *Red Alert* in the USA), and the second was *Fail-Safe* by Eugene Burdick and Harvey Wheeler. The George/Bryant book was originally published in the UK in 1958 and then in America in March 1959, whereas the Burdick-Wheeler novel appeared in late 1962. *Two Hours to Doom/Red Alert* achieved substantial sales, and it was widely circulated and admired amongst nuclear strategists, the military and policy-makers.[9] *Fail-Safe* became a best-seller immediately prior to, during and after the Cuban Missile Crisis of October 1962. The novel was serialised in the *Saturday Evening Post* and chosen as a Book-of-the-Month-Club selection.[10]

FROM *RED ALERT* TO *DR. STRANGELOVE*

As the previous chapters have shown, throughout the Cold War filmmaker Stanley Kubrick was absorbed in esoteric theories of nuclear strategy and stayed a keen observer of global geopolitics.[11] With post-production completed on *Lolita* he searched for a suitable subject for his next film and continually gravitated towards the 'thermonuclear question'.

As noted, during Kubrick's extensive research and after a recommendation by Alastair Buchan, Head of the Strategic Studies Institute in London, he read the novel *Red*

Alert.[12] Even before securing the rights to the book, Kubrick had commenced developing a screen treatment with business partner and producer James B. Harris.[13] Kubrick wrote to George in November 1961 and Harris-Kubrick Pictures purchased the rights to the book through an intermediary in early December 1962.[14] In a memo to one of the Harris-Kubrick attorneys, Jack Schwartzman, Kubrick advised that 'the new production will be referred to as "Operation Peacemaker"'.[15] Working over Christmas 1961 and into early 1962 Kubrick and Harris developed a new treatment and screenplay, with George as co-writer joining them in New York in January. The treatment/screenplay was originally given the working title *Edge of Doom* and then formally denoted as *The Delicate Balance of Terror* (*D.B.O.T.*).[16]

Within a few weeks a taut script was completed and Harris pushed hard to get a deal struck with Eliot Hyman from Seven Arts Productions.[17] Seven Arts had just released *Lolita* with MGM and required a second feature from the Harris-Kubrick team.[18] The persistence of Harris paid off and the producer, film deal in hand (and with Kubrick's encouragement) amicably ended their business partnership in order to pursue his own ambitions as director.[19]

Kubrick continued to work with George on the screenplay but by April 1962 the director had begun to trust his instinct and shift towards what he would term 'nightmare comedy', redrafting the script to ultimately become *Dr. Strangelove: or How I Learned to Stop Worrying and Love the Bomb*.[20] Peter George saw Kubrick's creative about-face as a virtuoso turn and recognised the move as inspirational. However, the departure from a straight thriller caught long-time collaborator James B. Harris by surprise and caused great dismay. The deal struck with Seven Arts evaporated as soon as Hyman learned of Kubrick's new approach. Harris recalls thinking, somewhat sardonically: 'Jee-zus, you turn your back on the guy for one minute ... and he immediately flushes his career down the toilet. I mean, he was *toast*!'[21]

While Wheeler protested that he had no knowledge of Peter George (Bryant) and *Red Alert* or its UK title *Two Hours to Doom*, the converse did not apply. On Boxing Day 1961, the same day that Harris-Kubrick accepted the deal through their intermediary to acquire all rights 'other than publication' for George's novel, Eugene Burdick wrote to the filmmakers, submitting an outline and partially completed version of *Fail-Safe* for their consideration.[22] According to Wheeler, Kubrick agreed to consider the book after a conversation with Perry Knowlton, Burdick and Wheeler's literary agent, during a flight to London.[23] By 19 January 1962 Kubrick had politely declined the offer and enclosed by registered mail a detailed film treatment and copy of George's book, 'pursuant to our agreement in connection with the exchange of literary materials' and 'other literary materials which we have heretofore prepared relative to our theatrical motion picture project'.[24]

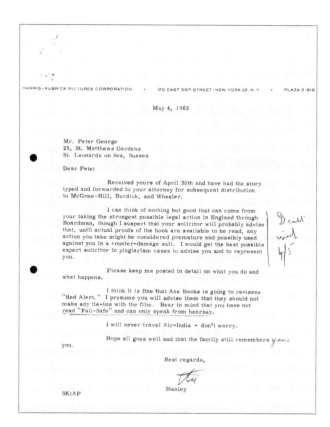

HARRIS-KUBRICK PICTURES CORPORATION • 120 EAST 56th STREET · NEW YORK 22, N. Y • PLAZA 2-816

May 4, 1962

Mr. Peter George
25, St. Matthews Gardens
St. Leonards on Sea, Sussex

Dear Pete:

Received yours of April 30th and have had the story
typed and forwarded to your attorney for subsequent distribution
to McGraw-Hill, Burdick, and Wheeler.

I can think of nothing but good that can come from
your taking the strongest possible legal action in England through
Boardman, though I suspect that your solicitor will probably advise
that, until actual proofs of the book are available to be read, any
action you take might be considered premature and possibly used
against you in a counter-damage suit. I would get the best possible
expert solicitor in plagiarism cases to advise you and to represent
you.

Please keep me posted in detail on what you do and
what happens.

I think it is fine that Ace Books is going to re-issue
"Red Alert." I presume you will advise them that they should not
make any tie-ins with the film. Bear in mind that you have not
read "Fail-Safe" and can only speak from hearsay.

I will never travel Air-India – don't worry.

Hope all goes well and that the family still remembers you,
you.

Best regards,

Stanley

SK:AP

On 14 April 1962, a full six months before the first printing of *Fail-Safe*, an industry gossip article by 'Whitefriar' in *Smith's Book Trade* raised plot and character similarities between *Red Alert* and *Fail-Safe*. When alerted to the clipping, George wrote to Kubrick asking his advice on whether he should take legal action, noting that Ace Books would cash-in on the controversy and reprint *Red Alert* in the US, even though his book was now 'far removed' from the current screen treatment.[25] George also noted that Hutchinson Publishing (UK) made a deal with McGraw Hill (US) to publish *Fail Safe* in September that year. The next day George's publisher, Tom Boardman Jnr, wrote to Kubrick enclosing the relevant clippings from *Smith's Book Trade*. Boardman promptly contacted Hutchinson's Managing Director, Robert Lusty, warning him of George's dismay at Whitefriar's allusion of plagiarism.[26] The same day George forwarded to Kubrick Boardman's letter to Lusty and outlined their legal strategy.[27] Kubrick immediately replied advising George to acquire 'a good plagiarism solicitor' and take 'the strongest possible legal action' against Burdick and Wheeler.[28]

A week later Hutchinson's Editorial Director, Harold Harris, blithely informed Boardman that he had simply purchased the UK rights to *Fail-Safe* 'from a synopsis' not having 'seen a page yet' but had been advised there was 'little similarity' between the two novels.[29] On 15 May 1962 Boardman wrote to Kubrick, attaching a copy of his correspondence with Harris warning of legal action if Hutchinson published *Fail-Safe*. Boardman also enclosed his own précis of the similarities of plot between both books to Harris.[30] These events, when coupled with the January 1962 exchange of literary materials between Harris-Kubrick and Burdick and Wheeler, and George's own correspondence with the American authors and publishers, makes Wheeler's 2000 assertion of ignorance of *Red Alert/Two Hours to Doom* implausible if not deliberately deceitful.

From June to October 1962, Kubrick and George continued to refine their screenplay, now re-oriented towards 'nightmare comedy'. Legal correspondence between Kubrick and Louis Blau on 20 June 1962 has the project titled 'Dr. Strangelove'.[31] Concerned that *Fail-Safe* would soon be optioned for filming, Kubrick advised Blau that a game plan be devised for just such a contingency, should the rights be sold. In the meantime, the script went through continuous modification during this period.[32] On 31 August 1962 the Kubrick and George final script was now formally titled and bound as *DR. STRANGELOVE Or: How I Learned To Stop Worrying And Love The BOMB* with the principal protagonists depicted as po-faced but playing for laughs while they prepared for global thermonuclear war.[33] Meanwhile the novel of *Fail-Safe* had yet to appear in either the USA or UK but from mid-to-late October it was serialised in the *Saturday Evening Post* over three installments. The timing was fortuitous for the publishers as President Kennedy announced on 22 October 1962 the discovery of Soviet Intermediate Range Ballistic Missiles (IRBMs) in Cuba and the superpowers lurched towards Armageddon.[34]

The book went into mass distribution shortly thereafter. With the release and publicity afforded *Fail-Safe*, George and Kubrick again sought advice on possible litigation in early November 1962. However, Louis Blau advised the situation be monitored and that 'now is not the time for a public protest'.[35] Given additional space to consider the implications of *Red Alert*, George wrote to his agent and Kubrick with his initial two-page comparison between his own book and *Fail-Safe*, squarely indicating plagiarism.[36]

Part of Columbia Pictures' 'due diligence' to protect their interest in *Dr. Strangelove* involved an objective study of the underlying work by a party not associated with the production in order to evaluate the veracity of the allegation of plagiarism against *Fail-Safe*. The studio asked Philip Charlot from the Story Department to undertake the analysis that was furnished to Columbia's Jack Fleischmann as a thirty-page report. Charlot first considered the similarities between Burdick and Wheeler's *Fail-Safe* and Wheeler's earlier short story 'Abraham 59' noting that while the plots had little in common, the characters and themes were shared.[37] Regarding the novels *Red Alert* and *Fail-Safe*, in his detailed summaries Charlot recognised that, even though 'plot similarities would be expected' because the premise of the books was essentially the same, it was 'more than coincidence' that multiple commonalities appeared across the novels. For Charlot this would support a case of plagiarism.[38] He concluded that Peter George did have a case in claiming his work was purloined, asserting that Burdick and Wheeler 'borrowed extensively' from *Red Alert* to create *Fail-Safe*.[39]

Charlot's report was sent to Kubrick while the co-writer, director-producer was in pre-production and beginning to cast *Dr. Strangelove*.[40] By mid-December 1962, he and lawyer Louis Blau were working up a briefing document in preparation of a legal suit against the authors and owners of *Fail-Safe*.[41] Kubrick supplied the exact phrasing of the major points alleging plagiarism in *Fail-Safe* for Blau to incorporate into a letter for George's legal challenge. On 20 December Blau cabled Kubrick informing him that the plagiarism lawsuit was officially filed and that *Fail-Safe* had not yet been sold. Ten days later Blau cabled Kubrick with the inevitable news, confirmed by Columbia, that Max E. Youngstein had 'agreed to purchase *Fail-Safe*', and that Blau had airmailed Peter George's draft press release to the studio.[42]

THE DISPUTE

Over the New Year holiday George finalised his formal statement alleging plagiarism, citing correspondence from experts Thomas Schelling (1960) and Herman Kahn (1961) whose unsolicited letters both praised the originality of his novel and noted how they were widely circulating copies of the book to their colleagues.[43] The statement outlined George's selling of the motion picture rights, claiming that the *Fail-Safe* plagiarism by the authors and their publishers had 'caused irreparable damage' to him, Kubrick and Columbia Pictures.[44] On 5 January 1963, the studio had dispatched George's statement to over two dozen influential media, relevant production and military contacts.[45]

It was a hectic time for the freshly minted producer, yet Kubrick skillfully pursued his options to the best advantage of *Dr. Strangelove*. One unexpected hiccup came during ne-gotiations with Sterling Hayden, who was offered the role of psychotic Air Force General, Jack D. Ripper.[46] Hayden had previously starred in the Harris-Kubrick *noir* feature *The Killing* (1955) and Kubrick sent him the *Strangelove* screenplay. Hayden accepted the part on 11 January 1963 with a terse but flattering reply via cablegram:

> Audacity of project equals brilliance of script strangely enough Burdick and I have been friends for years … congratulations.[47]

Kubrick was alarmed that some accidental or innocent communication between these West Coast pals might jeopardise his legal manoeuverings around Burdick, Wheeler and Youngstein. He fired off a cable same day:

Thank you for your kind words. Under no circumstances show script to anyone particularly Burdick as important law suit in works between Peter George author of novel *Red Alert* published 1958 upon which film is based and authors and publisher of *Fail-Safe* ... General Ripper will be long remembered.[48]

George's action against the publishers and authors was soon combined with Kubrick's own suit (via Polaris Productions and Hawk Films) when the inevitable film rights sale of *Fail-Safe* occurred. Kubrick liaised on the matter with Columbia's Head of Marketing, Bob Ferguson, after he learned that a former luminary at United Artists, Max E. Youngstein, had secured *Fail-Safe*. It was to be Youngstein's first independently financed production, the showcase of his new company, Entertainment Corp of America (ECA).[49] At a press conference held on 11 January 1963 Youngstein reported that Henry Fonda had signed to play the President and Sidney Lumet was attached as the director. Wheeler was also present and publicly refuted the plagiarism claim, stating his short story, which he maintained was the basis for *Fail-Safe*, was written in 1957.[50]

Events then moved rapidly from contingency plan to action. Kubrick's legal strategy was two-fold. Firstly, he wanted to protect his commercial interests in *Dr. Strangelove* against a competing, and allegedly plagiarised, literary work spawning another film property. This meant his film had to be released first, so injunctions were sought. Secondly, he saw the opportunity to generate significant publicity for his own film through a controversial lawsuit and its press coverage. On 15 January, he cabled Louis Blau:

Please call me at studio Wednesday with *Fail Safe* statement. [...] Am sure Frankovich will back us up on any aggressive line ... I definitely would like to make a press conference statement if at all possible jointly for myself and Columbia Pictures. This has the greatest chance to stop Max and make newspaper space. Important to get Frankovich's go ahead on joint action.[51]

Throughout the pre-production, casting and script revision with Terry Southern, Kubrick continued to liaise with Blau and George on their legal tactics. The opportunity to hold a press conference in the UK simultaneous with the US lodgment of the lawsuit appealed to the director and he pursued this idea repeatedly with his American attorneys.[52] Kubrick also relayed George's concerns that should the suit fail, the author would not be able to cover Blau's costs.[53] The matter was quickly resolved with George instructed to cable his lawyers in Los Angeles 'on the basis that Columbia finances entire lawsuit' with the studio 'empowered to dismiss lawsuit in its entirety', agreeing to pay his legal team a 25% contingency fee from any recovery against an agreed 60% split to Columbia and 40% to George.[54] Amidst this maelstrom of legal positioning, principal photography for

Dr. Strangelove commenced on 28 January 1963 at Shepperton Studios. Two weeks later, during a hectic shooting schedule, Stanley Kubrick was fronting a press conference at the Dorchester Hotel, London, alongside Peter Sellers, George C. Scott and Keenan Wynn. Kubrick took the opportunity to read from a prepared statement concerning the plagiarism suit against the authors and publishers of *Fail-Safe*, alleging that

> such appropriation and infringement of plaintiffs' copyrights and property will materially impair the value of the motion picture 'Dr. Strangelove', and that plaintiffs will be subjected to the impairment of several million dollars of potential distribution revenues.[55]

Film industry trade journals had reported that *Fail-Safe* would commence production on 1 May for a mid-August 1963 release.[56] Once the plagiarism suit was announced the fierce competition between the two productions received adjacent, front-page column inches, as detailed in *The Hollywood Reporter* of 12 February 1963. Headlining with 'Youngstein Sets Start Dates On 3 ECA Pix' the *Reporter* announced that *Fail-Safe* was now 'slated to roll April 15' with a release 'by September'. A parallel headline stated, 'Columbia Sues to Stop "Fail-Safe"' heralding that 'the war of the literary nuclear bombs reached court yesterday. [...] Charging copyright infringement and unfair competition', the plaintiffs sought a Federal Court injunction 'to stop ECA from producing, distributing or exploitation of a picture based on "Fail-Safe"'. *Daily Variety* the same day ran lengthier coverage of the lawsuit, detailing more fully the specifics of the charges.[57]

But Youngstein would not be deterred. Forty-eight hours later *Daily Variety* was quoting the producer as being assured by attorneys from McGraw-Hill, the publishers of *Fail-Safe*, that Peter George's plagiarism suit would 'pose no problems' for the ECA executive. Youngstein was moving 'full steam ahead', saying:

> From the title and what I've heard about the screenplay, 'Dr. Strangelove' appears to be something of a comedy. Ours is a serious drama, thus I don't see how the suit could stand up in court.[58]

The publicity made some impact on both sides of the Atlantic. *Paths of Glory* star and *Spartacus* star-producer, Kirk Douglas (replying to an unrelated Kubrick letter concerning *Seven Days in May*) wrote offering his support: 'What's happening with your lawsuit versus "Fail-Safe"? If there's any way that I could help, I wish you'd call on me.'[59]

With Columbia leading the action against *Fail-Safe*, the film's financial viability (chiefly $400,000 from the American Congress of Exhibitors) soon ebbed away, leaving both Youngstein's ECA and its parent company Television Industries Inc. (TVI) badly

exposed.[60] The damage from the legal challenge was so swift it led to ECA's complete collapse within a few days. *The New York Times* reported that ECA's proposed slate of future
productions was sold-off to major studios.[61] It is with some irony then that Columbia
– which had already begun negotiating with Youngstein – quickly acquired *Fail-Safe*.
Commenting on the Studio's rapid move *Daily Variety* observed:

> Facts behind Columbia's decision to take over film it originally tried to prevent being
> made are not clear. [...] As one wag put it yesterday, 'If Columbia doesn't get the pub-
> lic in to laugh at the bomb it now has a chance to see if they'll go for it as melodrama'.[62]

But the conflict did not end with Columbia becoming the 'parent' of both film projects.
The spectre of a counter-suit by the *Fail-Safe* authors and the original producers was
flagged in *The Hollywood Reporter*.[63] A little over six weeks into his principal photography, Kubrick knew that Lumet and Youngstein's New York-based production shoot and
post-production would be rapid (April to September). So the race was on.

THE SETTLEMENT

With Columbia bankrolling both films the studio moved to secure its interests and limit
potential damages. The competing productions would be staggered in their release.
But an agreement is never quite an agreement until executed and counter-signed. Blau
wrote to Kubrick on 8 March advising that, despite 'the understood terms' that *Fail-
Safe* would (a) not be released domestically until 1 June 1964, and (b) for outside the
USA delayed at least six months after *Strangelove*'s run (but no later than 1 December
1964), Youngstein's lawyer Harold Berkowitz was undermining that position directly
with the Studio.[64] Berkowitz's lobbying was paying off, as Blau now faced opposition
from Gordon T. Stulberg, Columbia's in-house lawyer, who felt Kubrick's position was too
harsh. Stulberg pushed Blau to rescind the release dates to 1 April (domestically) and
1 June (internationally). Irrespective of Columbia's proposed concession to *Fail-Safe*,
Youngstein's lawyer immediately upped the ante. Blau told Kubrick:

> Berkowitz came back in almost ultimatum form and said that Youngstein, in order to
> get financing, had to have the privilege of releasing no later than January 1, 1964,
> and if we didn't agree to that date he would lose his financing and we would be held
> accountable for damages, etc., etc. Naturally, I didn't acquiesce to the ultimatum.
> [...] At the moment, the settlement is presumably off.[65]

Kubrick cabled Blau with some good news a few days later. Columbia's head of UK operations, Mike Frankovich, was 'not worried about a counter-suit' and he had cabled Stulberg instructing him not to interfere with Blau's negotiations.[66] During this period, Columbia executives (including Frankovich) were viewing dailies from the set of *Dr. Strangelove* and the feedback 'was glowing'.[67] With *Fail-Safe* yet to commence filming the studio firmly backed its bird-in-the-hand, *Dr. Strangelove*.

On 27 March, while Columbia was still finalising its deal on *Fail-Safe*, Kubrick cabled Blau with important news:

> Understand *Fail Safe* beginning in April presumably under Columbia control. Frankovich and Joffe assured me this would only be done with my approval which I gave without any specific details discussed since it obviously not in Columbia's best interests to conflict pictures. However strongly believe you should insist part of Columbia agreement with Youngstein provides waiver of any counteraction by any of the defendants against George and myself.[68]

With these instructions Blau continued to press for a result irrevocably favouring Kubrick and George. However, the compromised draft settlement terms between the parties clearly troubled Kubrick. He cabled Lou Blau on 29 March 1963, expressing his concern that it might appear that Peter George 'was sold out'.[69] Blau's return cable the next day was unequivocal:

> Part of settlement includes five thousand for author. Peter George devinitely [sic] not sold out as matter of fact hes [sic] coming off smelling like a rose considering all circumstances and publication dates.[70]

A deal brokered through Columbia was finally struck on 12 April. The terms irrefutably advantaged Kubrick in respect of (a) the mandated delay to *Fail-Safe*'s American and international releases to be six months post-Strangelove's run; (b) that no *Fail-Safe* rushes, edited versions or portions be shown to the press, or to exhibitors for at least thirty days from *Strangelove*'s release domestically and abroad; and (c) no announcement of the settlement concerning *Fail-Safe* could be made without Stanley Kubrick's approval.[71]

A few days later Blau wrote to Kubrick and George enclosing the 'Mutual Release and Agreement' between all parties in the suit, for signing and exchange.[72] A check for $5,000 was made out to Peter George and an equal amount for attorneys Blau and Weber for their legal fees:

> You and Peter will note especially that the Release contains language clearly indicating that the offer of settlement was made to the GEORGE ET AL. group ... for 'good

and valuable consideration'. This was done in order to enlighten anyone reading the Release that lawsuit was not a 'frivolous' one, and a settlement favoring the George group resulted in the compromise settlement.[73]

Blau concluded with, 'Under all of the circumstances, I consider the settlement a good one from the standpoint of Peter and yourself', given that had it proceeded in court George would not have been able to challenge Wheeler's 'irrefutable affidavits' that his short story 'Abraham 59' was in circulation by March 1958 prior to its January 1959 publication.

Understandably Peter George was underwhelmed with and perhaps aggrieved by the result. He had asserted professional damage from the public revelation of plagiarism. Caught up in the whirlwind of Hollywood lawyers and studio publicity, with Kubrick and Blau advising him to take strong action to protect his copyrights in the UK and USA, George no doubt felt out of his depth. Initially, George and Kubrick's legal proceedings foregrounded damages in the millions and sought an injunction to prevent any further printing and distribution of *Fail-Safe* in the UK and USA. This, of course, was an ambit claim – something to be negotiated and the dispute ideally settled out of court, which it ultimately was.

Upon sighting the negotiated draft settlement terms, George wrote to Blau, graciously thanking him for his representation and his legal team's efforts, but clearly expressing his disappointment:

I must say at once to you, Louis, both as an attorney and as a friend, that I am not prepared to settle on these terms. Please do not be offended if I speak plainly, as I know you have my best interests in mind, and I appreciate that. But I feel that the figure of $5,000 is quite unacceptable. I don't doubt that Stanley has told you I feel very strongly in this matter, but I am prepared to consolidate this action on what I think to be a reasonable basis. This comprises:
  a) A sum of $25,000 cash to be paid to me
  b) A sum equating to five percent of the gross sums which Messrs. Eugene Burdick and Harvey Wheeler have received from the film rights of FAIL SAFE. Since Max Youngstein has announced this publicly as $500,000, I do not think this request is unreasonable.[74]

However, George was a pragmatist and recognised 'certain developments' in the suit (Wheeler's revelation about 'Abraham 59' and its pre-publication circulation) had the potential to minimise his case. He told Blau: 'I feel there has been gross plagiarism – which I agree would be difficult to prove against Harvey Wheeler', since there were other points of similarity between both books, not contained in the earlier short story. George had consulted widely amongst British lawyers, directors and editors 'who unanimously support me in my belief'.[75] Yet he was prepared to reach 'a favourable compromise ... in the interests of peace'.

George also related to Blau something of the physical and professional toll that the protracted plagiarism dispute was having on him personally, concluding with:

> Over the past fifteen months I have been constantly worrying about this lawsuit. This alone has cost me dearly in terms of novels which I had planned but have been unable to write because of the worry ... I cannot overestimate the strength of my feelings.

Around the same time Marc Jaffe and Grace Bechtold, editors at Bantam Books who were publishing the novelisation of *Dr. Strangelove*, sent the author a list of manuscript amendments they required to better reflect the film script. These were not a set of directions, no matter how minor or niggling, that George was pleased to undertake.[76] A month later George was hospitalised and unable to work. Kubrick was completing production at Shepperton but sent the writer a basket of fruit on behalf of the *Strangelove* cast and crew that George noted was much appreciated. The author recovered fully and, though initially heavily medicated, pressed on with the novelisation and his other manuscript projects. The rest and recuperation seemed to energise George who had become more sanguine concerning the plagiarism settlement. He wrote warmly to his US lawyers Blau and Schwartzmann, thanking them and acknowledging receipt of their cheque of $7,500 (with the agreed legal fee deducted prior).

However, a short time after all parties had executed the Agreement, Kubrick cabled Blau on 9 July to once again intervene on his behalf:

> Due to unforeseen uncontrollable technical delays new distribution date New York Los Angeles openings Christmas. Mass booking end January February. Vital you obtain agreement Columbia delay Fail-Safe from March 1st to July 1st.[77]

Fortunately Frankovich backed him and the director obtained his extension to 1 July 1964, quarantining *Fail-Safe* for six months after *Dr. Strangelove*'s general release. Even when adjusting his own schedule Kubrick remained ever vigilant in holding his adversaries to the terms of the Agreement. After seeing an August issue of *American Cinematographer* featuring an article on *Fail-Safe*, he cabled Blau: 'This is direct violation agreement not to publicize until Strangelove release ... it is serious precedent and should be strongly protested in writing by you to Jaffe Stulberg, etc.'[78]

Irrespective of the litigation and its protracted nature Kubrick remained pragmati-cally open to any idea that might maximise his box-office returns. In early 1965 he raised the idea of piggy-backing off the domestic *Fail-Safe* release, suggesting to Columbia that it could run *Dr. Strangelove* with *Fail-Safe* as a double bill.[79] Kubrick enthused to Columbia's New York-based Executive Vice President Leo Jaffe, that 'it would be one of the most talked about combinations in film history'. Jaffe's response to the 'bizarre' idea was muted, suggesting Kubrick wait for six months before any serious consideration be given, since the domestic run of *Fail-Safe* was still underway and a double-screen-ing would prejudice international box-office strategy.[80] Ultimately the double bill never eventuated from Columbia's marketing department.

The events recounted in this chapter demonstrate a key aspect of first-time studio producer Stanley Kubrick's attention to detail and his strident efforts to protect the copyright and intellectual property associated with the production of *Dr. Strangelove* and its underlying literary work. According to the relevant correspondence and legal files, throughout the plagiarism controversy Kubrick went to extraordinary lengths to ensure the favourable positioning of his movie over and above a competing studio production slated to be released first, despite an array of objection, obstruction and interference from multiple parties. Throughout these events, Kubrick appears considerably protec-tive of author Peter George's interests and rose to his defence as a mentor. Naturally, these moves served to advantage them both. However, the tenor of correspondence suggests the director wanted to do the right thing, aware of George's relative inexperi-ence and possible naivety negotiating with Hollywood's legal experts.

Despite Harvey Wheeler's attempted revisionism perhaps it is James B. Harris, Kubrick's former business partner, who has most succinctly summarised the outcome of the dispute: 'a deal was worked out – because they were both at Columbia, which *ab-solutely* fucked *Fail-Safe* – *Strangelove* had to be released first'.[81]

Regardless, the fierce competition between the producers of *Dr. Strangelove* and *Fail-Safe* revealed some remarkable parallelism. Both films were based on fictional literary works, and both screenplays (at least initially in *Strangelove*'s case) were approached generically as thrillers in semi-documentary style. Neither film sought, nor was granted, Pentagon approval or military assistance but instead used commercially available stock footage of jet-bombers.[82] Both films lost their initial financing only to find a mutual sup-porter in Mike Francovitch at Columbia. Both creators of the underlying literary works alleged plagiarism, where George's (ultimately successful out-of-court) claim was then rhetorically counter-challenged by Wheeler *et al*. With Columbia financing and distribut-ing each film, the studio funded the legal action between the competing productions but retained the right to 'dismiss, settle, discontinue or otherwise terminate' as it saw fit. All parties negotiated in good faith and a compromise was reached facilitated by the studio. Eventually this outcome entirely favoured Peter George and Stanley Kubrick despite the diminution of their final damages settlement.

Perhaps Wheeler felt satisfied that he had the last say on the matter in 2000. The chronology of events and associated analysis presented in this chapter should definitively settle that matter, as the out-of-court settlement is now a matter of public record.[83]

NOTES

1   Peter Krämer, 'Complete Total Final Annihilating Artistic Control', in *Stanley Kubrick: New Perspectives*, ed. Tatjana Liujic, Peter Krämer, and Richard Daniels (London: Black Dog, 2015), 49–60.

2   Peter Krämer has recently published two fine articles on *Dr. Strangelove* drawing from the Kubrick Archive holdings deposited at the University of Arts London. See: '"The Greatest Mass Murderer since Adolf Hitler": Nuclear War and the Nazi Past in Dr. Strangelove', in *Dramatising Disaster: Character, Event, Representation*, ed. Christine Cornea and Rhys Owain Thomas (Newcastle: Cambridge Scholar Press, 2013); and '"To Prevent Heat from Dissipating": Stanley Kubrick and the Marketing of *Dr. Strangelove* (1964)', *InMedia* 3 (2013).

3   A collection of scholarship based on this new access to Kubrick's Archive includes an earlier version of this chapter; see Mick Broderick, 'Reconstructing Strangelove: Outtakes from Kubrick's Cutting Room Floor', in *Stanley Kubrick: New Perspectives*, ed. Tatjana Liujic, Peter Kramer, and Richard Daniels (London: Black Dog, 2015), 150–73.

4   Harvey Wheeler, 'Fail-Safe Then and Now', *The Idler* 2, no. 32 (2000); www.the-idler.com.

5   Ibid.

6   See Peter George, 'Statement by Peter George Regarding Legal Action for Plagiarism Against Authors and Publishers of the Novel 'Fail-Safe'', 3 January 1963, 2. SKPC.

7   Wheeler, 'Fail-Safe Then and Now'.

8   Several authors get the chronology of events and/or the outcome wrong, often recycling the mythology. See, for example Kubrick biographers Lobrutto, *Stanley Kubrick: A Biography*, 89; Baxter, *Stanley Kubrick: A Biography*, 175; Rodney Hill and Gene D. Phillips, *The Encyclopedia of Stanley Kubrick*, Facts on File (New York: Checkmark Books, 2002).

9   Thomas Shelling (15 December 1960) and Herman Kahn (8 August 1961) wrote to Peter George, praising the novel, with Khan noting how he had handed it around to fellow nuclear strategists. Kubrick's initial letter soliciting George also notes Khan's mention of the novel in *On Thermonuclear War*.

10 Wheeler, ibid.

11 Christiane Kubrick, interview by the author, April 2005.

12 Lobrutto, *Stanley Kubrick: A Biography*, 227.

13 See 'Intended Screen Play Revisions for the Novel 'Red Alert'', 25 October 1961, submitted to Burdick & Wheeler by Registered mail (19 January 1962), in exchange for their offer of rights to an early pre-publication draft of the novel *Fail-Safe*. Surprisingly, this revision

uses the plot devices of the novel but alters the nuclear first strike from American to Soviet forces, SKPC.

14 Kubrick letter to George, 4 November 1961, PGA. Harris relates that he and Kubrick used Sig Shore as a go-between to secure the rights to get the book cheaper, rather than be represented as Harris-Kubrick. See correspondence between Sig Shore and Scott Meredith, 13–16 December 1961. SKPC.

15 Memo from Ben Reyes to Jack Schwartzman, 29 December 1961, SKA.

16 Script draft, *Red Alert*, 8 January 1962, SKA.

17 James B. Harris, phone interview with author, June 2004.

18 Ibid.

19 Coincidentally Harris went on to direct his own nuclear thriller, *The Bedford Incident* (1965), also for Columbia Pictures. He suggested Mike Frankovitch, who oversaw all three film projects, was a 'one-man world War III fan'.

20 On 'nightmare comedy', see Stanley Kubrick, 'How I Learned to Stop Worrying and Love the Cinema', in *Films and Filming* (June 1963), 12. Kubrick wrote to BBC producer David J. Webster on 23 April 1962, signaling that his project had now tuned away from a nuclear documentary style, believing it would no longer work. The move towards the nightmare comedy might be traced back to 21 March 1962 with Kubrick writing to Blau, requesting him to return the copy of the script 'The Delicate Balance of Terror', the earlier version of the script; both documents from SKPC.

21 Harris, ibid.

22 Burdick letter to Harris-Kubrick, 26 December 1961, SKPC.

23 Wheeler, 'Fail-Safe Then and Now'.

24 Kubrick letter to Burdick & Wheeler. The Harris-Kubrick treatment of *Red Alert* is dated 25 October 1961.

25 George letter to Kubrick, 30 April 1962, SKPC.

26 Boardman letter to Kubrick, 30 April 1962, SKPC.

27 George letter to Kubrick, 4 May 1962, SKPC.

28 Kubrick letter to George, 4 May 1962, SKPC.

29 Harris letter to Boardman, 11 May 1962, SKPC.

30 Boardman letter to Kubrick, 15 May 1962, SKPC.

31 Correspondence from Jack Schwartzmann suggests the title 'Dr. Strangelove' was registered by James B. Harris with Paramount Pictures on 25 May 1962. This also implies that Paramount was approached as a potential financier after the Harris-Kubrick deal fell through with Seven Arts and before Kubrick secured a deal with Columbia.

32 Kubrick letter to Blau, 21 June 1962, SKA.

33 Script, Harris-Kubrick Pictures, 31 August 1962, PGA.

34 On the Cuban missile crisis, see declassified documents and analysis at the online National Security Archive: http://www.gwu.edu/ffnsarchiv/nsa/cuba_mis_cri/index.htm

35 Blau letter to Kubrick and George, 9 November 1962, SKPC.

36 George letter to Tom Boardman Jnr and Kubrick, 22 November 1962, SKPC.

37 Philip Charlot letter and report to Jack Fleischmann, 27 November 1962, SKPC, 1–2.

38 Charlot report to Fleischmann, 27 November 1962, SKPC, 27.

39 Charlot report to Fleischmann, 27 November 1962, SKPC, 28–29.

40 Seymour Steinberg letter to Stanley Kubrick, 19 December 1962, SKPC.

41 Kubrick letter to Blau, 14 December 1962, SKPC.

42 Blau cable to Kubrick, 29 December 1962, SKPC. The cable has a series of options/questions hand written by Kubrick concerning his possible actions, such as his calling Youngstein, sending him a copy of *Red Alert*, or having Columbia handle the situation.

43 Statement by Peter George, 3 January 1963, SKPC, 1

44 Ibid, 2.

45 See list of names under title 'Peter George Legal Statement sent to', 5 January 1963, SKPC.

46 Hayden was not Kubrick's first choice. The initial offer went to Gene Kelly who declined.

47 Sterling Hayden cable to Kubrick, 11 January 1963, SKA, University of the Arts London.

48 Kubrick cable to Hayden, 11 January 1963, SKPC.

49 Ferguson letter to Kubrick, 14 January 1963, SKPC.

50 Nat Weiss cable to Kubrick, 11 January 1963, SKPC.

51 Kubrick cable to Blau, 15 January 1963, SKPC.

52 Kubrick cables to Blau, 16 January and 24 January 1963, SKPC.

53 Kubrick cable to Blau, 16 January 1963, SKPC.

54 Jack Schwartzmann cable to Kubrick, 31 January 1963. SKPC.

55 'Transcript of Remarks Made by Stanley Kubrick at Press Conference, Dorchester Hotel, 12 February 1963', SKPC, 2.

56 See *Daily Variety*, 7 February 1963, 1; *The Hollywood Reporter,* 7 February 1963, 1; *Motion Picture Daily*, 7 February 1963, 1.

57 'Claim "Fail-Safe" "Plagiarized" Brit. "2 Hours to Doom"', *Daily Variety*, 12 February 1963, 1, 4.

58 'Suit Won't Stall "Fail-Safe" Filming, Youngstein Avers', *Daily Variety*, 14 February 1963, 1, 4.

59 Kirk Douglas letter to Kubrick, 19 February 1963, SKA. Given the reported hostility from Douglas (at least in later years), this is certainly a friendly gesture, following on from Kubrick's own unsolicited but considered advice to Douglas.

60 'Fail-Safe Being Acquired by Col.', *The Hollywood Reporter*, 1 April 1963.

61 Howard Thompson, 'Movie Company to Be Dissolved', *The New York Times*, 6 April 1963.

62 "Winston' to 20th, 'Fail-Safe' to Col. As ECA Fold Nears', *Daily Variety*, 5 April 1963.

63 Kubrick letter to Blau, 18 March 1963, SKPC.

64 Blau letter to Kubrick, 8 March 1963, SKPC.

65 Ibid.

66 Kubrick cable to Blau, 11 March 1963, SKPC.

67 Blau cable to Kubrick, 27 February 1963, SKPC.

68 Kubrick cable to Blau, 27 March 1963, SKPC.

69 Kubrick cable to Blau, 29 March 1963, SKPC. Kubrick again raised his concerns when Columbia's lawyer Stulberg later confirmed to him that the Studio agreed to pay George $10,000 which seemed to contradict Blau's reporting of the agreement that provided only half that amount.

70 Blau cable to Kubrick, 30 March 1963, SKPC.

71 Columbia Picture letter to Polaris Productions and Hawk Films, 12 April 1963, SKPC.

72 Blau letter to Kubrick, 16 April 1963, SKPC.

73 Ibid, 2.

74 George letter to Blau, 22 April 1963, SKPC.

75 Ibid.

76 'Novelization manuscript of DOCTOR STRANGELOVE', 14 April 1963, SKPC.

77 Kubrick letter to Blau, 9 July 1963, SKPC.

78 Kubrick to Blau, 24 September 1963, SKPC.

79 Kubrick letter to Leo Jaffe, 13 April 1965, SKPC.

80 Jaffe letter to Kubrick, 20 April 1965, SKPC.

81 James B. Harris, phone interview with author, June 2004.

82 Sidney Lumet, interviewed by Naylor, 'Inside Dr. Strangelove'.

83 Recalling the sardonic coda to Kubrick's *Barry Lyndon* (and Thackery's novel), we should likewise observe of those fictional protagonists, 'they are all equal now'.

CHAPTER FOUR

Authentically Strange: Presidential Predelegation, Fail-safes and Doomsday Machines

At the time of *Dr. Strangelove*'s release there was serious speculation over the technical accuracy of the plot, production design and dialogue, especially in view of the grave secrecy and national security measures protecting disclosure of classified technologies and emergency war-fighting procedures. Production designer Ken Adam, who worked on designing bomb shelters during World War II before piloting Hawker Typhoons, has mentioned on several occasions that he and art director Peter Murton had to rely mostly on publicly sourced material from flight magazines and books to design the internal B-52 instrumentation.[1] This speculation has only increased over the years, when matched against what was then known publicly about nuclear strategy and systems of deterrence and what can now be ascertained from recent declassifications of US and Soviet documents.[2] The following dialogue, brief scene descriptions and corresponding analysis are drawn directly from the film.

In many film prints, video and DVD versions *Dr. Strangelove* opens with a silent and slow-rolling 'disclaimer' from the Pentagon, bold white sans serif text on a black background, asserting:

> It is the stated position of the United States Air Force that their Safeguards would
> prevent the occurrence of such events as are depicted in this film. Furthermore, it

should be noted that none of the characters portrayed in this film are meant to represent any real persons living or dead.

Although the movie did not receive formal (or informal) US military assistance, the disclaimer was nevertheless imposed on all film prints struck by Columbia Pictures shortly after the movie had commenced its domestic release in January 1964.[3] Audiences encountering this visual caveat – one that seeks to deny the veracity and foreground the fictional nature of the scenario – may have felt some lingering curiosity from reading this bold statement and, ironically, it could have served to heighten interest in scrutinising the Air Force's 'safeguards' while reflecting on the characters portrayed, potentially as corresponding with 'real' persons.

By cryptically disavowing association with the depicted events that follow, the military's public relations caveat of denial is likely counterproductive. Rather than reducing concern the enigmatic prologue may well raise curiosity amongst viewers for what is yet to be revealed, a point elaborated upon by Peter Krämer.[4] However, when the film is viewed for a second (or subsequent) time with the full cognitive knowledge of what is about to play out, the disclaimer can appear amusing, like another black joke, and elicit laughter from an audience. It can be interpreted retrospectively as deliberate and integral to the grotesque humour of the film, not separate from it as an officially sanctioned rider to what it proceeds. Regardless, only a couple of minutes later, the film's own standard production disclaimer, hand written by Pablo Ferro, states:

> The characters and incidents portrayed and the names used herein are fictitious and any similarity to the names, history and characters of any person is entirely accidental and unintentional.

Immediately following the Air Force text, the film fades up from black to reveal the familiar Columbia studio mannequin depicted as a classically attired woman atop a pedestal, holding a torch aloft in her right arm, standing in front of a backdrop of light and dark cumulous clouds. The first image of the film proper is of a metallic antenna jutting from the nose of a jet, with a narrow slit at its rounded tip, a penile eye at the head of monstrous phallus thrust forward to the instrumental strains of 'Try a Little Tenderness'.[5] The turbulent clouds of the Columbia logo segue to a montage of overlapping stock footage high above the cloud-tops, showing B-52s refuelling mid-air. It is a sexual *ballet mécanique* with the shaft from a KC-135 stratotanker penetrating the strategic bomber, before it breaks away, seemingly spent from the deposit of its aviation 'essence', its retracted aerodynamic boom and recipient B-52 swaying listlessly while the accompanying tune fades to silence.

Inside a computer room at Burpelson Air Force Base, Group Captain Mandrake receives a call from the Base Commander, General Ripper, and walks past a large row of static display boards, one of which states boldly in capital letters 'Peace is Our Profession'. Appearing at first like an Orwellian gag, where war is peace, freedom is slavery and ignorance is strength, the SAC motto was indeed authentic. Each SAC Wing had its own designated maxim such as 'Checkmate to Aggression', 'Deter or Destroy', 'Force for Freedom', 'Peace Through Strength', 'Sentinels of Peace', 'Guardian of Freedom', through to 'Death from Above'.[6] The aforementioned 'Peace is our Profession' was SAC's official motto and in some draft script documentation Kubrick had a large photo of a SAC security officer stationed beside a massive billboard with the text emblazoned across it. The soldier is from General LeMay's Air Police Squadron, or the 'Palace Guard of SAC HQ', and wears and stag-handled Smith & Wesson six-shooter. Similar postures and photographic compositions are replicated in Kubrick's mise-en-scène of Burpelson AFB during the exterior montage while Gen. Ripper addresses his troops using the base intercom.[7] One brief shot displays multiple versions of the signage at the entrance to the base where 'Peace is Our Profession', the 'Burpelson' Base name and the '843rd Bomb Wing' is followed by 'After the Wreck Comes the Reckoning', invoking both reprisal and Biblical wrath.

AIRBORNE ALERT

After the announcement of the success of Sputnik in 1957 SAC initiated an operational alert system where one-third to a half of its nuclear bombers were on standby and ready for a fifteen-minute takeoff. Concerned about vulnerability on the ground to Soviet ICBMs, the USAF maintained up to twelve nuclear-armed bombers airborne 24 hours a

An Air Police Squadron officer, or the 'Palace Guard of SAC HQ', outside Offutt AFB, 1959. (US National Archives)

day under various code names such as Head Start, Round Robin and Chrome Dome.[8] The Airborne Alert Program placed these dozen or so B-52 bombers, all carrying thermonuclear weapons, along designated flight-routes across Arctic air space, over Spain and the Mediterranean, and crossing the Pacific from Alaska to Japan.[9] The film's unseen narrator intones:

Narrator:
In order to guard against surprise nuclear attack, America's Strategic Air Command maintains a large force of B-52 bombers airborne 24 hours a day. Each B-52 can deliver a nuclear bomb load of fifty megatons, equal to sixteen times the total explosive force of all the bombs and shells used by all the armies in World War II. Based in America, the airborne alert force is deployed from the Persian Gulf to the Arctic Ocean, but they have one geographical factor in common – they are all two hours from their targets inside Russia.

This narration is almost exactly derived from Peter George's novel where the implied 'two hours to doom' forms the basis for the title of the British version of the book. However, despite the narration, it is highly unlikely that any B-52 in 1963–64 carried a composite load of 50Mt. Most B-52s had a payload ranging between two and four nuclear weapons including variations of approximately 1.1 Mt (B-28), 3.8 Mt (Mk-15/Mk-39), 9Mt (Mk-36/Mk-53) and up to 25Mt (Mk-41).[10] According to Eric Schlosser, during the Cuban Missile Crisis while the military was placed on DEFCON 2, every day 'about sixty-five of the bombers circled within striking distance of the Soviet Union. Each one carried a Hound Dog missile with a thermonuclear warhead, as well as two Mark 39 or four Mark 28 hydrogen bombs.'[11]

In *Dr. Strangelove*, when radio man Lt. Goldberg receives a coded message ('FDG135') from Burpelson, he alerts his Commander: 'Major Kong, I know you're gonna think this a crazy, but I just got a message from base over the CRM-114. It decodes as "Wing Attack Plan R". R for Romeo.' Goldberg ('Goldie') has little idea how 'crazy' his jocular allusion will turn out to be. Up to this point, and for the next few minutes of elapsed screen time, Kubrick is careful not to narratively telegraph the craziness of the command, or the insanity of the SAC Wing Commander who has issued the order. Indeed, Kubrick frames General Ripper in this opening sequence sitting behind his desk but carefully lights the set so that it barely illuminates the General's desktop nameplate, revealed to be 'Jack D. Ripper'. Shortly after this introduction it is revealed by one of the characters that General Ripper's bombers 'were airborne at the time as part of a special exercise we were holding called Operation Dropkick'.

PERMISSIVE ACTION LINKS

Inside the B-52 after Major Kong and another officer have opened two on-board combination lock safes (adorned with soft-core magazine pin-ups) to extract and distribute the sealed orders for Plan R. Major Kong calmly reads from the printed text like a convivial commercial airline pilot or flight attendant perfunctorily instructing passengers on procedures:

> **Maj. Kong:**
> This is your attack profile: to insure that the enemy cannot monitor voice transmission or plant false transmission, the CRM-114 is to be switched into all the receiver circuits. Emergency phase code prefix is to be set on the dials of the CRM. This'll block any transmission other than those preceded by code prefix. Stand by to set code prefix.

The above sequence in *Dr. Strangelove* depicts the 'two man rule' (TMR), or 'two person concept' (TPC) whereby two crewmembers had to individually undertake roles in order to prevent accidental or unauthorised use that, when combined, enabled the release of nuclear weapons. The TMR later became the bedrock of ICBM- and submarine-based missile systems.[12] As Thomas Jones reported in the November 2005 Smithsonian *Air & Space* magazine, B-52s crews during the Cuban Crisis remained orbiting at their 'positive-control turnaround points' listening to radio traffic. They pensively awaited

> the Emergency War Order from SAC headquarters in Omaha to come crackling over the bombers' long-range, high-frequency sets. At least two crew members were to copy the message, then compare its numbers and letters to onboard decoding documents. The voice messages would either recall them or commit them to strike their targets.[13]

Kubrick and his art department went to extraordinary lengths to ensure visual and verbal verisimilitude during the onboard B-52 flight procedures, drawn heavily from George's novel and his experiences as an RAF navigator. The camera zooms in to reveal astonishing instrument detail of all the (believed) relevant aircraft systems, still highly classified at the time.[14]

Concerns about unauthorised access and use of nuclear weapons peaked during a European inspection trip by members of the Congressional Joint Committee on Atomic Energy (JCAE) in December 1960.[15] The party was deeply troubled that US nuclear weapons held by NATO forces were kept under inadequate, and possibly illegal, command

and control. Encountering American nuclear weapons aboard NATO rapid reaction jets, piloted by foreign air forces, who could 'scramble' even without proper authorisation, prompted renewed Congressional interest in creating a mechanism to lock weapons and safeguard their unauthorised access and use.[16] Indeed, it was watching British V-bombers flying low overhead that spurred author Peter George to consider the possibility that any such flight may be nuclear armed and acting unilaterally, which led to his writing *Red Alert*.

As a result of these misgivings, alongside a raft of near cataclysmic US thermonuclear weapons accidents from the mid-1950s to early 1960s, an urgent audit was undertaken by the AEC and Pentagon to reconsider retrofitting devices that could better ensure safety. The JCAE report culminated in the Presidential directive of June 1962, the National Security Action Memorandum (NSAM) 160, which authorised the installation of Permissive Action Link (PAL) devices in all nuclear weapons dispersed in NATO commands.[17] Specific objectives for PAL's were listed as follows:

1. Safeguarding weapons against actions by an individual psychotic;
2. Meeting the legal and political requirements of US control;
3. Maintaining control against the unauthorised use of weapons by our own or allied military forces under conditions of high tension or actual combat; and
4. Assuring that weapons could not be used if forcibly seized by an organized group of individuals or by a foreign power.[18]

In the context of *Dr. Strangelove* it is significant that the first objective specifically foregrounds preventing 'an individual psychotic' from procuring and using nuclear warheads. While the JCAE looked to Europe and the UK to head their objectives list with fears over unauthorised use of nuclear weapons by an individual psychotic, others began to worry about American access at home and abroad. A crash programme was initiated to prioritise which weapons and delivery systems needed immediate attention. Technicians and designers created an arming device designated PAL, developed and deployed in the early 1960s. According to a former Department of Energy Assistant Secretary: 'The first PALs were manually-operated multiple-digit combination electromechanical locks which had to be opened before weapons could be armed. In some cases, arming codes were not carried on board aircraft but instead were to be transmitted from base after an attack order had been given.'[19] The PAL combination had to be 'set in the proper order before the weapon can be armed and either launched or dropped over its target'.[20]

Prior to the widespread deployment of 'sealed pit' thermonuclear weapons —where the plutonium cores and their high explosive triggers are pre-inserted intact — earlier atomic and H-bombs were manually armed in-flight. Having *prêt-à-porter* H-bombs easily

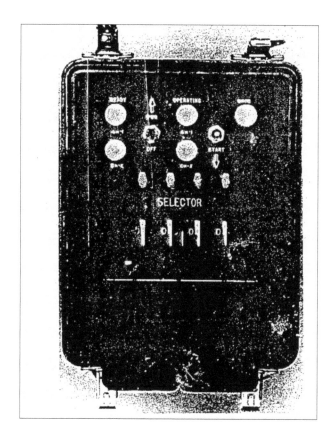

PAL-A four digit device controller for nuclear weapons (declassified 1994 Sandia Report 'PAL Control of Theater Nuclear Weapons', best image available).

armed and always at the ready to be deployed concerned civilian overseers of military matters, including JFK's Secretary of Defense, Robert McNamara. Soon after his appointment, when he was briefed on B-52 crashes and other nuclear weapons accidents, McNamara was horrified. In several instances multiple weapon safeguards failed, and in once case in January 1961, after a B-52 broke up mid-flight, two Mk-39 H-bombs plummeted towards Goldsboro, North Carolina where only a single safety mechanism – one of four, a 'simple, dynamo technology, low-voltage switch' – prevented a large chunk of the US east coast from becoming a smoldering radioactive crater, contaminating much of north east America with fallout from a four-megaton detonation.[21]

Riffing off Kubrick's film title, Parker F. Jones, the nuclear weapons safety department supervisor at Sandia National Laboratories, reassessed the accident in 1969 'to set the record straight' and titled his report 'Goldsboro Revisited, or How I Learned to Mistrust the H-Bomb'. Parker concluded that during the early Airborne Alert years the Mk-39 H-bomb (and the B28, B41 and B53 thermonuclear weapons) 'did not possess adequate safety' for use in these global B-52 patrols.[22] Perhaps it is even more worrying that Jones retrospectively identifies the B41 (Mk-41) hydrogen bomb as prone to the same fault, since this is the weapon (with a 25Mt yield) that closely matches the two devices depicted in *Dr. Strangelove*. According to the online Nuclear Weapons Archive, a PAL

> is an electronic (originally electro-mechanical) device that prevents arming the weapon unless the correct codes are inserted into it. Two different codes must be inserted, simultaneously or close together. This is the 'two man rule' principle – which requires it to be impossible to arm any nuclear weapon through the actions of a single individual. The codes are usually changed on a regular schedule. [...] Once the weapon is armed, 'environmental sensing devices' (ESDs) prevent detonation of the weapon unless it is properly delivered to the target.[23]

These ESDs detect environmental factors during 'the delivery process', such as the time of the bomb's descent, its acceleration, and the ambient temperature and pressure. Without these factors being detected in the correct order, and occurring within predefined parameters, the thermonuclear bomb should not detonate in the air or on the surface.[24]

Reading through his attack profile, Major Kong informs the crew:

Kong:
Primary target, the ICBM complex at Laputa. Target reference Yankee Golf Tango Three Six Zero. Thirty megaton nuclear device fused for airburst at ten thousand feet. Twenty megaton nuclear device will be used if first malfunctions. Otherwise proceed to secondary target, missile complex seven miles east of Barshaw. Target reference November Bravo X-Ray One Zero Eight. Fused airburst at ten, check, twelve thousand feet.

How big *were* the H-bombs carried on B-52s during the Cold War? At the time of the initial script writing in early 1962 through to film's January 1964 release, most American nuclear weapon yields remained highly classified. However, details have emerged from successive waves of declassifications and Freedom of Information requests. For example, the US Atomic Energy Commission (AEC) advised in 1962 that it had a 25Mt weapon in its arsenal.[25] A year later the AEC stated that it had the capability of deploying a 50–60Mt gravity bomb on B-52s, if required without further testing, as well as installing a 35Mt warhead on a Titan II ICBM. However, neither weapon option was actively pursued.[26] Such declassified announcements confirmed that the largest gravity bomb, designated Mk-41, with a hydrogen warhead using a 'dirty' fission–fusion explosion, yielded 25 megatons, or equivalent to 25 million tons of TNT in destructive nuclear force. It weighed

Mk-41 thermonuclear bomb, the largest deployed weapon in the US arsenal capable of delivering 25 Megatons of explosive force, and deployed from 1961.

just under 5,000 kilograms, was 3.8 metres long and nearly 1.3 metres in wide. This monstrous device could be carried in either the B-52 or the B-47 jet bombers. Between September 1960 and June 1962 approximately 500 Mk-41 bombs were built and then actively deployed until their full 'retirement' in July 1976. As in the fictional 20 Mt and 30 Mt bombs described in *Dr. Strangelove*, the Mk-41 did not have an adjustable yield, but came in two versions – the larger, 'dirty' type (Y1) of 25Mt used natural uranium and the smaller 'clean' version (Y2) at under 10Mt had a lead jacket to minimise fallout.[27]

To achieve the higher yield, the Mk-41 employed a 'dirty' configuration in the tertiary stage of detonation. While clearly not the movie's imagined cobalt-thorium G casing of the Doomsday Device, a substantial and lethal cloud of radiation would result from the Mk-41's detonation, with additional dirty fallout generated by any surface burst. According to the online, interactive *NukeMap*, detonating a 25Mt surface burst at the Kotlas airfield in Russia would have resulted in a massive fireball 9.5 kilometres wide, instantly vaporising or incinerating everything within an area of 65 square kilometres.[28] Up to a diameter of about eight kilometres the immediate, lethal prompt radiation at ground level – registering at 500rem – would kill approximately 80% of those exposed. However, anyone within this 52km² radiation zone who was close enough to receive that radiation dosage would still be *inside* the 10,000+ degree nuclear fireball. The explosion would leave a crater nearly three kilometres wide and a kilometre deep. The huge pressure wave produced by the blast (at 20psi) would flatten concrete buildings within a 12km diameter, essentially killing all inhabitants. Twice as far out, where the overpressure drops to 5psi, most residential buildings collapse, causing widespread fatalities, or overwhelming injuries across the 563km² affected zone. Thermal radiation ignites everything combustible within a staggering 5,340km², and anyone exposed up to a distance of over 40km from the explosion will instantly suffer third-degree burns. The resultant fallout would be catastrophic. Based on an average wind speed of 15mph, the most severe fallout at 1,000rads per hour (considered 100% lethal within two days to two weeks) would stretch over 55km in length and affect an area of approximately 15,200 square kilometres. As the fallout spreads further downwind the intensity and lethality decreases, so by twice the distance, at approximately 115km, the dose rate drops to the still significantly dangerous level of 100rad per hour, with the fallout contaminating well over 50,000km².

Although the Mk-41 was never fully tested, the largest US thermonuclear weapon detonated was the 15Mt Bravo test that irradiated 7,000 square miles of the Pacific with fallout raining down on Marshallese Islanders, American observers and the crew of a Japanese fishing boat (*Lucky Dragon No. 5*). To this day, a number of affected atolls in the Marshall Islands remain contaminated and uninhabitable.[29]

It should be noted that both the targets of Laputa and Barshaw (and Kodlosk) are fictitious Russian locations for the purpose of the film plot. They do not exist on any declassified SAC target lists. However, throughout the development of the screenplay Kubrick used George's underlying literary work to name the real Soviet city of Kotlas (500km north-east of Moscow at the junction of the Vychegda and Northern Dvina rivers) as the bomber's primary target: 'the I.C.B.M. base at Kotlass [sic]'.[30] Recently declassified target information from the *Atomic Weapons Requirement Study for 1959* – a report that assigned each and every SAC warhead to their Sino-Soviet bloc targets – contradicts the film's use of airbursts against a missile complex.[31] Regardless of the large destructive capability of either a 20Mt or 30Mt weapon, SAC mandated thermonuclear surface bursts for *all* such 'priority' targets. In reality there was no ICBM complex at Kotlas, however, there was an airfield 4km from the adjacent town housing 60,000 people. Written in 1956 and forecasting into 1959, SAC's *Atomic Weapons Requirement Study* planned to use six nuclear weapons against Kotlas, including ground burst H-bombs to destroy the runways (by 'cratering'). Less than three miles distance from the airfield, the city of Kotlas would have been obliterated (or 'smeared' as the B-52 crew say in the novel) from the blast, heat and radioactivity, with a high level of fallout generated by thermonuclear weapons hitting the ground, contaminating a vast area. Even if Kotlas was spared a direct hit, had SAC delivered its proposed apocalyptic (either retaliatory or pre-emptive) attack on the Soviets, the cities of Moscow and St. Petersburg were each assigned dozens of atomic and thermonuclear ground zeros. The fallout from these bombardments alone would have ensured that rural populations centres several hundreds of kilometres distant (such as Kotlas) would have been rendered barren and uninhabitable for generations.[32]

In *Dr. Strangelove* Major Kong says to his men after receiving the Go code, in classic understatement:

> I got a fair idea of the kind of personal emotions that some of you fellas may be thinking. Heck, I reckon you wouldn't even be human beins if you didn't have some pretty strong personal feelings about nooclear combat.

During the Cuban Missile Crisis combat crews similarly reflected on the apocalyptic importance of their roles, especially when SAC changed the global defense condition to DEFCON 2. One SAC airborne refueller, Gus Letto, recalled thinking at the time:

> It was unlikely that we would complete the entire mission … I decided that the world as we knew it would be at an end and that my family, if they were lucky, would not survive the initial nuclear exchange.[33]

Former B-52 First Lieutenant, Buck Shuler, remembers his principle war targets as prioritised strikes against the Soviet 'leadership', vividly recalling that 'the aiming point of the first weapon was the southwest corner of the Kremlin'.[34] B-52 crewman Clyde Ketcham felt 'it would be a one-way trip', echoing the combat contingencies depicted in the film:

> Even if not shot down, after flying through all the radioactivity, I don't think we would have lived very long, and on most missions, we had very little fuel left and really no friendly places to go after the last target. I think most crew members held down at the very bottom of their soul … that God wouldn't let this happen. That's how I kept my sanity.[35]

PRESIDENTIAL PREDELEGATION

When the bombardier, Lt. Lothar Zogg, queries Major Kong over the possibility of their attack order 'Go Code' being 'a test', the pilot assures the crew that

> ol' Ripper wouldn't be giving us Plan R unless them Rooskies had already clobbered Washington and a lot of other towns with a sneak attack.[36]

The logic of Plan R and its urgent execution is entirely understood by the B-52 crew to be in play only as *retaliation* following a pre-emptive Soviet nuclear strike 'clobbering' America. However, still two hours from their targets, shouldn't the *Leper Colony* crew consider that striking against ICBM sites would now be *redundant*, given Kong's comment that the Soviets had already obliterated key US cities? The ICBMs would be amongst the very first weapons used and the bases likely expendable after launch (even taking account of preserving a reserve force). The veracity of General Ripper's order is also questioned by his own Executive Officer, Group Captain Mandrake, when he hears civilian radio broadcasts:

> I'm afraid I'm still not with you, sir. Because, I mean, if a Russian attack was *not* in progress, then your use of Plan R, in fact your orders to the entire wing ... oh. Well I would say, sir, that there was something dreadfully wrong somewhere.

When Ripper demurs and asks for a drink, Mandrake finally understands the significance of the General's unauthorised action. Attempting to leave the locked office Mandrake musters his most deferential of Englishness to, almost apologetically, request the Wing's three-letter recall code: 'Have you got them handy, sir?' Kubrick presents Ripper menacingly, filmed from low-angle and shot in high-contrast black and white chiaroscuro. Drawing deeply on his cigar, Ripper reveals his pearl-handled .45 hand gun, a threatening action that confirms the suspicions of his seconded British 'bruvva officer'. Noting that only he knows the code, Ripper advises 'there's nothing anybody can do about this thing now', asserting boldly 'there is no possibility of recalling the wing', only 'total commitment'. Once the penny drops for Mandrake (and we the audience), not only does the General confirm that he has unilaterally initiated World War III, but it is an attack order predicated by deranged logic, a mania seemingly etched into the weathered contours of Ripper's face:

> I can no longer sit back and allow communist infiltration, communist indoctrination, communist subversion, and the international communist conspiracy to sap and impurify all of our *precious bodily fluids*.

Hence, the entire premise of Peter George's novel and the Kubrick-George-Southern film adaptation establishes as its primary plot device the veracity of an unauthorised command to attack Russia with thermonuclear bombs.

In the Pentagon's War Room, a hastily arranged meeting presents the US President and his key military chiefs alongside their civilian and service subordinate aides, all seated at a large circular table. They assemble before giant maps denoting the relative positions of B-52 bombers, and their primary and secondary targets. Air Force chief and four star general, 'Buck' Turgidson, quickly appraises the President of the situation, advising that Ripper's Wing of 34 B-52s – fully armed, each with forty megatons of nuclear weapons – are on their way to bomb the Soviets. An audible, collective gasp echoes throughout the cavernous War Room:

Muffley:
General Turgidson, I find this very difficult to understand. I was under the impression that I was the only one in authority to order the use of nuclear weapons.

Turgidson:
That's right sir. You are the only person authorised to do so. And, although I hate to judge before all the facts are in, it's beginning to look like General Ripper exceeded his authority.

Muffley:
It certainly does. Far beyond the point I would have imagined possible.

Turgidson:
Well perhaps you're forgetting the provisions of Plan R, sir.

Muffley:
Plan R?

Turgidson:
Plan R is an emergency war plan in which a lower echelon commander may order nuclear retaliation after a sneak attack if the normal chain of command is disrupted. You approved it, sir. You must remember. Surely you must recall, sir, when Senator Buford made that big hassle about our deterrent lacking credibility. The idea was for Plan R to be a sort of retaliatory safeguard.

Muffley:
A *safeguard*!

Turgidson:
I admit the human element seems to have failed us here. But the idea was to discourage the Russkies from any hope that they could knock out Washington, and yourself, sir, as part of a general sneak attack, and escape retaliation because of lack of proper command and control.

It is quite likely that this scenario is what prompted the US Air Force to require Columbia Pictures to insert the disclaimer at the head of the film. As the National Security Archive (NSA) has shown, a previously top secret directive initiated by President Eisenhower, and undertaken by successive Presidents throughout the 1960s, confirms that the principal plot device of *Red Alert* and *Dr. Strangelove* was entirely plausible. As early as March 1956, President Eisenhower – previously America's Commander-in-Chief in

Europe during World War II – sought Defense and State Department policy advice on establishing advanced Presidential authorisation for nuclear weapons use by senior commanders.[37] Later that year, Eisenhower approved advanced authorisation for air defense forces to employ nuclear weapons against any attack on the continental USA. By May 1957 Eisenhower had guidelines drafted for a pre-release authority of nuclear weapons 'expenditure' in at least two situations:

1)   when attacks by sea or by air on US territory and possessions provided no time for consultation with the President on defensive measures, or

2)   when 'enemy attacks' prevented a Presidential decision and it was necessary to protect US forces abroad, including those in international waters, or to launch SAC to retaliate to nuclear attack on the continental United States.[38]

After consultation with the Joint Chiefs of Staff (JCS), in late 1959 President Eisenhower issued revised 'predelegation' orders to his senior commanders, enabling them to immediately launch nuclear retaliation if the Soviets succeeded in a 'decapitation' attack on Washington, one that annihilated, or at least gravely disrupted, the national command authority including the President and his constitutionally approved successors.[39] The Joint Chiefs quickly instructed their 'lower echelon' commanders – the Commanders-in-Chief in Europe, the Atlantic and Pacific, and the Strategic Air Command – with a 'general statement of purpose' that authorised them to

expend nuclear weapons in defense of the United States, its Territories, possessions and forces when the urgency of time and circumstances does not permit a specific decision by the President or other person empowered to act in his stead.[40]

The JCS specifically advised the Commander-in-Chief, Strategic Air Command (CINCSAC), that he could approve nuclear release only in 'circumstances of grave necessity'. When releasing the documents online the NSA described these declassification revelations as 'one of the Cold War's deepest secrets', further suggesting that nuclear predelegation authority continued at least until the 1980s.[41] Importantly, and of direct relevance to the plot of *Dr. Strangelove*, in addition to the identified senior commanders, the revised predelegation orders (January 1959 and May 1960) permit *other* 'Authorised Commanders' to be:

Commanders of numbered armies, fleets, and air forces, and commanders of Joint Task forces and of other commands in equivalent stature to the numbered forces from time to time to be designated Authorizing Commanders.[42]

This revised order effectively enabled the JCS, or the SAC Commander-in-Chief, or sundry other subordinate senior commanders 'in equivalent stature' to be granted this authority 'from time to time', such as under the B-52 airborne alert exercises depicted in both the book and film.

On assuming office in January 1961, John F. Kennedy was quickly counseled by his White House aide, McGeorge Bundy, over the dangers of the predelegation order – one that Bundy felt inherently permitted a 'subordinate commander [to] start the thermonuclear holocaust on his own initiative if he could not reach you'.[43] Implicit in Bundy's warning to the incoming President was an acknowledgement that such a commander had the capacity to launch an attack *without* Presidential authorisation, whether predelegated or not. Regardless, Kennedy let the existing top secret arrangements stand, known only to a handful of military staff and those senior administration officials with Pentagon oversight. JFK's new Secretary of Defense, Robert S. McNamara, later came to the view that predelegation was 'not in the US interest', especially after the Hawkish Pentagon responses to the Berlin and Cuban Crises of 1961 and 1962.[44]

As William Burr has noted, Cold War Presidents from Eisenhower to Lyndon B. Johnson 'sought to avoid giving excessive leeway to military commanders to prevent their precipitously initiating a devastating US-Soviet nuclear exchange'.[45] Despite these reservations successive Presidents in the 1960s provided secret predelegation authority – precisely as depicted in *Dr. Strangelove* – to lower echelon commanders to use nuclear weapons supposedly in emergency situations. Effectively there was nothing to stop a madman at a senior command level from issuing unauthorised attack orders under the pretext of predelgation. In the case of the *Dr. Strangelove*, a scenario had to be invented, logically, to prevent a 'recall' from reaching the bombers. The damaged *Leper Colony* proceeds to bomb Russia after a Soviet missile detonates nearby and, as the bemused Lt. 'Goldie' Goldberg reports: 'All the radio gear is out, including the CRM-114. I think the auto-destruct mechanism got hit and blew itself up.'

FAIL-SAFE AND CRM-114

In the War Room an increasingly testy President Muffley verbally spars with his Air Force Chief, General Turgidson, becoming irritated at the seeming *fait accompli* he has been delivered as US Commander-in-Chief:

Muffley:
Well I assume then, that the planes will return automatically once they
reach their fail-safe points.

Turgidson:
Well, sir, I'm afraid not. You see the planes were holding at their fail-safe

points when the Go code was issued. Now, once they fly beyond fail-safe they
do not require a second order to proceed. They will fly until they reach
their targets.

Muffley:
Then why haven't you radioed the planes countermanding the Go code?

Turgidson:
Well, I'm afraid we're unable to communicate with any of the aircraft.

Muffley:
Why?

Turgidson:
As you may recall, sir, one of the provisions of Plan R provides that once the
Go code is received the normal SSB radios in the aircraft are switched into a
special coded device, which I believe is designated as 'CRM-114'. Now, in order
to prevent the enemy from issuing fake or confusing orders, CRM-114
is designed not to receive at all, unless the message is preceded by the
correct three-letter code group prefix.

Muffley:
Then do you mean to tell me, General Turgidson, that you will be unable
to recall the aircraft?

Turgidson:
That's about the size of it. However, we are plowing through every possible
three-letter combination of the code. But since there are seventeen thousand
permutations it's going to take us about two and a half days to transmit them all.

During the B-52 airborne alert procedure Single Side Band (SSB) position reports were regularly transmitted along the route, sometimes hourly, often avoiding the need for map coordinates. Frequent Foxtrot test messages ('no answer required') were relayed to the planes – any one of which could be 'an order sending the bomber to war [and] commit the crew to combat'.[46] The elaborate and detailed interior production design and mise-en-scène, captured by Kubrick's hand-held Arriflex camera and zoom lens, depicts the B-52 crew switching from normal SSB voice communication within the cockpit to CRM discriminators.[47]

After the first set of PALs were installed in 1961–62, other modifications led to the installation of PAL-B aircraft controllers installed in cockpits, designated MC1707, 'used to interrupt critical warhead circuits until the proper code is inserted by either aircraft or ground control equipment'.[48] It was a pair of black boxes (decoder and recoder) approximately eighteen cubic inches in size and weighing 2.2 lbs. This mechanism was redesigned in the late 1960s to prevent multiple attempts to numerically 'unpick' the

Later versions of a PAL cockpit control arming device (six numerical digit), with settings for ground or airburst, in either free fall or retarded/delay modes. (declassified 1994 Sandia Report 'PAL Control of Theater Nuclear Weapons', best image available)

lock by systematic or random combination in order to 'minimize the possibility of repeatedly trying codes until hitting the right one'.[49] *Dr. Strangelove's* B-52 'black box', as George and Kubrick conceptualised it, was a similar electro-mechanical device with three alphabetical coded wheels creating 26^3 possible combinations (i.e. 17,576). In reality, the PAL-B operated four numerical wheels producing 10^4 coded possibilities (i.e. 10,000). Kubrick was very keen to ensure that George's RAF experience and contacts in the military could unofficially confirm the veracity of this type of device, or one similar to it, connected to the plane's communications system, an essential element of the film's credible plot. Responding to Kubrick's desire for verification, George wrote:

> I had been at work contacting various former colleagues, who have in turn made certain inquiries with regard to the matter we were discussing. The chief source on which I am relying is our very highly placed person in the Department which specialises exclusively in communications and allied problems regarding world wide movement of aircraft. Based on his and another expert's opinions, I am of the opinion that there is in fact no practical way of demonstrating inability to recall the bombers other than by the introduction of a device such as the CRM-114. This does not altogether surprise me since when I originally wrote the book this was obviously a problem with which I had to grapple. I was at the time at a unit where there were several high ranking and specialist communication officers, and I remember going into the matter with them exhaustively in those days. The position has not changed. I do not think therefore that it is possible to demonstrate inability to recall other than through some mechanical device. And I do not think it is possible to do it better than

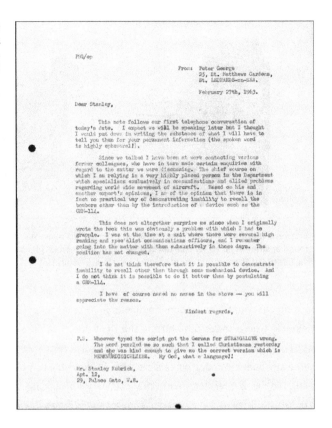

by postulating a CRM-114. I have of course named no names in the above – you will appreciate the reason.[50]

The prudent note of caution at the end is understandable. The unit to which George refers is most likely the UK early warning and radar defense post at RAF Neatishead in East Anglia where he was stationed in the early 1960s; a part of England that also hosted five US military and communication bases.

Somewhat closer to the film's fictional CRM-114 was a six-digit Security Container System (SCS) that controlled the arming and access of nuclear warheads carried by B-52s. As a rationally imagined, though fictional, device for safeguarding communications with the strategic bomber in flight, the CRM-114 combines the function of radio transmission with a mechanism to authorise crew access for nuclear 'expenditure'. According to Ken Adam:

The only thing we didn't know was that failsafe device, called the CRM in the film. We didn't know what that looked like and we came up with an idea and it seemed to be pretty realistic. [...] Way into the shooting the publicity people invited some American Air Force personnel to look at the shooting we did. And they literally went white when they saw the inside of the B-52 because they said it was absolutely correct even to the little black box, which was the CRM. So the next day I got a memo from Stanley, hoping that I got all my research from legal sources or justifiable sources otherwise I, or he, could be in serious trouble, with a possible investigation by the FBI.[51]

Inside the War Room General Turgidson informs the President that base commander Ripper had called SAC headquarters 'shortly after he issued the Go code'. Coincidentally, Ripper's call entirely conforms with the top secret Presidential predelegation authority procedures outlined earlier. A testy President Muffley instructs Turgidson to read aloud the 'partial transcript of that conversation':

Turgidson:
The duty officer asked General Ripper to confirm the fact the he had issued the Go code and he said, 'Yes gentlemen, they are on their way in and no one can bring them back. For the sake of our country and our way of life, I suggest you get the rest of SAC in after them, otherwise we will be totally destroyed by red retaliation. My boys will give you the best kind of start, fourteen hundred megatons worth, and you sure as hell won't stop them now.'

General Turgidson smirks and chuckles to himself as he reads the last line with apparent self-satisfaction. This text closely mirrors General Quinten's conversation outlined in *Red Alert,* with the added comic emphasis of 'fourteen hundred megatons worth', a likely embellishment from Terry Southern.[52] Originally each B-52 squadron, or strategic Wing, comprised 45 planes, but after the launch of Sputnik fears of Soviet ICBMs meant large concentrations of B-52s were vulnerable to missile attack with little warning, hence SAC began to disperse their Wings into smaller allotments of 3 x 15 bombers per Wing, totaling 42 Squadrons of B-52s. If each bomber held a payload of 50Mt, as the opening narration intimates, then Wing Commander Ripper's 1,400 megatons would account for 28 bombers. Turgidson informs the President that the Wing has 34 bombers with an average of 40 Mt per plane, which at 1,360 Mt is close enough to Ripper's impudent qualification, rounded out to 1,400 Mt.

Turgidson continues to read from the transcript, slowing his delivery towards the end, almost faltering at each word, staccato-like, seemingly in disbelief – the staggered cadence heightening the bizarre, incongruity of the passage.

Turgidson (cont.):
'So let's get going. There's no other choice. God willing, we will prevail in peace and freedom from fear, and in true health, through the purity and essence of

our natural ... *fluids*. God bless you all.' Then he hung up.

We're still trying to figure out the meaning of that last phrase, sir.

HUMAN RELIABILITY

Kubrick kept in his *Strangelove* files a press clipping from the 2 April 1962 edition of *Newsweek*. It reported that experts were worried that any one of the thousands of personnel responsible for atomic munitions could 'go berserk and start a private nuclear war'.[53] The article noted that in order to prevent such an occurrence, SAC General Curtis E. LeMay ordered 'that all 50,000 airmen with any possible access to nuclear weapons be rescreened for a "human reliability certificate"'.

As Eric Schlosser suggests the US Air Force Human Reliability programme was designed to weed out mentally unbalanced or disturbed individuals in the lower ranks, not the senior echelons.[54] In fact, it was up to commanders to make the judgement of a subordinate's 'reliability' (or otherwise) and not all soldiers under review were examined by a 'psychological professional'.[55] A number of reports in the late 1950s and early 1960s drew attention to the possibility of a psychologically unstable soldier gaining access to nuclear weapons. Fred Iklé's RAND report on the risk of accidental or unauthorised nuclear detonation concluded that existing safety procedures did little to deter 'deliberate, unauthorized attempts to detonate a nuclear weapon'.[56] At the time few safeguards could prevent trained personnel familiar with nuclear fusing and firing mechanisms from using nuclear weapons. Schlosser recounts that Iklé worked with psychiatrist Gerald J. Aronson. They discovered that Air Force staff working with nuclear weapons required a top secret clearance but no 'psychological screening'. Alarmingly, Iklé and Aronson found that individuals with 'transient psychotic disorders' were permitted to join the USAF, and up to twenty airmen per year employed on nuclear weapons details were 'expected to have a severe mental breakdown'.[57] The researchers detailed a range of chilling case histories involving Air Force officers – pilots who were paranoiacs and schizophrenics – who suffered regular anxiety attacks, hostile sexual fantasies and delusions of grandeur. Some presented with paranoid delusions and believed they were 'invested with a special mission that sets them apart from society'.[58] Given this, the depiction of General Jack D. Ripper in *Dr. Strangelove*, obsessed by bodily fluids and communist conspiracies, seems less far-fetched than one might assume.[59]

In *Strangelove*'s War Room, the President doesn't mince words:

Muffley:
There's nothing to figure out, General Turgidson. This man is obviously a psychotic.

Turgidson:
Well, I'd like to hold off judgment on a thing like that, sir, until all the facts are in.

Barely suppressing his rising anger, the President fires back at Turgidson's apologist and evasive rejoinder.

Muffley:
General Turgidson, when you instituted the human reliability tests, you assured me there was no possibility of such a thing ever occurring.

Turgidson:
Well I don't think it's quite fair to condemn a whole program because of a single slip up.

Turgidson's comic disavowal aside, there were plenty of high-ranking 'slip ups' in the US Air Force command at the time of *Dr. Strangelove*. According to Gene Healy, throughout the Cold War General Curtis E. LeMay deliberately sought to provoke an international incident that would provide a pretext for him to deliver his 'Sunday punch', a massive pre-emptive air attack, delivering hundreds of atomic and hydrogen bombs that would cause tens of millions of Soviet fatalities. One example of such provocation occurred in 1954 when LeMay ordered nuclear-armed bombers to fly across Russia, and commented to his aides, 'well, maybe if we do this over flight right, we can get World War III started'.[60]

If General LeMay was considered a bellicose 'sonofabitch' by military subordinates, politicians and bureaucrats alike, his successor as head of SAC, four-star General Thomas

A reference photo of Gen. Curtis E. LeMay found in the *Dr. Strangelove* files held at the Stanley Kubrick Archive. (US National Archives)

SAC Commander in Chief, General Tomas Power standing before a Big Board display, 1960. (US National Archives)

Power, was deemed by many as dangerous and possibly deranged. According to Power's own deputy, General Lauris Norstad:

> I used to worry about General Power. I used to worry that General Power was not stable. I used to worry about the fact that he had control over so many weapons and weapon systems and could, under certain conditions, launch the force. Back in the days before we had real positive control [PAL locks], SAC had the power to do a lot of things, and it was in his hands, and he knew it.[61]

Power was similarly characterised by General Horace Wade, commander of SAC's 8th Air Force, as 'mean ... cruel ... unforgiving ... I used to worry that General Power was not stable'.[62] Even LeMay felt Powers was unstable and a 'sadist', describing his protégé as 'cold, hard and demanding ... an autocratic bastard'.[63] Power infamously fumed to a nuclear strategist, who had the temerity to counsel restraint during a 1960 SAC briefing, 'Restraint! ... Why are you so concerned with saving *their* lives? The whole idea is to kill the bastards ... Look: at the end of the war, if there are two Americans and one Russian, we win!' The strategist fired back, 'well, you'd better make sure that they're a man and a woman'.[64]

True to form, both LeMay and Power aggressively sought to compromise President Kennedy during the Cuban Missile Crisis in order to goad the Soviets into a nuclear war, by initiating unauthorised actions in and around Soviet airspace, or by conducting nuclear tests at time of heightened hostility. As Gene Healy has surmised:

> That Presidents advised by such men had in their hands the means to kill millions should be unsettling to people of normal human sensibilities. That Presidents showed restraint while in possession of such power gives us cause for thanks, but it is, at best, an uneasy source of comfort.[65]

It is little wonder, then, that Khrushchev constantly painted American military leaders as 'madmen'. When the SAC airborne alert was announced the Soviet Premier warned of the dangers that an airman 'through nervous mental derangement' might 'drop his deadly load on the territory of some country'. According to Eric Schlosser, 'the mental instability of SAC officers became a recurrent theme in Soviet Propaganda.'[66]

Ironically, during the Cuban Crisis, Khrushchev had to counter the irrational plea from Fidel Castro, that if an American attack or invasion should take place, then the Soviet Union must launch an immediate nuclear assault on the imperialist Americans and destroy them forever.[67] Castro's letter seems desperate, even slightly unhinged:

> If ... the imperialists invade Cuba with the aim of occupying it, the dangers of their aggressive policy are so great that after such an invasion the Soviet Union must never allow circumstances in which the imperialists could carry out a nuclear first strike against it. [...] [This] would be the moment to eliminate this danger forever, in an act of the most legitimate self-defense. However harsh and terrible the solution, there would be no other.[68]

Fortunately for the world, Khrushchev ignored the revolutionary leader's ideological zeal and negotiated a withdrawal of ballistic missiles with Kennedy, while secretly retaining the already deployed battlefield nuclear weapons and cruise missiles, undiscovered by the Americans. After Castro's near apocalyptic adjuration, any chance of those weapons remaining on the island and potentially within Cuban control was unimaginable.[69]

PRE-EMPTION, MEGADEATH AND MASS MURDER

A bullish and adversarial General Turgidson presses on with his hawkish agenda:

Turgidson:
Mr. President, there are one or two points I'd like to make, if I may.

Muffley:
Go ahead, General.

Turgidson:
One, our hopes for recalling the 843rd bomb wing are quickly being reduced to
a very low order of probability. Two, in less than fifteen minutes from now the
Russkies will be making radar contact with the planes. Three, when they do,
they are going to go absolutely *ape*, and they're gonna strike back with everything they've got. Four, if, prior to this time, we have done nothing further to
suppress their retaliatory capabilities, we will suffer virtual annihilation.

During this lengthy monologue, Turgidson mixes his quotidian vernacular with the sophisticated and disingenuous discourse of 'nukespeak'.[70] He then pauses to smirk and
wink at his colleagues, continuing with:

> Now ... five ... if, on the other hand, we were to immediately launch an all-out
> and coordinated attack on all their airfields and missile bases we'd stand a
> damn good chance of catching 'em with their pants down. Hell, we got a five-to-
> one missile superiority as it is. We could easily assign three missiles to every
> target, and still have a very effective reserve force for any other contingency.

The general quickly grabs a nearby folder, previously depicted as either SAC *War Alert
Action Book* or *World Targets in Megadeaths,* the former item based on a public domain
photo sourced from the US National Archives:[71]

> Now, six ... an *unofficial* study which we undertook of this eventuality, indicated
> that we would destroy 90 per cent of their nuclear capabilities. We would there-
> fore *prevail*, and suffer only *modest* and *acceptable* civilian casualties from
> their remaining force, which would be badly damaged and uncoordinated.

Shocked at General Turgidson's plan to follow Ripper's B-52 Wing in an all-out, coordinated counterforce nuclear attack on Russian airbases and missile sites, the President
asserts:

Muffley:
General, it is the avowed policy of our country never to strike first with
nuclear weapons.

Turgidson:
Well, Mr. President, I would say that General Ripper has already invalidated
that policy.

That was not an act of national policy and there are still alternatives left open to us.

How accurate was this belief in national policy – that the US would not strike first? Throughout the Cold War Presidents Truman, Eisenhower and Kennedy each drew up multiple plans for first strikes during their terms in office. In the midst of the 1961 Berlin confrontation JFK requested all military options available for deterring Soviet aggression. These included serious consideration during the months of September and October for a pre-emptive, though limited, strike on Soviet nuclear forces to avoid retaliatory attacks on US urban-industrial targets, let alone a full strike on major American cities.[72] First-strike logic informed some of the earliest military planning for an overwhelming attack on the Soviets. At the top secret 1950 SAC conference, held a few months after the Soviet A-bomb explosion was revealed, Air Force General Vandenberg quoted Clauswitz (as does General Ripper) and spoke of annihilating Soviet war fighting capability before the 'inevitable' strike against America, using a USAF war plan designated Operation 'Offtackle' (similar to *Dr. Strangelove*'s 'Dropkick').[73] Vandenberg considered the numerical superiority and near monopoly of the US atomic bombs as an 'illusory ... wasting asset' unless they were used.[74] Whereas the new acquisition of atomic bombs 'made the Soviet Union more fanatic and aggressive in pursuit of its objectives'. So Vandenberg counselled a first and fast strike.[75]

By the late 1950s the prospect of America 'expending' the majority of its strategic arsenal in a coordinated attack meant thousands of weapons. A declassified memo from Policy Director, Gerard C. Smith, to Secretary of State, John Foster Dulles, highlights the alarming level of nuclear *overkill* that SAC would inflict in a retaliatory nuclear strike. After a NSC briefing to Eisenhower, Smith railed against SAC's plan to 'over-destroy targets', since 100 megatons ('equivalent of 5,000 Hiroshima-type bombs') would be used against Moscow alone. Smith was incredulous. The Air Force attack would come *after* – as a follow up – an initial devastating US nuclear assault: 'I was advised ... Moscow would be hit with IRBMs, fleet ballistic missiles, air-to-surface missiles, and ICBMs *before* being hit by SAC airplane delivered bombs' [emphasis mine]. Smith continued acerbically:

> You will note the heavy fatalities from fall-out. This will not be limited to the Soviet Union and China. Leaving aside the question of the morality of this type of general destruction of the Soviet Union, I have serious doubts as to the morality of a retaliation against the Soviet Union which would have serious effects on non-belligerent nations. [...] We used to be advised that a doctrine of 'restraint' governed the planning of our strategic bombing operations. It is difficult to see any fruits of such doctrine in this briefing.[76]

Smith's reminder of 'restraint' emphasised the discord amongst White House policy-makers and their colleagues in the Pentagon, such as SAC Commander-in-Chief General Thomas Power.

During the Cuban Missile Crisis, General Curtis E. LeMay strongly advocated military intervention in Cuba, arguing against JFK's blockade and political negotiation, asserting that Kennedy's approach was 'almost as bad as appeasement at Munich' predicting the Soviets would seize the chance to swiftly move on Berlin.[77] LeMay warned Kennedy: 'If we don't do anything in Cuba they're gonna push on through to Berlin and *push real hard!*' U-2 spy photos revealed the missiles in Cuba could reach SAC's southeastern airbases and, if nuclear armed, they would cause mass civilian deaths. For LeMay, a pre-emptive first strike on Cuba was inevitable, otherwise America would 'just drift into a war under conditions that we don't like ... I just don't see any solution other than direct military intervention *right now.*'[78]

Ironically, JFK prepared for just such a contingency, as a release from the JFK Presidential Library confirms, including a reference to the very same appeasement in Munich that LeMay chastisingly invoked. A draft media statement was created in the event the US launched airstrikes against Cuba:

> My fellow Americans, with a heavy heart, and in necessary fulfilment of my oath of office, I have ordered – and the United States Air Force has now carried out – military operations with conventional weapons only, to remove a major nuclear weapons build-up from the soil of Cuba. [...] The United States of America need not and cannot tolerate defiance, deception and offensive threats on the part of any nation, large or small. Nuclear weapons are so destructive, and ballistic missiles are so swift, that a sudden shift in the nature of their threat can be deeply dangerous – especially when the trigger appears to be in the hands of a violent and unstable revolutionary leader. [...] If the 1930s taught us any lesson at all, it was that aggressive conduct, if allowed to grow unchecked and unchallenged, will ultimately lead to war. This nation is opposed to war – but it is true to its word.[79]

According to some accounts Kennedy's speechwriter, Ted Sorensen, who was staunchly opposed to airstrikes, refused to write the speech so it was drafted by National Security Advisor McGeorge Bundy.[80] While Kennedy appeals for US citizens to remain calm and calls for talks with Soviet Premier Nikita Khrushchev to discuss the situation, it is quite possible that this speech, if delivered, would have marked the beginning of a nuclear war. The White House and Pentagon were unaware that nuclear weapons were *already* delivered and operational in Cuba, and that battlefield commanders had predelegation authority from the Kremlin to use them in case of an American attack, conventional or otherwise.[81] According to documents by the National Security Archive: 'It was the understanding of the field commanders that tactical nuclear weapons would be used to repel a US attack on Cuba [and] in all likelihood, tactical nuclear weapons would most definitely be used in a first salvo if US forces had landed in Cuba'.[82]

> **Turgidson:**
> Mr. President, we are rapidly approaching a moment of truth both for ourselves as human beings and for the life of our nation. Now, the truth is not always a pleasant thing, but it is necessary now to make a choice – to choose between two admittedly regrettable, but nevertheless, distinguishable post-war environments – one where you got 20 million people killed, and the other where you got 150 million people killed.

Turgidson's rhetoric coincidentally echoes the classified National Security Council's 1962 *Report of the Net Evaluation Subcommittee* that 'wargamed' scenarios of a Soviet counterforce attack. Facing such an assault the report casually notes that 7.3 million US and European civilian fatalities 'would appear to be within acceptable limits'. In this modelling two-thirds of the deaths resulted from blast effects and the remaining third from fallout.[83] In a parallel scenario, the NET Subcommittee assumed Soviet retaliation, using 529 warheads totaling 4,443 megatons, and averaging at 9Mt per weapon, would cause 64 million casualties and kill one third of the US population. The report estimated that only 12% of Americans would die from fallout due to the (seemingly heroic) assumption that within a few years time 'there would be substantial improvement in the protection against fallout and in the training of most of the population as to proper behavior in nuclear attack'.[84] However, neither national indoctrination nor the necessary major fallout infrastructure was ever undertaken.

> **Muffley:**
> You're talking about mass murder, General, not war.
>
> **Turgidson:**
> Mr. President, I'm not saying we wouldn't get our hair mussed. But I do say no more than 10 to 20 million killed, tops. Er ... depending on the breaks.
>
> **Muffley:**
> I will not go down in history as the greatest mass murderer since Adolf Hitler!
>
> **Turgidson:**
> Perhaps it might be better, Mr. President, if you were more concerned with the American people, than with your image in the history books.

President Muffley's concern over mass murder can nevertheless be read ambiguously. Is he concerned with the first-strike homicide of millions of Russians, or the responsibility of 'acceptable civilian casualties' at home implied in Turgidson's 'unofficial' plan? Or both? Certainly there is no discussion of European and British fatalities, or Soviet satellite countries and China, let alone other 'non-belligerent' countries.

More sobering statistics can be found in the February 1962 evaluation presented to Robert McNamara predicting future fatalities from two first-strike options, where either the US or USSR attacked pre-emptively. The modelling for a 1966 war provided four alternate scenarios for each of the two nation's first-strikes, designating targets as 'a. Urban-Industrial, b. Military and Urban-Industrial, c. Military (Groundburst), and d. Military (Airburst vs Soft)'.[85] An American strike with either 'No Warning for USSR' or 'Usable Warning for the USSR' assumed only a counterforce attack, not the deliberate targeting of Soviet cities, and vice-versa. Yet even this scenario (b.) would result in 70 million Russian deaths (with or without 'usable' warning). The Soviet retaliatory attack caused 38 million deaths in the USA and 40 million in Western Europe. The modelling notes that a war four years into the future assumes both nations (but not Western Europe) would have 'improved fallout protection for 80 per cent of the population'. The plan concedes, however, 'without fallout protection, the casualties in the US and Soviet Union would increase by from 50% to 80%, depending on the strike option'. This equates to between 105–126 million Russians killed in a first strike, and 57 to 68 million Americans in retaliation. Hence the initial scenario greatly underestimates the projected fatalities.

Calculated at the time Kubrick and George were developing their script, for an imagined war two years after the film's 1964 release, the top secret document confirms that a 'pre-emptive' or 'preventative' first-strike by America on the Soviet Union would not only be the single, greatest act of mass murder in history, but, rather than Turgidson's optimistic and cheery surmise of getting 'our hair mussed', it would decimate the American homeland, where between 25–40% of the population would be killed outright in 'red retaliation'.

DOOMSDAY MACHINES AND COBALT BOMBS

Regardless of plans to develop these revolutionary nuclear deterrent devices from the late 1950s the AEC was advising the Pentagon that it could easily produce lighter weapons but with significantly larger yields. 60Mt bombs could be mass produced for B-52 bomber delivery. Echoing Edward Teller's monstrous Manhattan Project ruminations on the Gigaton 'Backyard' device (see chapter two), in March 1958 the USAF Chief of Staff requested a study to be conducted on the feasibility of utilizing 'weapons with a yield of 100 to 1,000 MT'. According to USAF historian George F. Lemmer:

> The Air Staff concluded that it might be feasible but not desirable to use a

1,000-megaton weapon. Since lethal radioactivity might not be contained within confines of an enemy state and since it might be impractical even to test such a weapon, the Air Force Council decided in April 1959 to postpone establishing a position on the issue.[86]

In the War Room, the Russian Ambassador concludes his conversation with the Soviet Premier over the Pentagon 'hotline' and bids him a glum 'Dasvidanya'. His deep voice is sombre and his expression dour.

De Sadesky:
The fools … the mad fools.

Muffley:
What's happened?

De Sadesky:
The Doomsday Machine.

Muffley:
The Doomsday Machine? What is that?

De Sadesky:
A device which will destroy all human and animal life on earth.

Muffley:
All human and animal life?

The despondent and increasingly grim Soviet Ambassador continues:

De Sadesky:
When it is detonated, it will produce enough lethal radioactive fallout so that within ten months, the surface of the earth will be as dead as the moon.

Turgidson:
Ah, come on, De Sadesky, that's ridiculous. Our studies show that even the worst fallout is down to a safe level after two weeks.

De Sadesky:
You've obviously never heard of cobalt-thorium G.

Turgidson:
No, what about it?

De Sadesky:
Cobalt-thorium G has a radioactive half-life of 93 years. If you take, say, 50 H-bombs in the hundred megaton range and jacket them with cobalt-thorium G, when they are exploded they will produce a *doomsday shroud* – a lethal cloud of radioactivity which will encircle the earth for 93 years!

Turgidson's interjection, above, presents a highly specious claim concerning fallout and safety. Even at the time it was ludicrous to suggest that fallout from either a limited or mass nuclear strike would be 'safe' after a couple of weeks.

Muffley:
I'm afraid I don't understand something, Alexi. Is the Premier threatening to explode this if our planes carry out their attack?

De Sadesky:
No sir. It is not a thing a sane man would do. The Doomsday Machine is designed to trigger itself *automatically*.

Muffley:
But surely you can disarm it somehow.

De Sadesky:
No. It is designed to explode if any attempt is ever made to untrigger it.

Over the past decade details have emerged about a Soviet 'Doomsday-machine-like system' ostensibly conceptualised in 1964, and built and tested in the 1980s 'to preserve a retaliatory capability' due to deep concerns over 'the vulnerability of their C3 systems to a US first strike'.[87] The ultra-secret Soviet 'Perimeter' nuclear warning/nuclear strike system sought to minimise 'human safeguards' in the command and control process. If the US initiated a decapitating strike, aimed at the Soviet political leadership and its central control systems, Perimeter could launch a semi-automatic nuclear strike under pre-determined conditions, such as the severing of communication with political or military leaders, or nuclear weapons detonation detection.[88] Following these pre-ordained triggers, a few military personnel deep in an underground bunker could launch emergency command and control rockets, which in turn would automatically transmit launch orders to ICBMs in their silos.[89]

In a series of interviews with former Soviet military leaders after the demise of the Soviet Union, it was revealed that the Soviets also contemplated an *automatic* Doomsday system, sometimes called 'The Dead Hand', where 'triggering sensors were to launch the command missiles when excited by the light, or seismic shock, or radiation, or atmospheric density resulting from an incoming nuclear strike'.[90] One interviewee, General-Colonel Andran Danilevich, declared that the military had explored the possible system deployment but they evaluated the posture as 'too dangerous and unreliable and halted their development'. However, many others interviewed on the subject stated that the 'automatic trigger system was deployed, but would be activated only during crises'.[91] Commenting on the automated versus human command and control of Perimeter/Dead Hand, *Washington Post* contributing editor David Hoffman claims, 'The Soviets did look briefly at [a] totally computer driven automatic system and they decided against it', instead opting for 'a human firewall in a deep, safe bunker'.[92]

Muffley:
But this is absolute madness, ambassador. Why should you *build* such
a thing?

De Sadesky:
There are those of us who fought against it, but in the end we could not keep
up with the expense involved in the arms race, the space race, and the *peace*
race. And at the same time our people grumbled for more nylons and washing
machines. Our Doomsday scheme cost us just a small fraction of what we'd
been spending on defence in a single year. But the deciding factor was
when we learned that your country was working along similar lines,
and we were afraid of a Doomsday *gap*.

Muffley:
This is preposterous. I've never approved of anything like that.

De Sadesky:
Our source was *The New York Times*!

De Sadesky's sharp rebuke was remarkably accurate. Indeed, as early as 1954 William L. Laurence was reporting in *The New York Times* that US experiments in the Pacific had made the previously theoretical concept of a doomsday Cobalt bomb possible. Laurence quoted Albert Einstein from 1950 who said of a cobalt hydrogen bomb, 'If successful, radioactive poisoning of the atmosphere, and hence annihilation of any life on earth will have been brought within the range of technical possibilities'. Laurence noted that the successful tests at Eniwetok Atoll 'have thus brought Professor Einstein's prophecy into the realm of fact'. Since the 'cobalt bomb could be exploded from an unmanned barge in the middle of the ocean' it could virtually be made to an unlimited size, with an explosion producing 'a deadly radioactive cloud 320 times more powerful than radium' that could drift thousands of miles across 'the North American Continent'.[93]

Similarly, it was Bruce G. Blair who revealed the Soviet Doomsday device 'Perimeter' to the world in *The New York Times* in October 1993.[94] In a follow-up *Times* report, Blair said 'the system works with little or no human oversight, can send coded messages over thousands of miles to military forces and can launch nuclear-armed missiles with no human assistance', adding 'that it is, by nature, prone to error'.[95] De Sadesky's rebuke over a 'Doomsday gap' was a topical reference for an American audience in the early 1960s.[96] The illusion of a strategic 'gap' in both bomber and missile production was used to great advantage by opponents of Eisenhower, and later Vice President Nixon, during political debates.[97] Eisenhower and Nixon were privately furious that they could not divulge the truth, showing the opposite – that America had numerical superiority in both domains – because the U-2 spy plane reconnaissance photos proving the matter were classified top secret.

Unexpectedly President Muffley asks an as yet unseen (except tangentially and in long-shot from across the War Room table) and unrecognised character for his expert opinion.

Muffley:
Dr. Strangelove, do we have anything like that in the works?

Strangelove propels himself back from the War Room table, automaton-like, to reveal that he is seated in a wheelchair. Strangelove struggles with the locomotion and begins speaking as he rolls towards the President.

Strangelove:
A moment please, Mr. President. Under the authority granted me as director of weapons research and development, I commissioned last year a study of this project by the Bland Corporation. Based on the findings of the report, my conclusion was that this idea was not a practical deterrent, for reasons which, at this moment, must be all too obvious.

Strangelove's comments can be directly attributed to former RAND Corp. analyst Herman Kahn, who noted in his landmark 1961 book *On Thermonuclear War* that such a device would ultimately be 'an unsatisfactory basis for a weapons system'.[98] Kahn maintained that although it was 'disquieting [that] more than a few scientists and engineers seem attracted to the idea', a Doomsday Machine was inherently *not* controllable, and the consequences for error enormous and irreversible: 'a failure kills too many people and kills them too automatically. There is no chance of human intervention, control, and final decision.'[99]

Muffley:
Then you mean it is possible for them to have built such a thing?

Strangelove's right hand, covered in a black glove, trembles while holding a cigarette. His bare left hand determinedly plucks the cigarette away from the gloved hand's clutch as he answers:

Strangelove:
Mr. President, the technology required is easily within the means of even the smallest nuclear power. It requires only the *vill* to do so.

Muffley:
But, how is it possible for this thing to be triggered automatically, and at the same time impossible to untrigger?

Strangelove:

Mr. President, it is not only possible, it is essential. That is the whole idea of this machine, you know. Deterrence is the art of producing in the mind of the enemy, the *fear* to attack. And so, because of the automated and irrevocable decision making process which rules out *human* meddling, the Doomsday Machine is 'terrifying'. It's simple to understand ... and completely credible, and convincing.

Turgidson:

Gee, I wish we had one of them Doomsday Machines, Stainesy.

Kubrick's cut-away to Turgidson (and Presidential aide, Staines) listening, appearing enthralled by the prospect of an ultimate deterrent, provides opportunity for comic commentary but also enabled Kubrick and editor Tony Harvey to match various takes of Sellers where the actor had delivered more interesting performances from different angles and set-ups.

Strangelove's elucidation is a concise précis of Herman Kahn's description of several Doomsday Machine variants, something Kahn describes as 'idealized (almost caricatured) devices'.[100] Under Kahn's discussion of the 'desirable characteristics of a deterrent', the RAND analyst prioritises as number one the characteristic: 'frightening'.[101] As with Strangelove's clenched-grin invocation of 'terrifying', Kahn explains that the Doomsday Machine is 'as *frightening* as anything that can be devised'. Doomsday Machines are also more 'inexorable' because they can be made essentially indestructible. Their operation is simple and reliable, and their automated function 'eliminates the human element', such as being subject to 'humanitarian' considerations, threats by the enemy or any other 'loss of resolve'. The alignment with Strangelove's rationale, above, is further apparent in Kahn's discourse, when he adds that the Doomsday Machine

is certainly *persuasive*. Even an idiot should be able to understand their capabilities. Most likely such machines would be *cheap* compared to present weapons expenditures.[102]

This economic rationale is also demonstrated in Ambassador De Sadesky's earlier rebuttal of the President.

Strangelove's explanation shocks Muffley. The President's director of weapons research and development alignment of 'deterrence' with 'fear' closely matches Herman Kahn's view, who called deterrence a 'psychological problem', and quoted Thomas Schelling's observation that both sides worried over 'the reciprocal fear of surprise attack'.[103]

Muffley:
But this is fantastic, Strangelove. How can it be triggered automatically?

Strangelove:
Well, it's remarkably simple to do that. When you merely wish to bury bombs,
there is no limit to the size. After that they are connected to a gigantic
complex of computers. Now then, a specific and clearly defined set of circumstances, under which the bombs are to be exploded, is programmed into
a tape memory bank.

Kahn notes in *On Thermonuclear War* that his 'entirely hypothetical' Doomsday Machine required protection from enemy attack by being installed deep underground with secure connection to a computer. Prefiguring the Internet, Kahn's design necessitated that the computer be networked with a reliable communications system, and fed by hundreds of environmental sensory devices.[104] The computer is then programmed to respond to information alerting that the predefined number of nuclear weapons ('say, five nuclear bombs') have been detonated within a prescribed area. The transmission of the data irrevocably triggers the Doomsday Machine resulting in 'the earth destroyed'.[105] For Kahn, the device represented an 'ideal' deterrent.

Strangelove:
[continuing]
But the ... whole point of the Doomsday Machine ... is lost ... *if you keep it a
secret! Vy didn't you tell zee vorld*, eh?

De Sadesky:
It was to be announced at the Party Congress on Monday. As you know,
the Premier loves surprises.

De Sadesky's perfunctory acknowledgment confirms the well-established fact that the Soviet Premier indeed loved surprises. In reality Nikita Khrushchev rejoiced in catching his adversaries and party opponents off-guard. A political trickster, the Premier shocked the Soviet Communist Party in 1956 with his speech denouncing Stalin, calling him a violent tyrant who created a cult of personality.[106] As *Life* magazine headlined in 1958, 'Khrushchev Basks in New Surprises', noting that the Premier anticipated and relished the uproar his surprise announcements made within diplomatic circles.[107] After the shock of Sputnik's launch, and 'applying the lessons of strategic surprise to the international image of their strategic capabilities', the Premier constantly sought to rattle America and NATO with claims that the USSR had more than enough A- and H-bombs and missiles 'to wipe out from the face of the earth any country that dares to attack the Soviet Union'.[108] Two of the biggest surprises of the Eisenhower and Kennedy years were, respectively, Khrushchev's unilateral announcement of a ban on nuclear testing in the atmosphere in March 1958, and the surprise resumption and detonation of a 50MT weapon, air dropped over the Arctic, called 'Tsar Bomba', and capable of being upgraded to 100Mt.[109]

ALTERNATE TARGETS AND LOW FLYING B-52S

Flying low over the frozen Russian terrain was an important aspect of the *Dr. Strangelove* plot in order to demonstrate how initiative might enable a B-52 crew to evade detection and assault.

> **Kong:**
> Now, boys, we got three engines out; we got more holes in us than a horse trader's mule, the radio's gone and we're leaking fuel, and if we's flying any lower, why, we'd need sleigh bells on this thing. But we got one little budge on them Rooskies, at this this height, why, they might harpoon us but they dang sure ain't gonna spot us on no radar screen.

The sequence is entirely accurate, as General Turgidson's inappropriate enthusiasm will soon reveal. In November 1959 SAC altered the operational requirements of B-52s to fly low to avoid Soviet Surface to Air Missiles (SAM).[110] Most of the bombers' combat capabilities were modified, including an 'advanced Electronic Counter Measures (ECM) suite' and, crucially, to 'perform the all-weather, low-altitude interdiction mission' below 500 feet (or 150 metres).[111]

> **Navigator:**
> Sir, if we continue to lose fuel at the present rate, I estimate we only have thirty-eight minutes flying time which will not even take us as far as the primary.

Kong is impenitent and argues with the navigator, demanding to find a way to reach their assigned primary or secondary target. But the navigator's calculus is irrefutable and final.

> **Kong:**
> Well ... *shoot*. We ain't come this far just to dump this thing in the drink. What's the nearest target opportunity?
>
> **Navigator:**
> Sir, if the rate of loss does not increase, we have a chance to reach target three eight four, grid coordinate zero zero three six nine one, and possibly make it from there to the tango delta weather ship.

Kong:
What kind of a target is that, anyhow?

Bombardier:
Sir, that's the ICBM complex at Kodlosk.

This sequence recalls the 'unlucky' atomic bombing of Nagasaki. Three days after the first atomic bomb ('Little Boy' with a uranium gun assembly) was dropped on Hiroshima, the crew of 'Bockscar' flew towards Japan armed with a plutonium implosion bomb ('Fat Man').[112] The primary target of Kokura was obscured by ground haze and smoke and impossible to bomb optically. The crew was expressly forbidden to use radar for the bombing mission so they moved on to their secondary target, the city of Nagasaki. It was a difficult mark, spread out within a long valley and surrounded by hills. The B-29 crew encountered mechanical problems and the plane was running low on fuel. The bombardier peered through the clouds and found a brief opportunity to drop his bomb. It detonated one kilometre off-target.[113] The plane made a single circle above the incinerated city before quickly leaving for Okinawa.

Despite Kong and his crew showing great initiative in avoiding radar and missiles, it is unlikely that they would have permission to use their discretion to bomb another target. Yet there would be nothing stopping the crew from undertaking this unilateral action given that all communications had been severed. Narratively, however, this surprise move provides a credible rationale for why the plane succeeds in reaching its new target – the President strongly advises all Soviet defensive systems to be directed towards the plane's pre-authorised Plan R target.

After speaking with the Soviet Premier, Muffley is resolute in providing the Russians all possible assistance in destroying his own B-52 bomber, 'The Leper Colony', which has inexplicably evaded detection despite being initially reported shot down by Soviet missiles. Realising that even a single thermonuclear detonation will trigger the Doomsday Machine, the President looks for reassurance from his Joint Chiefs:

Muffley:
General Turgidson, is there really a chance for that plane to get through?

The General stands next to military colleagues and civilian aides with his jacket off and shirtsleeves rolled up, listening intently. He pauses to consider the question and answers with increasing enthusiasm, spreading his arms, wing-like and laughs:

Turgidson:
If the pilot's good, see. I mean, if he's really sharp – he can barrel that baby
in so low... You oughtta see it sometime, it's a sight. A big plane, like a '52...
vroom! There jet exhaust fryin' chickens in the barnyard!

Muffley:
Yeah, but has he got a chance?

Turgidson:
Has he got a chance? Hell Ye... ye...

Turgidson halts mid-sentence, raising his hand to his mouth, realising the gravity and inappropriateness of his spirited reply. The General's misplaced enthusiasm was, however, quite justified. As mentioned above, in order to improve the B-52's combat capabilities in a rapidly changing strategic environment, such as interception by Soviet SAMs, most B-52s were quickly modified to enable improved, low-level flying at high speed.

POST-NUCLEAR SURVIVAL, MINE-SHAFTS AND GDP

After the tense build-up of the final B-52 bomb-run sequence, resulting in Major Kong releasing a thermonuclear weapon, riding it down rodeo-style and emitting war-whoops, before it blindingly detonates over the ICBM complex, Kubrick cuts back to the sullen War Room. Strangelove swings his wheelchair around rapidly to perform an about-face, moving away from the Big Board. He slowly rolls towards Muffley, announcing:

Strangelove:
Mr. President, I would not rule out the chance to preserve a nucleus of human specimens. It would be quite easy ... heh, heh ... at the bottom of ... ah ... some of our deeper mineshafts. The radioactivity would never penetrate a mine some thousands of feet deep. And in a matter of veeks, sufficient improvements in dvelling space could easily be provided.

Muffley:
How long would you have to stay down there?

Strangelove reaches into his jacket expecting to extract his circular bomb effects calculator, which is already held in his gloved right hand and he performs a quick set of manipulations and calculations before snatching the device away with his other hand.

Strangelove:
Vell let's see now ... ah, cobalt-thorium G. Radioactive half-life of uh ... hmm ... I would think that uh ... possibly uh ... one hundred years.

Muffley:
You mean, people could actually stay down there for a hundred years?

Strangelove:
It would not be difficult, *mein Führer*! Nuclear reactors could ... heh... I'm sorry, Mr. President. Nuclear reactors could provide power almost indefinitely.

Greenhouses could maintain plant life. Animals could be bred and *slaughtered*. A quick survey would have to be made of all the available mine sites in the country. But I would guess that, ah … dvelling space for several hundred thousand of our people could easily be provided.

Throughout the Cold War (and still operating today) President Eisenhower initiated a plan for the 'continuity of government' should the US Executive be eliminated in a sneak attack. Eisenhower established a number of underground facilities for this purpose, including the Greenbrier bunker in West Virginia, large enough to hold representatives from both Congressional chambers, Representatives and the Senate.[114] Eisenhower also gave approval for SAC to build hardened underground defence bunkers for communications. Similarly the Kennedy administration instituted a nation-wide strategy for communal fall-out shelters, announced publicly in *Life* magazine, but it failed dismally.[115] JFK did lead by example, building a personal fallout shelter, at public expense, in Palm Beach Florida. Ten months before the Cuban Missile Crisis the Kennedy family procured a 'bunker' at the Lorida residence where they spent many weekends, including the one immediately before JFK's assassination in November 1963.[116]

Muffley:
Well I … I would hate to have to decide who stays up and who goes down.

Strangelove:
Vell, zat would not be necessary Mr. President. It could easily be accomplished with a compu-dah. And a compu-dah could be set and programmed to accept

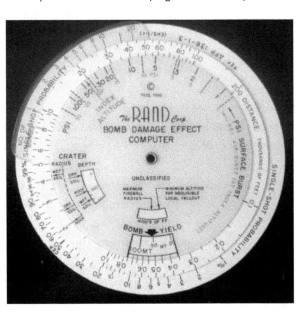

RAND Corp. 'Bomb Damage Effect Computer'. This circular slide rule is similar to the one used (made by the Lovelace Institute and included in *The Effects of Nuclear Weapons*) by Dr. Strangelove inside the War Room. It was advertised to film exhibitors in the movie's press kit as a novel 75 cent item to stimulate local interest in the screenings: 'They make sensational giveaways to VIP's – editors, critics, radio and television personalities.'

factors from youth, health, *sexual* fertility, intelligence, and a cross section of necessary skills. Of course it would be absolutely vital that our top government and military men be included to foster and impart the required principles of leadership and tradition.

Strangelove slams his left fist violently onto his gloved right hand which instantly propels itself into a Nazi salute. The Doctor groans as his left hand grabs his rebellious right forearm and thrusts it back towards his groin.

Naturally, zey vould breed prodigiously, eh? There vould be much time, and little to do, he he. But, ah, vith the proper breeding techniques and a ratio of say, ten females to each male, I vould guess that they could then verk their vay back to the present gross national product within say, twenty years.

Strangelove's estimate draws from Kahn and others commentators on national survivability and projections of post-holocaust GDP (see chapter two). Kahn asserts: 'Postwar restoration may even be faster … because we are likely to work harder and consume less.'[117] Using tabulated, quantifiable data by the RAND analyst's calculus 'we will have an economy able to restore most of the prewar gross national product relatively rapidly'.[118]

Muffley:
But look here Doctor, wouldn't this nucleus of survivors be so grief stricken and anguished that they'd, well, envy the dead and not want to go on living?[119]

As the President speaks Kubrick cuts away to Strangelove, his gloved hand mischievously rolling back his right wheel before his other arm intervenes, beating his right hand until it final goes limp, causing the Doctor to slump sideways.

Strangelove:
No sir … Excuse me … Also when … when they go down into the mine everyone would still be alive. There vould be no shocking memories, and the prevailing emotion will be one of *nostalgia* for those left behind, combined with a spirit of *bold curiosity* for the adventure ahead! Ha!

Strangelove's excitable right arm shoots out into a Nazi salute and he again pulls it back towards his lap. His left fist repeatedly pounds on the rebellious one. In medium close-up his gloved hand gives Strangelove an uppercut to the lower jaw but he reflexively turns and bites down on it hard, then groans in pain. Still biting, his left hand grapples with the other but it breaks away and clutches at his throat, strangling him.

Strangelove's dialogue echoes the optimism of Herman Kahn who repeatedly down-played the vicissitudes of post-holocaust life. In a 1962 article Kahn blithely announced that 'objective studies' indicated that after a nuclear war 'though the environment will be hostile to human life for possibly thousands of years, it will not be so hostile as to pre-clude normal and happy lives for the survivors'.[120] Kahn believed that survivors would pitch in and work harder in the extended, post-war emergency period. As for dismissing survivors envying the dead, the response is taken in summary from one of Kahn's major chapters titled 'Will the Survivors Envy the Dead?' and subtitled 'How Much Tragedy is "Acceptable"?'.[121]

The entire War Room has watched on, unperturbed by Strangelove's violent and bi-zarre spectacle, while Turgidson nonchalantly enquires:

Turgidson:
Doctor, you mentioned the ration of ten women to each man. Now, wouldn't that necessitate the abandonment of the so-called monogamous sexual relationship, I mean, as far as men were concerned?

Strangelove:
Regrettably, yes. But it is, you know, a sacrifice required for the future of the hu-uman ra-ace. I hasten to add that since each man will be required to do prodigious … [in mid-close up, Strangelove looks down, off camera, to his lap, shifts uncomfortably and removes his gloved hand, before continuing] service along these lines, the women will have to be selected for their sexual characteristics which will have to be of a highly stimulating nature.

De Sadesky:
I must confess, you have an astonishingly good idea there, Doctor.

Buoyed by the prospect of America's senior political and military leadership not only sur-viving the Doomsday Machine's radioactive shroud, but abandoning the status quo for a promiscuous programme of breeding with dozens of attractive young women, the nar-rative rapidly descends into militarist grand-standing and squabbles over competitive repopulation, preserving a nuclear deterrent underground, and ensuring there will be no post-holocaust 'mine-shaft gap!'. Still clutching his bomb effects calculator Strangelove rises from his wheelchair and limps towards the President. He comes to a rapid a halt, realising his newfound mobility, exclaiming: 'Mein Furhrer. I can *valk*!' Kubrick cuts imme-diately to a volley of atomic and hydrogen bombs detonating, symbolic of the Doomsday Machine's triggering, syncopated to Vera Lynn's 'We'll Meet Again'.

This chapter has sought to illuminate both the prescience and veracity of Kubrick's film, yet it would likely require another book to comprehensively cover all aspects of the movie's technical accuracy, including debates about Fluoridation, the explosive impact of a surface-to-air (SAM) missile on a B-52, the Electronic Counter Measures (ECM), B-52 crew survival kits, and the underground War Room design. The alignment of *Dr. Strangelove*'s fictional plot, dialogue and production detail to the then (and in some cases still) secret American nuclear policy and classified technology, was at the time unprecedented. George and Kubrick successfully created a scenario of heightened realism, juxtaposed against biting and absurdist satirical dialogue, but mostly restrained theatricality to demonstrate life in the Cold War as authentically strange.

NOTES

1   Ken Adam interview transcript, ibid.
2   Taylor Downing, 'War on Film – Dr. Strangelove', *Military History* (2014); http://www.military-history.org/articles/war-on-film-dr-strangelove.htm.
3   Lawrence H. Suid, *Guts and Glory: The Making of the American Military Image in Film* (Lexington, KY: University Press of Kentucky, 2015), 232.
4   Krämer, *Dr. Strangelove*.
5   As Kate McQuiston points out, audiences familiar with the lyrics of 'Try a Little Tenderness' would further appreciate the sexual innuendo of the sequence, *We'll Meet Again: Musical Design in the Films of Stanley Kubrick* (New York: Oxford University Press, 2013), 24. The inspiration for this sequence came from compilation editor Pablo Ferro and Kubrick finding instant agreement on the inescapable sexual nature of machine design. Pablo Ferro interview with the author 2004.
6   https://en.wikipedia.org/wiki/List_of_USAF_Bomb_Wings_and_Wings_assigned_to_Strategic_Air_Command
7   LeMay personally oversaw these troops acquiring Smith & Wesson six-shooters, see http://www.smithandwessonforums.com/forum/s-w-revolvers-1857–1945/38302-chrome-nickeled-victory-m-p-used-sac.html
8   Global Security, 'Weapons of Mass Destruction: Strategic Air Command'; http://www.globalsecurity.org/wmd/agency/sac.htm
9   Hans M. Kristensen, 'Secrecy on a Sliding Scale: US Nuclear Weapons Deployments', (1999); http://oldsite.nautilus.org/archives/nukepolicy/Denmark/index.html
10 http://www.strategic-air-command.com/weapons/nuclear_bomb_chart.htm
11 Eric Schlosser, *Command and Control: Nuclear Weapons, the Damascus Accident, and the Illusion of Safety* (Penguin Press, 2013), 292.
12 See recent US Air Force instructions at: https://fas.org/irp/doddir/usaf/afi91-104.pdf
13 Thomas Jones, 'A Full Retaliatory Response', *Air & Space*, November 2005.
14 Post Cold War, this once classified instrumentation can now be bought as scrap online at auction; see http://www.b-52parts.com/b52interior.htm, and http://www.boneyard2u.com/boneyard2u.html.
15 'The JCAE and the Development of the Permissive Action Link'; http://www.brookings.edu/about/projects/archive/nucweapons/box9-2.

16 Sandia Laboratories, *Command and Control Systems for Nuclear Weapons: History and Current Status* (1973), 9.

17 John F. Kennedy, 'National Security Action Memorandum Number 160: Permissive Links for Nuclear Weapons in Nato', (1962); http://www.jfklibrary.org/Asset-Viewer/DOwYUab4bOmVeDyLvL58jQ.aspx.

18 Sandia Laboratories, *Command and Control Systems*, 7.

19 See 'Transcript of questions & answers between Representative Fazio and W. Graham Claytor', May 1991, at https://cryptome.org/nuke-fuze.htm

20 Peter Stein and Peter Feaver, *Assuring Control of Nuclear Weapons: The Evolution of Permissive Action Links* (Lanham, MD: Center for Science and International Affairs, Harvard University, 1987); Ashton B Carter, John D. Steinbruner, and Charles A. Zraket, *Managing Nuclear Operations* (Washington DC: The Brookings Institution, 1987) at https://cryptome.org/nuke-fuze.htm.

21 On the Goldsboro accident see Schlosser, *Command and Control*, 245–48; National Security Archive, 'New Details on the 1961 Goldsboro Nuclear Accident'; http://nsarchive.gwu.edu/nukevault/ebb475/.

22 The Guardian, 'Goldsboro Revisited: Account of Hydrogen Bomb near-Disaster over North Carolina – Declassified Document', (2013); http://www.theguardian.com/world/interactive/2013/sep/20/goldsboro-revisited-declassified-document.

23 Nuclear Weapons Archive, 'Principles of Nuclear Weapons Security and Safety', (1997); http://nuclearweaponarchive.org/Usa/Weapons/Pal.html.

24 Ibid.

25 US Department of Energy Office of Declassification, 'Restricted Data Declassification Decisions 1946 to the Present (Rdd-7)', (2001); http://www.fas.org/sgp/othergov/doe/rdd-7.html#I49.

26 Robert Johnston, 'The Largest Nuclear Weapons: Multimegaton Weapons', (1999); http://www.johnstonsarchive.net/nuclear/multimeg.html.

27 See Nuclear Weapons Archive, 'The B-41 (Mk-41) Bomb: High Yield Strategic Thermonuclear Bomb'; http://nuclearweaponarchive.org/Usa/Weapons/B41.html.

28 NukeMap; http://nuclearsecrecy.com/nukemap/

29 Comprehensive Nuclear-Test-Ban Treaty Organisation, 'Castle Bravo on 1 March 1954, Bikini Atoll: Largest US Test in Terms of Yield and Fallout', (2012); https://www.ctbto.org/specials/testing-times/1-march-1954-castle-bravo/.

30 Peter George, *Red Alert* (Ace Books, 1958), 28.

31 Strategic Air Command, 'Atomic Weapons Requirement Study for 1959', (1956).

32 See Federation of American Scientists, 'Nuclear Weapon Radiation Effects', (1998); http://fas.org/nuke/intro/nuke/radiation.htm.'Meteorological conditions will greatly influence fallout, particularly local fallout. Atmospheric winds are able to distribute fallout over large areas. For example, as a result of a surface burst of a 15 Mt thermonuclear device at Bikini Atoll on March 1, 1954, a roughly cigar-shaped area of the Pacific extending over 500 km downwind and varying in width to a maximum of 100 km was severely contaminated. Snow and rain, especially if they come from considerable heights, will accelerate local fallout. Under special meteorological conditions, such as a local rain shower that originates above the radioactive cloud, limited areas of heavy contamination may be formed.'

33 Leto quoted in Jones, 'A Full Retaliatory Response'.

34 Shuler, ibid.

35 Ketchman, ibid.

36 While 'clobbering' is a colloquial term used comically in this context, Peter George employs the term in *Red Alert* and Herman Kahn casually (or semi-comically) refers to it in *On Thermonuclear War*.

37 National Security Archive, 'First Documented Evidence That US Presidents Predelegated Nuclear Weapons Release Authority to the Military', (1998); http://nsarchive.gwu.edu/news/19980319.htm.

38 Ibid.

39 National Security Archive, 'Instructions for the Expenditure of Nuclear Weapons in Accordance with the Presidential Authorisation Dated May 22, 1957', (Revised as at 28 January 1959); nsarchive.gwu.edu/NSAEBB/NSAEBB45/doc3.pdf.

40 'First Documented Evidence That US Presidents Predelegated Nuclear Weapons Release Authority to the Military'.

41 Ibid.

42 Archive, 'Instructions for the Expenditure of Nuclear Weapons in Accordance with the Presidential Authorisation Dated May 22, 1957', 20.

43 McGeorge Bundy to JFK, January 1961, 'First Documented Evidence That US Presidents Predelegated Nuclear Weapons Release Authority to the Military'.

44 Ibid.

45 William Burr, 'Newly Declassified Documents on Advance Presidential Authorisation of Nuclear Weapons Use', (1998); http://nsarchive.gwu.edu/news/predelegation2/predel2.htm

46 US Air Force, 'Operation Headstart', *Film 242.FR.33* (1959); https://www.youtube.com/watch?v=GDWS_9uS9IM.

47 Curtis E. LeMay oversaw the transfer of voice communications from AM radio transmission to SSB for the new B-52s in the mid-1950s and personally tested the equipment on two lengthy flights to Okinawa and Greenland. See Gil McElroy, 'Amateur Radio and the Rise of Ssb', *QST* (2003), www.arrl.org/files/file/Technology/pdf/McElroy.pdf.

48 Sandia Laboratories, *Command and Control Systems*, 9.

49 Ibid.

50 Peter George to Stanley Kubrick, 27 February 1963, PGA.

51 Ken Adam interview transcript, 'Inside Dr. Strangelove'. At the time of writing, after a lengthy delay, the FBI had initially responded to the author's Freedom of Information (FOI) request stating that no records could be found on Kubrick or *Dr. Strangelove*. Following an FOIA appeal, the FBI has advised it has located 'potential' records of relevance, as yet unseen by the author and too late for this book.

52 George, *Red Alert*, 34.

53 'Air Force HQ', 1962, *Newsweek*, 2 April, SKPC.

54 Schlosser, *Command and Control*, 190–95.

55 Louis Rene Beres, 'Nuclear Errors and Accidents', in *Search for Sanity: The Politics of Nuclear Weapons and Disarmament*, ed. Paul Joseph and Simon Rosenblum (Boston: South End Press, 1984), 150.

56 Schlosser, *Command and Control*, 10.

57 Ibid., 193.

58 Ibid., 192–93.

59 For a comprehensive overview of the military Personnel Reliability Program, see Herbert L. Abrams, 'Sources of Human Instability in the Handling of Nuclear Weapons', in *The Medical Implications of Nuclear War*, ed. Solomon F. Marston (Washington DC: National Academies Press, 1986); http://www.ncbi.nlm.nih.gov/books/NBK219146/.

60 Gene Healy, *The Cult of the Presidency: America's Dangerous Devotion to Executive Power* (Washington DC: Cato Institute, 2009), 96.

61 Steven M. Bellovin, 'Permissive Action Links, Nuclear Weapons, and the History of Public Key Cryptography', (2005); http://web.stanford.edu/class/ee380/Abstracts/060315-slides-bellovin.pdf

62 Quoted in Martin Hellman, 'Fifty Years after the Cuban Missile Crisis: Time to Stop Bluffing at Nuclear Poker', *Federation of American Scientists* (2012), www-ee.stanford.edu/ffhellman/publications/76.pdf

63 Richard Rhodes, *Dark Sun: The Making of the Hydrogen Bomb* (Simon & Schuster, 1996), 451.

64 Quoted in Kaplan, *The Wizards of Armageddon*, 246.

65 Healy, *The Cult of the Presidency*, 97.

66 Schlosser, *Command and Control*, 188–89.

67 See 'Castro-Khrushchev Letters on First Strike', *American Experience*; http://www.pbs.org/wgbh/americanexperience/features/primary-resources/jfk-attack/

68 Letter from Fidel Castro to Nikita Khrushchev, 26 October 1962, ibid.

69 Svetlana Savranskaya, 'Cuba Almost Became a Nuclear Power', *Foreign Policy* (2012); http://foreignpolicy.com/2012/10/10/cuba-almost-became-a-nuclear-power-in-1962/.

70 On the discursive properties of 'nukespeak' by the military-industrial complex, see Crispin Aubrey, *Nukespeak, the Media and the Bomb* (Comedia, 1982); Stephen Hilgartner, Richard C. Bell, and Rory O'Connor, *Nukespeak* (Penguin, 1983); Paul A. Chilton, *Language and the Nuclear Arms Debate: Nukespeak Today* (London: Francis Pinter Publishing, 1985).

71 The Stanley Kubrick Archive production file SK/11/3/5, has several such images from SAC, NORAD and B-52 schematics.

72 William Burr, 'First Strike Options and the Berlin Crisis, September 1961', (2001); http://nsarchive.gwu.edu/NSAEBB/NSAEBB56/

73 According to Sportingcharts.com, 'Offtackle is a running play on offense where the running back will endeavor to get outside of offensive tackle prior to turning up field to gain yards. Offtackle plays rely on athletic blockers who can get to the wide side of the field to make blocks, and on a running back who is capable of making a quick cut upfield to take advantage of any holes that open in the defense. Offtackle plays are more likely to result in big plays, since they run away from the strongest part of the defense, but they are also more likely to result in a loss of yards because the running back waits longer before attacking the line of scrimmage.' See http://www.sportingcharts.com/dictionary/nfl/off-tackle.aspx

74 General Vandenberg, 'Transcript of the Commanders Conference', (1950), 4–7.

75 Ibid.

76 http://www.seas.gwu.edu/nsaarchive/nsa/NC/nh2_2.gif

77 A recording of this exchange can be heard here: http://www.history.com/topics/cold-war/cuban-missile-crisis/speeches/lemay-and-kennedy-argue-over-cuban-missile-crisis?m=52af5724c3c2e&s=undefined&f=1&free=false

78 Ibid.

79 http://ipolitics.ca/2013/08/02/the-doomsday-speeches-we-never-heard/

80 Richard Solash, '"With A Heavy Heart...": Secret JFK Speech Could Have Signaled Start Of WWIII', Radio Free Europe, 19 October 2012; http://www.rferl.org/content/speech-that-wasnt-kennedy-prepared-speech-cuban-missile-crisis/24744628.html

81 See Robert McNamara's admissions in The Fog of War, 2009, Directed by Errol Morris.

82 Svetlana Savranskaya, Thomas Blanton and Anna Melyakova, 'New Evidence on Tactical Nuclear Weapons: 59 Days in Cuba', National Security Archive (2013); http://nsarchive.gwu.edu/NSAEBB/NSAEBB449/.

83 National Security Council, 'Report of the Net Evaluation Subcommittee', (Washington DC, 1962), 22.

84 Ibid., 32.

85 See National Security Archive, 'Summary of Population Fatalities from Nuclear War in 1966', (1962); http://nsarchive.gwu.edu/nukevault/ebb281/

86 George F. Lemmer, 'The Air Force and Strategic Deterrence 1951–1960', USAF Historical Division (1967); http://nsarchive.gwu.edu/nukevault/ebb249/doc09.pdf

87 Interviews conducted with 1995 post-Soviet military leaders describe Dead Hand as conceived in 1964 and becoming operational in the 1970s; see National Security Archive, 'Declassified Pentagon History Provides Hair-Raising Scenarios of US Vulnerabilities to Nuclear Attack through 1970s', (2012); http://nsarchive.gwu.edu/nukevault/ebb403/

88 David Hoffman, The Dead Hand: The Untold Story of the Cold War Arms Race and Its Dangerous Legacy (New York: Anchor Books, 2009).

89 See http://nsarchive.gwu.edu/nukevault/ebb371/

90 William Bur and Svetlana Savranskaya, 'Previously Classified Interviews with Former Soviet Officials Reveal US Strategic Intelligence Failure Over Decades', 11 September 1999; http://nsarchive.gwu.edu/nukevault/ebb285/

91 Ibid.

92 David Hoffman, quoted in Armin Rosin, 'A Spherical Bunker in Russia Was the Most Secure Place in the Entire Cold War', Business Insider (2015); http://www.businessinsider.com.au/a-spherical-bunker-in-russia-was-the-most-secure-place-in-the-entire-cold-war-2015–3?r=US&IR=T.

93 William L. Laurence, 'Now Most Dreaded Weapon, Cobalt Bomb, Can Be Built', The New York Times, April 7 1954; http://www.reformation.org/ny-times-cobalt-bomb-article.html

94 Bruce G. Blair, 'Russia's Doomsday Machine', ibid., October 8 1993, A35.

95 William J. Broad, 'Russia Has 'Doomsday' Machine, US Expert Says', ibid.; http://www.ny-times.com/1993/10/08/world/russia-has-doomsday-machine-us-expert-says.html

96 'Bomber Gap', Cold War Museum; http://www.coldwar.org/articles/50s/bomber_gap.asp

97 Dwayne A. Day, 'Of Myths and Missiles: The Truth About John F. Kennedy and the Missile Gap', The Space Review (2006); http://www.thespacereview.com/article/523/1

98 Herman Kahn, On Thermonuclear War (Princeton: Princeton University Press, 1960), 147.

99 Ibid.

100 Ibid.

101 Ibid., 146.

102 Ibid., 147.

103 Ibid., xvii and 16.

104 'The Bomb Alarm Display System [BADS], operational from 1961–1967, was designed to confirm whether nuclear weapons had detonated in the mainland US or at missile early warning radar sites in Alaska, Greenland and the United Kingdom. Knowing whether a nuclear attack had actually happened would help leaders decide how to response, and would help avoid launching missiles by mistake. The bomb alarm network, made by the Western Union Telegraph Company, monitored about a hundred military sites and US population centres using sensors like the one above. As Strategic Air Command, the North American Air Defence Command, the Pentagon, and other military headquarters, large electronic maps displayed the whole network. Sensors were mounted on building or telephone poles and placed several miles apart around cities and bases. If a nuclear blast occurred, the unit would send a warning signal to a control centre before the sensor was destroyed. The bomb alarm was not sensitive to lightning, sunlight or electrical surges. Photocells inside the glass lens reacted only to the flash of a nuclear explosion. Western Union designed the Bomb Alarm Display system beginning in 1959 and in 1962 the network was complete. One drawback was that it responded only after an attack – it did not give advance warning. Another drawback was that it relied on commercial telephone lines, which could be damaged in an attack. Though the bomb system made military decision making more reliable, better communication systems and satellites made the network unnecessary in the late 1960s.' See http://coldwar-ct.com/Bomb_Alarm_Network.html

105 Ibid., 145.

106 Chris Early, 'February 25, 1956: Khrushchev Launches Surprise Attack on Stalin', (2015); http://home.bt.com/news/world-news/february-25-1956-khrushchev-launches-surprise-attack-on-stalin-11363964039873

107 Anon, 'Khrushchev Basks in New Surprises', *Life*, 4 August 1958, 10.

108 Khrushchev, quoted in John Gooch and Amos Perlmutter, eds, *Military Deception and Strategic Surprise* (New York: Frank Cass, 1982), 47.

109 See William Burr and Hector L. Montford, 'The Making of the Limited Test Ban Treaty, 1958–1963', *National Security Archive* (2003); http://nsarchive.gwu.edu/NSAEBB/NSAEBB94/. According to the authors: 'The Soviets, who had been calling for a test ban since the mid-1950s, took a major initiative in early 1958 when they called for an American-British-Soviet test moratorium. At the end of March, the Soviets announced that they were unilaterally halting nuclear tests. [However] Khrushchev was also under pressure from the Soviet military to break the moratorium and he made the first move on 1 September 1961. The moratorium collapsed during an unfolding US-Soviet crisis over the status of West Berlin.'

110 See https://medium.com/war-is-boring/these-madmen-flew-b-52-bombers-at-wave-top-heights-8edc7e055980#.a6q2weicq

111 Marcelle Knaack, *Post-World War Ii Bombers, 1945–1973* (Washington DC: Office of Air Force History, 1988); Lori S. Tagg, *Development of the B-52: The Wright Field Story* (Dayton, OH: History Office Aeronautical Systems Center, Air Force Materiel Command, Wright-Patterson Air Force Base, United States Air Force, 2004).

112 Alex Wellerstein, 'Nagasaki: The Last Bomb', *The New Yorker*, 7 August 2015; http://www.newyorker.com/tech/elements/nagasaki-the-last-bomb

113 Ibid.

114 Rose, *One Nation Underground: The Fallout Shelter in American Culture*, 114–15.

115 See cover story, 'The Drive for Mass Shelters', *Life*, 12 January 1962.

116 Tom Vandebilt, *Survival City: Adventures Among the Ruins of Atomic America* (New York: Princeton Architectural Press, 2002), 144.

117 Kahn, *On Thermonuclear War*, 79.

118 Ibid., 83.

119 'Nucleus of survivors' was to be the name of Peter George's follow-up novel, but it was subsequently published in 1965 as *Commander-1* (Hienemann).

120 Kahn, as quoted in Kahn, *On Thermonuclear War*, xviii.

121 Ibid., 40.

CHAPTER FIVE

Reconstructing *Strangelove*: Outtakes from the Cutting Room Floor

Director-producer and co-writer Stanley Kubrick faced a range of creative opportunities and artistic challenges in the editing of *Dr. Strangelove.* Over the years a number of myths concerning the production of the film have circulated, stories that only a forensic analysis of Kubrick's production files can comprehensively evaluate. Amongst these claims is the degree to which Peter Sellers ad-libbed his lines, with the belief that he created significant amounts of new dialogue. For example, 'Continuity Girl' Pam Carlton has said that apart from delivering the first scripted line the actor ad-libbed the rest of his dialogue during the two 'hotline' phone calls with the Soviet Premier.[1] Interviews with several production associates and crew-members, who were present on set, have related that Kubrick shot endless takes. While Kubrick biographer Vincent LoBrutto gives credence to the ad-lib contributions, John Baxter claims erroneously that Kubrick 'always used at least three' cameras for any Sellers scene in order to capture the range of his improvisations.[2] Studio Daily Continuity Reports, however, show that only two cameras at any given time were trained on Sellers, and then only those in the War Room sequences. On a rare occasion three cameras were used to simultaneously cover the now deleted 'pie-fight' scenes.[3] In reality, Kubrick always acknowledged the contribution of actors to his scripts.[4] In relation to *Dr. Strangelove* Kubrick is quoted by Gene D. Phillips as saying: 'Some of the best dialogue was created by Sellers himself.'[5] However, such comments have been later misconstrued; this does not mean that a *lot* of dialogue was created, only 'some of the best'.[6]

THE STRANGELOVE OUTTAKES

The following scenes, as recorded in the Daily Continuity Reports, were originally scripted, rehearsed and then filmed, usually with multiple takes and in some instances multiple camera angles, from late January to mid-May 1963. As was standard industry practice, only key takes were printed. Fluffed dialogue lines, camera mechanical failure or other technical glitches, alongside the qualitative appraisal of the acting by the director, dictated which takes were ordered for printing. Although there are exceptions, usually only a single take (rarely two) would be chosen from the half a dozen or so that were usually filmed, on average, per scene.

These printed (out)takes were included in the initial rough edit assembly of sequences, but ultimately failed to make it into Kubrick's final release print. As editor Tony Harvey has related, the chronological sequencing of the script when translated onto film was in many ways 'a mess' and sometimes appeared disorienting or illogical: 'sometimes what you put on film doesn't always gel'.[7] The first assembly edit ran the risk that the audience would be lost if it was constructed literally as written. Furthermore, Harvey recounts: 'I remember we ran the first cut and we were both enormously depressed … it had no tension, no excitement and something was deeply missing from it.' As with Kubrick's earlier film, *The Killing*, the editing strategy of cross-cutting was once again employed but this time the narrative progression was linear and chronological, rather than *The Killing*'s selective repetition of the same action shown from different perspectives. Early in the edit Kubrick and Harvey set about re-arranging the sequences to make better sense of the chronology, action and characters. Harvey recalls that after the last day of shooting, he and Kubrick were devastated by their first cut: 'It didn't really work very well and I remember Stanley did this brilliant thing of cutting up the script, and everything was put on cards on an enormous board, and we reconstituted the whole thing and started from scratch.'[8]

Regardless of the editing process, the reasons for abandoning the array of scenes described here may vary considerably. Accordingly, some decisions are suggestive and entirely speculative, though mostly deductive. Some are consistent with what is already on the public record, while others contradict a number of assertions that continue to fuel the mythology around *Strangelove*'s production. Hence, this chapter draws from a range of primary sources – daily continuity reports, multiple script versions, set design and production stills, and key interviews – to reconstitute filmed sequences that failed to make the final cut. Despite some of the intrinsic problems with reconstructing the sequencing (e.g. chronologies of scenes, takes and dates) they are arranged here according to alphanumeric script numbering, location and narrative sequencing as best can be deduced in relation to the final release print.[9]

THE WAR ROOM (THE PENTAGON)

In several early takes the US President is portrayed suffering from a cold. Although these scenes were later re-edited to remove the portrayal of a sickly Commander-in-Chief, in some scenes and in production stills the inhalers are evident, as is Muffley shuffling a handkerchief up his sleeve.

In Scene 30R, filmed in medium-shot across the War Room table, the President rises into frame and is then seated between aides Staines and Frank. President Muffley then reaches for a large inhaler with his left hand.[10] Holding the inhaler up to his nose, coughing, the President says: 'Good morning gentlemen. Please sit down.' As they sit Muffley places the inhaler down next to him. The President asks Staines if everyone is present. As the aide describes who is missing, Muffley takes out a handkerchief and blows his nose, replacing it in his left sleeve.

An unapologetic and contrarian General Turgidson flexes his hawkish credentials before the President. At the War Room table standing next to Muffley, who holds inhalers in both hands, Turgidson leans forward, towering over his direct superior and patronisingly asserts his authority.[11]

Turgidson:
All the contingencies are being considered and you can rest assured that the departments concerned are on top of this. Now we all understand what a terrible strain you've been under, particularly just being rousted out of a sickbed. And if I may suggest, sir, we're all on the same side here. We are all trying to accomplish the same thing, and why don't you have a little confidence and let us pros handle it.

The President puts the large inhaler down on the table.

Muffley:
Now look here, General Turgidson, I want one thing understood and understood very clearly. I am running this — I am running this to the end. It is my right, my responsibility and anyone here who feels that his professional talents are not receiving the recognition they deserve is at liberty to ... to hand in his resignation which will be instantly accepted.

Turgidson stands upright, at attention.

Turgidson:
Mister President, we're all here to help you, sir, and you may rest assured that there was no offence meant by that remark.

Muffley:
Alright, I'll accept that. Now ... now let us ... let us all sit down.

In the following scene Staines and the President are shot in close-up across the War Room table.[12] After General Faceman brushes aside General Turgidson's concerns over casualties from any attack by Army Rangers against the Air Force base, Staines asks: 'Mister President, What do you think about civil defence? Shall we let the matter mature for a bit, sir?' Muffley has an inhaler shoved up a nostril, replying: 'Yes, yes. I think that's the best thing to do, yes.' The conclusion of the relevant Daily Continuity Report notes on the various takes that were printed: 'Match on President with inhalers and position of hands – OK'd by director. This scene was also covered by slates 95 and 97 but takes on these slates are being held. Different performance by Mr. Sellers.'[13] Obtaining a range of takes, often from differing angles and set ups, enabled Kubrick to cut around the eccentricities of Seller's performances.

Production designer Ken Adam recalls: 'The whole stage at Shepperton was in tears because Peter played it so he was suffering from asthma and a very bad cold. So he asked for an inhaler and the whole two days we shot, he played it with this inhaler and his terrible cold and it was hilariously funny.'[14] Because of the reorienting of Sellers' portrayal of the President, away from being sickly, these scenes were removed. Some fragments of this affected performance are still evident, for example in one of the widest long shots of the War Room table (when Turgidson is advising that there is a transcript of Ripper's phone call) at the bottom right of the frame, nearly obscured by the ring of overhead lights, Muffley can be seen using the nasal inhaler and coughing.

BURPELSON AIR FORCE BASE (INTERIOR GENERAL RIPPER'S OFFICE)

Group Captain Mandrake and General Jack D. Ripper are inside the General's office. Mandrake is framed in close shot at a small office bar, walking past bookshelves, holding a glass in each hand.[15]

Mandrake:
You know, Jack I'd be very interested to know why you've done this? (He turns to pour.)

Ripper:
Because I thought it was proper. Why else do you think I would do it? I've given it a great deal of thought, Mandrake. Don't think I haven't.

Mandrake:
I'm sure you have, sir. Apparently you're right out of rainwater (holds up bottle). Will distilled be alright?

Ripper:
That'll be fine.

Mandrake:
Good.

> **Ripper:**
> We've come a long way since Pearl Harbor and all the lessons
> we've learned are in Plan R.
>
> **Mandrake:**
> I'm sure they are, sir.
>
> **Ripper:**
> You're damned right they are.
>
> **Mandrake:**
> Would you care for some ice?
>
> **Ripper:**
> No, I like it a body temperature.

This deleted exchange shows both the incongruity of Mandrake's civil decorum at a time when the British officer desperately needs information, alongside his delicate discursive dance around a murderous psychotic – a madman whom the Group Captain is attempting to loosen-up by plying him with alcohol. Furthermore, Ripper's exposition concerning Pearl Harbor may espouse an understandable strategic rationale. The remark resonates with the option, later expressed by General Turgidson as an act of nuclear pre-emption, that the Americans should catch the Russians 'with their pants down'. It is ironic, however, that Turgidson is the one caught literally with *his* pants down. The news of Ripper's attack against the Soviets is relayed to him by his secretary, Miss Scott, while he is sitting on a hotel room toilet.

TURGIDSON'S HOTEL ROOM (INTERIOR)

A medium-shot from a crane looks down to Turgidson's secretary lying on the hotel bed, on the phone, smoking.[16] Continuity notes that this scene is 'to be intercut with shot of Turgidson in War Room in sc. 36 during Randolph speech to President'.

> **Turgidson (Off camera):**
> I told you not to call me at this number.
>
> **Secretary:**
> I'm sorry, Buck, are you going to be much longer?
>
> **Turgidson:**
> I don't know.
>
> **Secretary:**
> Well, what do you want me to do?
>
> **Turgidson:**
> Watch television.

Secretary:
The Late Late Show has been over for hours ... I just did, twice ... You know,
Buck, I don't think you love me at all ... You know, Buck, I don't think
you miss me at all.

It is interesting that Kubrick didn't intercut this scene, despite the recorded Continuity notes. All of the phone conversations in the film, except for the exchange between Ripper and Mandrake in the opening sequence, are presented in the final print as monologues (Mandrake/operator at Burpelson, the President/Soviet Premier on the War Room Hot Line, Turgidson's Secretary in the hotel room/General Puntridge, and General Turgidson in the War Room). Much of Kubrick's editing strategy pays off comically since the silences, pauses and gaps only add to the hilarity. It leaves audiences the space to imagine what is being said at the other end. What, for example, are we to imagine that the Secretary has just done, twice?[17]

THE LEPER COLONY (B-52 INTERIOR)

Inside the nuclear-armed B-52 'Leper Colony', on its way to bomb Russia, a crew member radios over the headphones to pilot Major 'King' Kong that there is a missile track at sixty miles 'coming in at Mack 3'. Kong acknowledges and takes the plane off autopilot and begins evasive manoeuvres. Kong nonchalantly starts to sing a song, one of apocalyptic patriotism, steeped in cowboy/frontier mythology that unconsciously draws from Christian Revelation both as dream and prophecy.[18] In mid-shot Kong steers the plane to the right.

Kong:
Last night as I lay on the prairie (left turn)
And looked at the stars in the sky
I wondered if ever a cowboy
Would drift to that sweet (right turn) bye and bye
Now the road to that bright happy region
Is a damn (left turn) narrow region so they say
But the road that leads to perdition
(right turn) is posted and blazed all the way
Roll on Roll on Roll on little doggies Roll on
Roll on Roll on Roll on little doggies Roll on
(left turn) now they say there will be a great roundup
And the cowboys like doggies will stand
(right turn) to be marked by the riders of judgment

Who are posted and know every brand.

I'm scared that I'll be a stray yearling

A maverick unbranded on high (left turn)

And get caught with the bunch of the Ruskies

When the boss of the riders goes by

But they say that he'll never forget you

That he knows every action and look

But for safety you'd better get branded

(right turn) get you name in that great tally book

Roll on Roll on . . .

This cowboy ode was written by country and western singer Eddy Arnold, who also composed 'The End of the World' and 'Make the World Go Away', further adding to this musical genre's apocalyptic desire for erasure. The song was re-released in 1963 on the album *Cattle Call*. It is interesting to speculate what the impetus was for the song's initial inclusion, its slight tweaking ('Ruskies'), and Slim Pickens' drawling, laconic performance. The song was not in any of the earlier scripts. Quite possibly, like Malcolm McDowell's casual humming of 'Singin' in the Rain' while rehearsing the assault in the Writer's home in *A Clockwork Orange*, perhaps cowboy Pickens absent-mindedly sang this tune while rehearsing on set and Kubrick spontaneously incorporated the improvisation.[19] Alternatively, it may have been a contribution made by Texan hipster Terry Southern, as this was filmed in early May after Sellers had declined to play Kong (due to injury or otherwise) and Pickens was brought in.[20] Yet there is no concrete indication that this is the case. Although an occasional visitor to the set, Southern had departed at pre-production, and his limousine script conferences with Kubrick were well over when this sequence was filmed. Furthermore, unlike 'We'll Meet Again' there is no evidence that Kubrick sought the rights for the song. Its ultimate deletion may well have been due to the scene's length and pacing, inevitably slowing down the rising (documentary) tension of the B-52 mission and working against Laurie Johnston's arrangement of 'When Johnny Comes Marching Home Again'.[21] Another reason for this scene's removal may have been the exaggerated performance. As Pam Carlton recollects, 'Stanley had to tone [Pickens] down a bit at times because he did go over the top.'[22]

BURPELSON AIR FORCE BASE (EXTERIOR)

Shot at dawn on the location of the fictitious Burpelson Air Force base, the sequence was actually filmed on an outer studio lot.[23] Using a hand-held Arriflex, director Kubrick filmed underneath a lorry in the foreground of the frame, tracking alongside Bat Guano as he crawls on his elbows, rifle in hand. In the background a jeep approaches from screen right, stops and a team of soldiers hop out. Guano halts at the rear of the lorry with another soldier (Rothman) behind him holding a loudhailer.

Three soldiers cross quickly in the foreground, left to right, as Guano reaches around behind him for the speaker that he holds to his mouth:

Col. Guano:
This is Colonel Bat Guano, 701st airborne ranger battalion. Why are you
men firing on us? ... This is Colonel Bat Guano. We are on a mission from the
President of the United States. We want to enter the base and speak with
General Ripper ... This is Colonel Guano. You are firing on your own men. If you
don't surrender in sixty seconds, I am under orders to return your fire.

While this excised scene served to introduce Col. Guano, the action and dialogue is redundant, as the hand-held combat footage and fire-fight from inside Gen. Ripper's office demonstrate. The motivations for this action had already been established in the War

Kubrick directing a scene featuring the inter-service battle to capture Burpelson Air Force Base. On the ground Colonel Bat Guano (Keenan Wynn) uses a loud hailer to plead with the opposing American troops to surrender. The scene was eventually cut from the film. (Stanley Kubrick Archive)

Room discussion. The deletion also makes Guano's first appearance and confrontation with Mandrake all the more surreal.

THE WAR ROOM

Of all the sequences shot for *Dr. Strangelove*, Scene 46 appears to have one of the largest number of takes, totaling fifteen in this instance. Of these, Kubrick chose to print only take '5' and '15'.[24]

The Soviet Ambassador has been granted entry into the War Room. From behind the buffet Ambassador De Sadesky is filmed in long shot walking towards President Muffley. General Turgidson and the other officials are in the background, seated at the large War Room table, with some standing to the side in pairs or a group. The camera tracks back as De Sadesky and Muffley walk together.

> **De Sadesky:**
> You are very clever, Mister President. You send planes to destroy Russia.
> You call me in here and tell me that the planes are coming but it's an accident.
> So you expect the peace-loving people of the Soviet Union to believe you.

De Sadesky circles around the President, who takes a handkerchief out and blows his nose.

> **De Sadesky (continues):**
> Hah, just sit back – and KER-BANG – you destroy us. Mr. President, your trick
> is very clever, but one thing you forget. We are chess players, and in chess,
> there are no tricks, just traps, and only beginners fall for traps.

The President returns his handkerchief to his sleeve and follows De Sadesky who has moved off in front of him.

> **Muffley:**
> You are choosing to misunderstand, Mr Ambassador.

> **De Sadesky:**
> Misunderstand? I understand only too well. Who could fail to understand
> such a clumsy trick? A trick at the expense of the peace-loving peoples of the
> Soviet Union. One ... last ... gigantic ... trick.

> **Muffley:**
> Anger will not help us now, Mr. Ambassador.

> **De Sadesky:**
> Nothing will help us now, Mr. President. We are not fooled by this fantastic lie.
> I am not fooled. The Premier will not be fooled. We are not such fools

as you may think, Mister President.

The Ambassador stands in the foreground as the President approaches him and places his hand on De Sadesky's shoulder.

Muffley:
Alexi. I have always had the greatest respect for your intelligence, your shrewd judgment of character and your ability to handle a crisis. When I speak to your Premier on the telephone, he must be able to authenticate what I say to him. So you understand why your presence here is perhaps the single most important hope to avoid a final and complete catastrophe. That is why I brought you here – that is why I revealed to you, Alexi, all our closely guarded and highly classified procedures.

This deleted confrontation nevertheless helps to set the scene for the belligerence of the two parties and the ridiculousness of the Ambassador repeating the ideological rhetoric of the 'peace-loving' communists. As several Kubrick scholars have identified the prevalence of the 'chess' motif throughout the director's *oeuvre* is common, so removing this overt and direct foregrounding in the dialogue is curious.[25] Certainly the brief shot of Muffley blowing his nose could easily have been cut around, as is the case with other such scenes.

In long shot from behind the buffet in Scene 46B the camera follows, tracks and pans back alongside Presidential aide Frank, who picks up a tray of vodka and glasses and joins the Ambassador and Admiral Randolf at the long table.[26]

FRANK:
Excuse me sir, would the Ambassador care for a drink?

Muffley (pours):
Yes, what about that, Alexi?

De Sadesky:
You would put anything in it?

Muffley:
Alexi.

De Sadesky:
I cannot be too cautious.

Muffley (pours another drink):
Of course not. Frank, can you show the Ambassador some breakfast.

Whether De Sadesky's concern here is about a foreign substance being introduced to his vodka as a doping agent or poison, the ironic implication is that it confirms General

Ripper's later (seemingly paranoid) assertion that 'under no circumstance will a commie drink water'. The sequence also recalls Timothy Cary in *Paths of Glory* sitting down to eat a last meal before his execution, pausing and ironically asking the two other condemned men, 'Do you think they put anything in it?' before violently spitting out his first mouthful. By cutting this exchange, Ripper's actions and sentiments only appear more deranged.

Upon the arrival of De Sadesky in the War Room, in long shot, General Turgidson walks towards the camera, still clutching his top secret books close to his chest. In the background everyone else is seated at the enormous circular table.[27] As the Presidential aides try and reach the Soviet Premier on the phone the Russian Ambassador has just belittled one of the American officials who offered him a non-Cuban cigar. De Sadesky rejects the offer as the product of 'capitalist stooges'. Turgidson then attracts the President's attention, in a harsh whisper:

Turgidson:
Mister President. Pssst. Are you gonna let that lousy communist punk
vomit all over us like this?

Muffley moves in front of Turgidson and stands to his right, they both look off camera, left, in the direction of De Sadesky.

Muffley:
Listen Buck, I know how you feel about this thing. How do you think I like it?
But we need this guy and there's one helluva lot riding on that phone call.
So why don't you just cool off and leave it alone now.

In the background, off-camera Staines interrupts, saying the Russians can't reach Premier Kissoff, they don't know where he is, and that he won't be back for two hours.

Showing President Muffley diplomatically calming down Turgdison at this point would have minimised the narrative and dramatic tension between the hawk (military) and dove (politician). It would have also presented the pair operating as a conciliatory team, not as antagonists, something the final film version serves to reinforce.

BURPELSON AIR FORCE BASE (INTERIOR)

During a lull in the fire-fight, where Army Rangers are trying to take control of the Burpelson Air Force base, Mandrake sits on a long couch in Ripper's office, leaning forward while nervously folding a silver gum wrapper, pensively looking at his wristwatch.[28]

Mandrake:
Jack, has it occurred to you that there are bags and bags of your boys being
killed out there?

Ripper:
Mandrake, any American boy who is not willing to die for his country
is not worth worrying about.

Mandrake:
True, very true, Jack. They say, you know, this little scene of yours is quite
brilliant. I must confess, I salute it. Quite Brilliant. But you know what
they say, Jack, the best laid plans of mice and men sometimes go astray,
and the snag is you see – of course I realise it's me, I'm dense. Just an old
dense fool, and I was wondering ... to help ... to save me in the situation,
make me look a bit more on the ball, as you say, if you could ...
could tell me why you're doing it, Jack?

Ripper moves alongside Mandrake and puts his arm around him. The General asks if
Mandrake has ever seen a commie drink water...

During a return to the intense, exterior the fire fight, as bullets rip through the office,
Ripper summons Mandrake to help him.[29]

Ripper:
The Red Coats are coming...

Mandrake, rises up off the couch.

Mandrake:
I'll probably only ruin it for you, Jack (rising). Anyhow Tally-Ho!

Mandrake joins Ripper who has raised a leg to steady himself while loading the machine
gun. Ripper strikes alight a book of matches and throws them out the window, while
chewing on his cigar the whole time. Much has been made of Sellers ad-libbing the hilarious line (actually only a single word change) about the 'string' in his leg being gone,
making the inclusion of this British rallying cry redundant.[30]

THE WAR ROOM

As indicated earlier, President Merkin Muffley was initially depicted as suffering from
the effects of a heavy head cold. After Kubrick watched the initial War Room rushes he
decided that having President Muffley played as a weak, effete humanist was the wrong
approach and he instructed Sellers to abandon the affectation of the cold.[31] Rather, he
asked that Sellers portray the President as one of the few rational characters in the film
and a stabilising, if ultimately ineffective, voice of reason. Hence, the early scenes were
either deleted from the cut or re-edited and trimmed to remove any obvious aspect of

this performance within the mise-en-scène. However, in some set-ups the inhalers can still be seen and Muffley is shown shuffling a handkerchief up his sleeve.

One of the more complex, and lengthy, War Room takes involved dialogue concerning the revelation of the Soviet Doomsday Machine and the veracity of its apocalyptic capacity.[32] At the end of the hotline conversation (unseen and unheard), Premier Kissoff reveals over the phone to De Sadesky that the Doomsday Machine is 'a device that will kill all human and animal life on earth', to which President Muffley responds: 'All human and animal life? Oh, but ... but there's no point in using such a thing. He must be mad.'

In a close shot the President is looking right to an off-camera De Sadesky. Although only two takes were filmed, in each take these lines of dialogue were repeated and slightly varied in their delivery.[33] The exchange is perfunctory but the President's (Sellers') response, a mastery of comic understatement.

Muffley:
Then, Alexi, if our planes get through that would mean the end of the world?

De Sadesky:
I'm afraid so, Merkin.

Muffley:
Gee, that's terrible.

In the final variation of this line of dialogue, Muffley expands:

Muffley:
Well, I mean we can't let that happen, can we? The whole human race relies on you
and I. I can't imagine anything more catastrophic than ... Gee, that would be terrible.

During the sequence where Turgidson makes a derogatory aside about Strangelove's 'Kraut' name to Presidential aide Staines, the doctor starts to speak in the background. The expository detail that Strangelove outlines is mostly lost in the final cut.[34] While the take focuses on Turgidson, Strangelove is heard continuing:

Strangelove:
...connected to a gigantic complex of computers. A specific and clearly
defined set of circumstances under which the bombs are to be exploded is
programmed into the tape memory banks. A single roll of tape can store all
the information, say, in a twenty-five volume encyclopedia, and analyse it in
fifteen seconds. In order for the memory banks to decide when such
a triggering circumstance has occurred...

The level of confusion and incompetence within the War Room is also evident in the excised scene where the President, De Sadesky and General Faceman are gathered around the buffet.[35] The President turns to Faceman and asks for the name of the officer 'who called me up from Burpleson'. Faceman replies, erroneously and ironically, that it was 'Colonel Guano', side-lining Mandrake either through error or ignorance. The President promptly orders: 'I want that officer promoted to Brigadier General and flown to Washington. I want to decorate him personally.'

In Scene 58D all present are jubilant that the entire nuclear bomber wing has been recalled, avoiding war and the prospect of a Doomsday detonation. When General Turgidson summons a communal prayer of thanksgiving, '...delivered us from the forces of evil', the Soviet Ambassador turns abruptly to leave.[36]

De Sadesky:
Excuse me but I'm afraid I have far more urgent matters to attend to.
But before I leave I wish to state unequivocally that my government will not
be satisfied with a polite note of regret over this violent aggression against
the peace-loving people of the Soviet Union.

Muffley:
Damn you, Sadesky! Damn you! That was the result of one man. A mentally
unbalanced person, and we have no monopoly on lunatics.

De Sadesky:
It is very convenient to place the blame on a dead man.

Muffley:
How dare you address me in such a manner!

De Sadesky:
Don't shout, Mr President!

Muffley:
I've warned about this danger for ages. I've stuck my neck out at Geneva
time and time again.

De Sadesky:
Bah! You never wanted disarmament, it would wreck your economy.

Muffley:
That's nonsense, we could spend just as much on schools, highways and space.

De Sadesky:
All you ever wanted to do was spy on our country.

Muffley:
That's a lie, De Sadesky. That's a damn lie. You wouldn't expect us to destroy our weapons without having the faintest idea of what you were doing inside your country.

De Sadesky (in the background the planes are receding across the Big Board maps):
And you, Mr President, would not expect us to let you spy in our country
before you destroyed your weapons.

> **Muffley (stepping forward, putting his hands on his hips):**
> Now listen to me, De Sadesky. Despite total distrust and suspicion we both
> place an incredible trust in each other – a far greater trust than disarmament
> or inspection would ever require. We trust each other to maintain the balance
> of terror. To behave rationally and to do nothing that would cause a war by
> accident or miscalculation or madness. Now this is a ridiculous trust because
> even assuming we both had perfect intentions we can't honestly guarantee
> anything. There's too many fingers on the buttons. What a wonderful thing for
> the fate of the world to depend on – a state of mind, a mood, a feeling of anger,
> an impulse, ten minutes of poor judgment, a sleepless night.

De Sadesky's allegations of American spying recalls the then contemporary scandals of U-2 flights over the Soviet Union and the 1960 shooting down and capture of pilot Francis Gary Powers. However, the charge is comically hypocritical since the Ambassador is shown (at least twice) secretly photographing the War Room interior. This was not so far from the reality of diplomatic spy-craft. Declassified CIA Daily Intelligence Checklists to President Kennedy two weeks before the Cuban Crisis noted a US naval attaché was 'roughed up' in Leningrad as reprisal for America ousting two Soviet diplomats from New York. The CIA report mentions the naval commander had his miniature 'minox camera, mini tape recorder and notes confiscated' – all caught on camera by a TASS photographer.[37]

Muffley's dialogue also paraphrases John F. Kennedy's famous 'Sword of Damocles' speech to the UN General Assembly.[38] While this Presidential soliloquy is rhetorically quite stirring it is ultimately theatrical and out of place with the overall tone of the film. It is pure exposition. Kubrick's scripted words, voiced here by Sellers, were retained across multiple treatments and script versions, but simply did not advance the narrative so were excised accordingly. The tenor of this discursive rationalising and its variation is continued in the next filmed scene with added dialogue.[39]

President Muffley continues to debate nuclear strategy and foreign policy with De Sadesky.[40]

> **De Sadesky:**
> You conveniently ignore the reality of force which is the only currency
> great nations have for negotiation.

> **Muffley:**
> The great nations of the world have always acted like gangsters and the small
> nations like prostitutes. And unless we can learn to replace this system that
> we politely call nuclear power politics with a new system of law and moral-
> ity between nations we will surely exterminate ourselves as we almost did

today. You see the bomb has become a great enemy to every nation than
they have ever been or could ever be to each other.
Don't you see that, De Sadesky?

This dialogue is followed immediately by Staines advising, 'Mr President, they've got the Premier on the phone'. The call acknowledges the failure of the Soviets to shoot down the B-52, 'Leper Colony', that is still believed headed to its primary target. Again, retaining this lengthy and earnest Presidential exposition would have slackened the dramatic tension and detracted from the overall 'nightmare comedy'.

Kubrick also cut from Scene 74 a discussion amongst the American military officials concerning the omnicidal implications of the Doomsday Machine.[41] While the bathetic exchange illustrates the assembled characters' individual and collective despondency it also provides Turgidson an opportunity to further rationalise acceptable levels of 'megadeath'.[42] After listening to Dr. Strangelove on the irrevocable end of the world if the Doomsday machine is automatically activated, the camera focuses on General Turgidson, in long-shot, and tracks back as he walks past officials seated at the buffet. Turgidson moves forward and sits next to the President, now in mid-shot, on the long buffet seat.

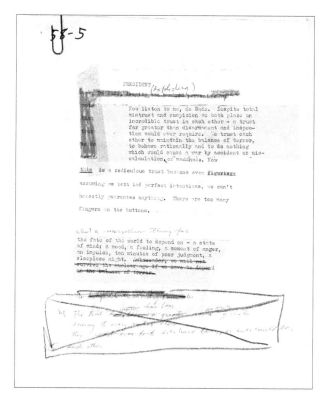

Multiple, layered, late script revisions and annotations, appearing as a palimpsest. Despite the intensive work this dialogue was not included in the final film. (Stanley Kubrick Archive)

Turgidson:
It's wrong. Dead wrong.

General Faceman:
It's not right.

Turgidson:
I don't care what anyone says, it just doesn't make sense that all human life
on earth should be ended.

Admiral Randolf:
I suppose the fishes will be alright — at least some of them.

Faceman:
What a horrible thought.

Turgidson:
It's all so pointless. I mean a man spends his whole life fighting for something
and this is what he gets. I can see twenty, forty, even a hundred million killed,
but everybody? It's just a damned shame and I don't mind saying so.

Turgidson places his arm around the President's right shoulder and leans his head down
on the President's left shoulder. Presidential aide Staines is seated on the other side of
the President, holding a stiff drink in both hands.

Staines:
Mr President, when are we going to break the news to the people?
I mean, sir, this is going to do one hell of a thing to your image.

Muffley (taking a drink):
Yeah. Alexi, how long is it going to take?

De Sadesky (off camera):
Four — maybe six months in the northern hemisphere. Perhaps a year in
the southern latitudes.

De Sadesky's prognosis is similar to the premise of the book and film versions of *On The Beach*, released only a few years earlier. In the 1957 novel, it is clear that cobalt-laced H-bombs are responsible for the annihilation of the species through a war of escalation. In Stanley Kramer's 1959 film adaptation (set in 1964, the year of *Strangelove*'s international release) there is no specific mention of this scenario other than to speculate on the proliferation of nuclear weapons.[43] The glib comment by Staines also reflects and contrasts with Turgidson's early slur that the President would be better served being more concerned with the American people than with his 'image in the history books'.

Recalcitrant Nazi Dr. Strangelove, however, provides a glimmer of hope to avoid the lethal long-lived radioactive fallout from the Doomsday Machine's cobalt-thorium

G. In Scene 74K, the scientist's upbeat scenario for underground survival, spanning generations, is partly based on his repugnant evaluation and dismissal of the 'wretched concentration camp survivors' who endured far worse conditions.[44] When asked by the President if people could survive in a shelter for a hundred years, the doctor replies:

Strangelove:
Huh! Mister President, man is an amazingly adaptable creature. After all, the conditions would be far superior to the so-called Nazi concentration camps where there is ample evidence that the wretched creatures clung desperately to life.

After impulsively calling Muffley 'Mein Führer' and promoting the need to survey the availability of deep mine shaft space throughout the USA, to be populated by a select few, the President responds to Strangelove's prognosis:

Muffley:
A couple of hundred thousand. But everybody would want to go down there. There'd be rioting and absolute chaos.

Strangelove:
Well, I'm sure that the armed services could deal with any disobedience.

Strangelove fleshes out his plan with a brutal, fascist logic, mentally computing how survivors could last a hundred years, by breeding prodigiously, with 'much time and little to do, ha ha'. The discourse closely follows the calculus of Kahn's *On Thermonuclear War*, described earlier, who liaised with Kubrick during the development of the script.[45]

Strangelove:
I should estimate the progeny of the original group of two hundred thousand would emerge in one hundred years' time at well over one hundred million. Naturally the group would have to continually engage in enlarging their original living space. But when they emerge a great deal of machine tools and real estate would be easily recoverable if they were moth-balled in advance. I would guess that they could then work their way back to the present gross national product within, say, twenty years.[46]

It is unclear why Kubrick removed much of this scene, other than on the page it appears as more unnecessary exposition. However, given Sellers' extraordinary performance as Dr. Strangelove, the rendering of these lines may have indeed been hilarious.[47]

The following cut scene indicates how prominent Strangelove becomes late in the crisis and the potential, future post-holocaust environment. When the War Room erupts into chaos Strangelove takes swift control of the situation. He finds a willing military ally in Turgidson, who promptly intervenes to further marginalise civilian political authority.

Turgidson (hands on hips, summoning):
Aye, gentlemen. I think, er … I think if mankind is going to survive here, it certainly owes a big deal of gratitude to Doc Strangelove's wonderful idea about the mineshaft. I think we ought to give him, um … well, er … three cheers. What d'you say? Hip hip hooray … Hip hip hoo-ray … Hip hip hoo-ray…**(singing)** For, he's a jolly good fellow … For, he's a jolly good fellow … For, he's a jolly good fellow … Which nobody can deny.

The general takes out a stick of gum and continues singing.

Which nobody can deny.
Which nobody can deny.
Which nobody can deny.
For, he's a jolly good fellow
For, he's a jolly good fellow
For, he's a jolly good fellow … ha, ha…
Which nobody can deny
Which nobody can deny
Which nobody can deny
For, he's a jolly good fellow
For, he's a jolly good fellow
For, he's a jolly good fell-ow
Which nobody can deny
Which nobody can deny
Which nobody can deny.

At the end of this sequence and buoyed by Strangelove's forecast of ten women to every man, Turgidson shouts at Muffley: 'Mister President — we must not allow a *mine-shaft gap*!' Suddenly, fallout calculator in hand, Strangelove rises from his wheelchair: 'Sir, I have a plan. *Mein Fürher*, I can valk.' After a couple of steps he falls, while Turgidson looks left off screen. Again, the lengthy repetition of Turgidson singing these lyrics may have diminished the narrative and plot momentum, appearing flat and cumbersome.

In Scene 74D Ambassador De Sadesky is wrestled to the ground by Turgidson, this time caught with a concealed camera while photographing the Big Board.[48]

Turgidson:
Aha. I caught you at it red-handed this time you dirty red. I caught him red-handed this time, Mr President – the dirty rat.

Muffley:
Ambassador De Sadesky – your attempts to photograph the War Room with a series of tiny cameras is a most serious breach of diplomatic courtesy it has ever been my misfortune to behold. Furthermore...

De Sadesky:
This is preposterous. There is such a thing as diplomatic immunity, Mr President.

Turgidson:
Mr President, if you ask me, this is all dummy stuff, just to throw us off the track. The real stuff is hidden somewhere on his person.

Turgidson hands over several miniature devices, all cameras, including one from De Sadesky's ankle.

Turgidson (continuing):
`Here ... here ... look at this.

Muffley:
What's this?

Turgidson:
Here's another one, look at that. I think he ought to get a first-rate frisking.

Muffley:
Quiet please. Yes, I quite agree with you, General Turgidson. In view of the seriousness of the situation and the ... the tinyness [sic] of his equipment, I think a complete body search would be in order, yes.

De Sadesky:
How dare you suggest such a thing. You will return me to my embassy at once.

Turgidson (sitting up from the floor):
Come on boys. Let's take Mr. Red upstairs and search his garments and person for tiny camera[s] and similar equipment.

As the officials murmur in the background, De Sadesky gets up and runs off, passing Turgidson and leaving the President and the gathered group behind him, looking on.

This deleted scene is also a remnant of a scripted, but unfilmed, sequence where 'all seven' of the Ambassador's 'bodily orifices' are to be searched. De Sadesky slowly does the math starting with his mouth, nostrils and ears, counting out each opening, then with dread and outrage realising what orifice six and seven means.

THE WAR ROOM PIE FIGHT

Making his escape, De Sadesky tries to leave the War Room but only encounters locked doors. The military and officials advance and the Russian seeks cover at the buffet from where the pie-fight erupts, and President Muffley is struck first. The 'pie-fight' has been previously discussed at length by several commentators including Terry Southern, Anthony Harvey, Ken Adam, Samuel Wigley, John O'Brien and Glenn Kenny.[49]

Kubrick's wife Christiane has observed that the decision to cut the famous pie-fight sequence was both heart-breaking for the director, but also liberating. After spending a few days shooting the scenes and constructing the sequence, when it came to the final edit, Kubrick undertook a very difficult decision. Christiane explains:

> The editing was great. It was very good; best pie fight ever. But in the wrong film. [...] He *loved* the pie fight sequence. It is indeed very funny and very good. And he looked at it over and over and he said, 'you know what, I could cry, but it doesn't fit. Fuck!' That's what he said. And he said, 'it really just is over-the-top; it doesn't belong in the story ... it doesn't end at the right point'. He felt it wasn't homogenous with the rest of the story. [...] And yes, he was very sad that he had to cut it out, absolutely. And then happy that he had done it. Sad that it had gone, but very happy that it was much better, much better.[50]

In the War Room during the melée as pies are hurled around, in medium shot, the President is suddenly covered in cream when Turgidson and others duck behind the President and the buffet.[51] Turgidson moves forward and holds onto Muffley.

Turgidson:
Mister President ... Mr. President ... Gentlemen, our beloved President has just
been infamously struck down with a pie in the prime of his life.

The crowd ad-lib exclamations of indignity. Although this scene was filmed in late March 1963, the line uncannily anticipates the assassination of JKF eight months later. Had the sequence remained in the final cut, it is likely Turgidson's comment would have been removed, like Major Kong's quip about having 'a pretty good time in Dallas'.

Turgidson:
Are we going to let that happen?

The crowd ad-libs 'No!' Turgidson continues as the President slides to the floor.

Turgidson:
Massive retaliation!

Turgidson and other officials rush to the buffet, pick up pies and hurl them off camera (right) while the President is left lying on the floor behind them.

For Scene 74U Turgidson and officials are framed in medium shot by the buffet as the camera tracks towards them.[52] They back away, arms raised (Turgidson, initially defiant with arms folded) as pies are thrown at them. The camera reverse tracks as Turgidson and the US officials advance, picking up pies and throwing them back with gusto to screen right, while fallen President Muffley remains in the background on the floor.

Scene 74V was filmed using a two-camera set up.[53] Camera A is a medium close-up of Turgidson and officials shooting from behind the buffet, and camera B has the General in close-up. Pies are being thrown at the group from behind the two cameras, back and forth, with the dialogue punctuating the action.

Turgidson moves towards the camera with a large pie in his right hand and a smaller one in his left, while the others remain near the buffet still throwing pies.

Turgidson:
I see you, De Sadesky, trying to sneak away. You'll never make it...
I got you this time, De Sadesky ... ha ha-ha ha-ha.

As this sequence shows, the mood of the film had shifted from nightmare comedy and satire towards farce and slapstick. According to composer Laurie Johnson this sequence was 'an experiment done before I came on the scene. It was just something [Kubrick] wanted to try out like a silent film. It was an alternative ending with a pianist [who] used to play in silent theatre.'[54] Pablo Ferro recalls the multiple variations that he and Kubrick undertook while editing to maximise the comic pacing:

> What was happening in that sequence was that it was slowing the film down. Slowing down even when it was long versions so Stanley had me do three different speeds with it, a 9 framer, a 12 framer and a 16 framer and probably a 20 framer because it was a slow one too. [...] And then we tried to cut it together and I liked the 8 framer the best when we cut that one up. And even when we did that, it still slowed the film down. Still it was a wonderful sequence, it was great, you laughed and we put the piano there, a regular piano, tring, ding, ding, because just when the President gets hit with the pie it starts the whole thing and we're going through this pie sequence which was... We all hated to see it go because it was so wonderful but if it slowed the film down, it was no good.[55]

Ferro also recalled that he and Kubrick experimented with but abandoned the idea of an animated bouncing ball above of the song's superimposed lyrics to enable an audience sing-along to accompany Vera Lynn's singing.[56]

The barely suppressed laughter that infected the cast and crew from Sellers' often *tour de force* comedic performances – evident in actor Peter Bull's smirking, downward gaze while Strangelove's rebellious arm and hand attacks the scientist – flows into the discourse with Turdigson's manic laughter. Shot from high on a crane, the camera for Scene 74BB lowers towards De Sadesky and the President (both covered in cream) sitting on the War Room floor making 'mud' pies out of the cream and cake.[57] De Sadesky takes off his hat and begins covering the inside with cream, building up the contents. The President gestures that he should flip it over, like building a sandcastle. The Ambassador does so and they begin to fill the hat again with cream and remnants of piecrust.

In Scene 74HH Strangelove is filmed in mid-shot, still seated on the floor next to his upturned wheelchair.[58] He takes a luger pistol from inside his jacket and raises the gun in his right hand, firing a single shot above his head into the air, then lowers his arm. Terry Southern has described this scene as showing Strangelove's rebel arm stealthily removing the gun from his jacket and holding the pistol to his right temple: 'the pistol is seized at the last minute by the free hand and both grapple for its control. The hand grasping the wrist prevails and is able to deflect the pistol's aim so that when it goes off with a tremendous roar' missing his head.[59]

Dr. Strangelove (Peter Sellers) fires his luger pistol, interrupting the pie fight inside the War Room. (Stanley Kubrick Archive)

Strangelove:
Gentlemen, you must stop these childish games. There is much work to do.

From camera left General Turgidson runs in to help Strangelove on the floor next to his wheelchair, still holding his gun.[60]

Strangelove:
Ah ... General...

Turgidson:
Ah ... Um ... Could I, err, offer you some assistance sir, Doctor?

Strangelove:
Well that's most kind of you, General. Most kind of you.

Turgidson (helping Strangelove get up):
Just take it ... Just take it easy now ... Put your weight on me.
There we go in the chair.

Strangelove (sits in the chair):
Yes ... yes. Thank you. Thank you, General.

Turgidson begins to brush the right shoulder of Strangelove with his hand, then stands back with both hands on the back of the wheelchair.

Turgidson:
I'm sorry I got that stuff all over you.

Strangelove:
Oh, it's nothing. You know I think the strain must have snapped their minds.
Perhaps it would be good if they were institutionalised.

Two cameras in close-up then show Strangelove as he 'gets plastered with pies'.[61] The crane-mounted camera peers down onto Strangelove as he struggles, pushing himself forward, trying to get back into his wheelchair. As he nears the chair a foot kicks the chair away to the left.

Strangelove:
You fools, I want to save you.

Another volley of pies hit Strangelove from left and right of screen, as he squirms on the floor, eventually motionless on his back. Apart from the slapstick impact of the pies, it's likely that this kind of emphasis on Strangelove's physical impairment may have unintentionally elicited spectator sympathy for the ex-Nazi. Despite the satirical nature of the scene, this was something Kubrick presumably wanted to avoid.[62] From this farce of infantile War Room violence and reprisals, the sequence then to cut to the famous

Daily Continuity
Report, 28 March
1963, describing a War
Room scene during the
Pie Fight, filmed but
ultimately removed by
Kubrick from the final
cut. (Stanley Kubrick
Archive)

Daily Continuity Report, 28 March 1963, describing a War Room scene during the Pie Fight, filmed but ultimately removed by Kubrick from the final cut. (Stanley Kubrick Archive)

montage of Atomic Energy Commission and Department of Defense stock footage show-casing Pacific and Nevada thermonuclear and atomic weapons detonations, syncopated to Vera Lynn's 'We'll Meet Again'.

This chapter has drawn from a range of primary sources to demonstrate what an ex-tended and alternative version of *Dr. Strangelove* may have looked like. While not every scene variation or struck print is described here, the majority of key filmed outtakes are recounted and analysed. From this reconstruction of deleted scenes it is clear that Kubrick was not an indulgent writer-director-producer, at least as far as *Strangelove* is concerned. Irrespective of the time, labour and costs associated with the scripting, re-hearsal, set construction and filming, he was rigorously focused and self-critical enough to make extremely tough decisions concerning overall narrative economy and aesthetic consistency. All told, had the film retained all of these excised elements, *Dr. Strangelove* would have run a further 20–30 minutes, pushing it towards two-hours, and unlikely to have pleased Columbia Pictures or, possibly, a paying audience.

It is also evident from the minor variation in dialogue, across takes and the repetition of scene set-ups and coverage, that Sellers and the other cast members quantitatively added very little to the shooting script. However, *qualitatively*, those variations in performance, no matter how slight – a few words here, an inflection or a nuanced reading there – often made all the difference. As with Terry Southern's *outré* suggestions for character names and enhanced dialogue, one facet of the genius of Kubrick was his creating an environment that encouraged and accepted inspired artistic intervention when it manifested.

Furthermore, claims of endless takes are not supported by documents in the production files. The actual studio shooting-ratio was close to average by Hollywood standards of the time. Nor were there multiple cameras continually trained on Sellers to cover his acting prowess. Whilst it has long been recognised that much of the film's humour stemmed from the script, its discursive word-play and from the actors' bravura performances, by examining the Continuity reports, alongside historical interviews with key personnel, it is abundantly evident that the editing and re-editing was crucial in making the film a comic success. Kubrick was not afraid during editing to discard substantial script elements and entire production sequences, just as he continued to improve and refine his film right up to the point of final cut and release.

NOTES

1   According to Pam Carlton: 'Sellers had two long telephone conversations, during the course of the movie. [...] And, though the conversations were actually scripted, Peter started, but only really delivered the first line of the script, and after that he just improvised and we just shot ten-minute takes and Peter just talked, and talked, and talked.' Pam Carlton interview, 'Inside Dr. Strangelove'.

2   Lobrutto, *Stanley Kubrick: A Biography*, 242; Baxter, *Stanley Kubrick: A Biography*, 185. Alexander Walker has also claimed that Kubrick 'kept two or three cameras running on Peter for the duration of those parts that he played', however, this is contradicted by Pam Carlton and disconfirmed by the Daily Continuity Reports. See Walker interview, 'Inside Dr. Strangelove'.

3   Many of these same individual scenes were covered from different angles, with different lenses and in varying degrees of closeness, as *separate* takes and set-ups, frequently shot on different days.

4   See Bernstein, 'How About a Little Game?', 35; Hill and Phillips, *The Encyclopedia of Stanley Kubrick*, 148.

5   Kubrick, quoted in Phillips, *Stanley Kubrick: Interviews*, 319.

6   As Tony Harvey relates about Sellers: 'In *Strangelove* he did this extraordinary improvisation in the war room with [gestures with hands] and the actors just broke up. You could hardly get

your scissors between the cuts. [...] But improvisation and that kind of thing has to be used very sparingly in the cutting room otherwise it shows. So it has to be kind of with a discipline of a script. You know when to cut'. See Harvey interview for 'Inside Dr. Strangelove'.

7 Tony Harvey, 'Inside Dr Strangelove'.

8 Ibid.

9 Kubrick made several alterations to the release print after the film was completed. For example, when JFK was assassinated on the day of one of the film's select previews, Major Kong's reference to having a good time in 'Dallas' was later looped over in post-production and changed to 'Vegas'. At the request of the US Air Force, a running leader at the start of the film rolled text silently to state it was the position of the Air Force that the events and people depicted were fictional.

10 Daily Continuity Report, *Dr. Strangelove*, Scene 30R; 19 February 1963; all the continuity reports referred to here are in SK/11/3/4. The author first accessed these and other *Strangelove* papers at the Kubrick residence (SKPC), Childwickbury, April 2005.

11 Daily Continuity Report, *Dr. Strangelove*, Scene 32, 19 March 1963.

12 Daily Continuity Report, *Dr. Strangelove*, Scene 30M, 18 February 1963.

13 Repeating the earlier set up for Scene 30M, the President holds a small inhaler in both hands while asking General Faceman if there are any Army units near Burpleson. Later when his aide Staines asks about civil defense, the President has a large inhaler up to his nose. Daily Continuity Report, *Dr. Strangelove*, Scene 38, March 1963.

14 Ken Adam interview, 'Inside Dr. Strangelove'.

15 Daily Continuity Report, *Dr. Strangelove*, Scene 34K, 31 January 1963. A brief snippet from this scene is shown in the director's self-narrated demonstration reel to exhibitors included in the 2016 Criterion Collection release of *Dr. Strangelove*.

16 Daily Continuity Report, *Dr. Strangelove*, Scene 36, 8 February 1963.

17 A series of later takes has the Secretary on the phone to Turgidson, adding the lines: 'I don't think you love me either. I don't think you respect me either. No you don't, it's just physical.' Daily Continuity Report, *Dr. Strangelove*, Scene 36, 8 February 1963.

18 Daily Continuity Report, *Dr. Strangelove*, Scene 43, 3 May 1963.

19 See Malcolm McDowell on improvisation, 'A Clockwork Orange quotes'; http://www.malcolmtribute.freeiz.com/aco/acoquotes.html

20 Hill, *A Grand Guy: The Art and Life of Terry Southern*, 107–27.

21 On the comedy versus the gradual, rising suspense inside the B-52 bomber Johnston observed: 'Every time a little comedy is played out on the screen, each step, each time one returns to the bomber, the audience have to feel that it's a step nearer to whatever's going to happen at the end. The tension had to mount very, very, slightly and gradually over that', 'Inside Dr. Strangelove'.

22 It should be noted, in contrast, that George C. Scott felt Kubrick only used the takes where he played Turgidson 'over the top'. Pam Carlton, 'Inside Dr. Strangelove'.

23 Daily Continuity Report, *Dr. Strangelove*, Scene 41E, 13 February 1963.

24 Daily Continuity Report, *Dr. Strangelove*, Scene 46, 4 March 1963.

25 On Kubrick's chess motif see Norman Kagan, *The Cinema of Stanley Kubrick*, 3rd ed. (New York: Continuum, 2000); Michel Ciment, Gilbert Adair and Martin Scorsese, *Kubrick: The Definitive Edition* (New York: Faber & Faber, 2001); Walker, *Stanley Kubrick, Director: A Visual Analysis*.

26   Daily Continuity Report, *Dr. Strangelove*, Scene 46B, 4 March 1963.

27   Daily Continuity Report, *Dr. Strangelove*, Scene 46C, 1 March 1963.

28   Daily Continuity Report, *Dr. Strangelove*, Scene 51, 1 February 1963.

29   Daily Continuity Report, *Dr. Strangelove*, Scene 60, 8 February 1963.

30   On the substitution of the word 'string' see interview with Sellers' friend and colleague, Joe McGrath interview, 'Inside Dr Strangelove'.

31   See Alexander Walker's interview on Sellers' initial, 'limp-wristed' characterisation, 'Inside Dr Strangelove'. On Kubrick's revision of Sellers performance Ken Adam has said: 'As we were driving back after two days shooting, I don't know if it was I, or Stanley, or Victor Lyndon, who was associate producer – somebody said, "but isn't the part of the President the more or less sane part in this crazy picture?" And Stanley said, "You're right, you know. He mustn't be satirised to that extent." So we had to re-shoot it all and Peter had to play it more seriously', Ken Adam interview, 'Inside Dr Strangelove'.

32   Daily Continuity Report, *Dr. Strangelove*, Scene 52A, 21 February 1963 .

33   Daily Continuity Report, *Dr. Strangelove*, Scene 55F, 11 March 1963.

34   Daily Continuity Report, *Dr. Strangelove*, Scene 55I, 12 March 1963.

35   Daily Continuity Report, *Dr. Strangelove*, Script 58A, 12 March 1963.

36   Daily Continuity Report, *Dr. Strangelove*, Scene 58D, 14 March 1963.

37   CIA Daily President's Intelligence Checklist, 4 October 1962; https://www.cia.gov/library/readingroom/document/0005995963

38   John F. Kennedy, 'Address at U.N. General Assembly, 25 September 1961'; http://www.jfklibrary.org/Asset-Viewer/DOPIN64xJUGRKgdHJ9NfgQ.aspx

39   Daily Continuity Report, *Dr. Strangelove*, Scene 58J, 15 March 1963.

40   Daily Continuity Report, *Dr. Strangelove*, Scene 58D, 14 March 1963.

41   Daily Continuity Report, *Dr. Strangelove*, Scene 74, 18 March 1963.

42   Contrary to the literature, the term 'megadeath' was not coined by Herman Kahn while at RAND. In his 1969 preface to the paperback edition of *On Thermonuclear War*, Kahn states unambiguously 'Not only is the term 'megadeaths' *not* used in the book, but I have never heard a professional analyst use it.' Kahn also repudiates the allegation that he 'recommended Doomsday Machines', vii. In one take used for the Exhibitor's showreel, narrated by Kubrick, General Turgidson uses 'megadeaths', but it was not in the final cut.

43   Concerning *On The Beach*, see Mick Broderick, 'Fallout on the Beach', *Screening the Past*, no. 36 (2013); http://www.screeningthepast.com/2013/06/fallout-on-the-beach/

44   Daily Continuity Report, *Dr. Strangelove*, Script 74K, 28 March 1963.

45   Christiane Kubrick, ibid. See also Kahn, *On Thermonuclear War*, 83.

46   Some of this excised performance can be seen in the director's self-narrated demonstration reel to exhibitors on the 2016 Criterion Blu-ray edition.

47   A document comparing the two endings – one with the pie fight and one without – an unidentified author suggests to Kubrick that he should not even retain the 'Mein Führer, I can walk!' outburst fearing audiences will: 'Laugh at the vaudeville pyrotechnics and Nazi send-up without grasping the "strategic" send up', SK/11/9/68.

48   Daily Continuity Report, *Dr. Strangelove*, Scene 74 D, 20 March 1963.

49   Southern, 'Notes from the War Room'; Samuel Wigley, 'Rare Images of the Dr Strangelove Custard Pie Fight Rare Images of the Dr Strangelove Custard Pie Fight', (2014); http://www.

bfi.org.uk/news-opinion/news-bfi/features/rare-images-dr-strangelove-custard-pie-fight; Ken Adam, 'Dr. Strangelove: The Missing Pie Fight'; http://www.webofstories.com/play/ken.adam/86; Glenn Kenny, "Mein Führer! I Can Walk!': Dr. Strangelove' Editor Anthony Harvey on the Lost Ending', (2009); https://mubi.com/notebook/posts/mein-fuhrer-i-can-walk-dr-strangelove-editor-anthony-harvey-on-the-lost-ending; 'Dr. Strangelove 'Pie Fight' Alternate Ending (1963)'; http://lostmedia.wikia.com/wiki/Dr._Strangelove_%22Pie_Fight%22_Alternate_Ending_(1963). And John O'Brien *Strangelove's Weegee*, Vancouver: Presentation House Gallery, 2013. Despite this substantial body of analysis and description already in press and online, the Kubrick Archive donors and legal representatives remain curiously resistant to acknowledging the circulation of this material as *already* in the public domain. It is entirely understandable that Kubrick's executor, Jan Harlan, fulfills his brother-in-law's request by refusing access to the remaining pie fight print(s), but the Trust's attempts to prevent disclosure, or the re-circulation of discussion about this history seem futile and ultimately counter-productive.

50   Christiane Kubrick, ibid.

51   Daily Continuity Report, *Dr. Strangelove*, Script 74&, 25 March 1963.

52   Daily Continuity Report, *Dr. Strangelove*, Scene 74U, 25 March 1963.

53   Daily Continuity Report, *Dr. Strangelove*, Script 74V ,25 March 1963.

54   Laurie Johnson, transcript, 'Inside Dr. Strangelove'.

55   Pablo Ferro, transcript, 'Inside Dr. Strangelove'.

56   Pablo Ferro, interview with the author, Los Angeles 2005.

57   Daily Continuity Report, *Dr. Strangelove*, Scene 74BB, 27 March 1963.

58   Daily Continuity Report, *Dr. Strangelove*, Scene 74HH, 28 March 1963.

59   Terry Southern, 'Notes from the War Room', ibid.

60   Daily Continuity Report, *Dr. Strangelove*, Scene 74 JJ, 28 March 1963.

61   Daily Continuity Report, *Dr. Strangelove*, Scene 74Q, 22 March 1963.

62   According to Nile Southern, Terry claimed to have written much of this the sparse dialogue.

Sons of *Strangelove*

How to follow a film where you have destroyed the world?

Kubrick's next project was the sublime and pioneering *2001: A Space Odyssey*. Superficially, the film was seen as a major departure from the director's work up to that point; however, a number of Strangelovean themes resonate throughout. Chief amongst these is the unexplained imagery of satellites orbiting above the Earth in the year 2001. Kubrick's famous jump-cut from man-ape Moonwatcher's animal bone, now used as a murderous tool and thrown into the air in slow motion, and spliced atemporally to match a nuclear weapons platform orbiting the future Earth, was not made explicit. The various satellites on view may simply be interpreted as civilian or otherwise benign spacecraft, evident in the Pam Am shuttle docking with Space Station 5. Arthur C. Clarke's novelisation, however, describes these initially seen 'satellites' as orbital bomb carriers, explained at the conclusion of the novel when astronaut Dave Bowman returns as the post-human, embryonic Starchild and detonates the circulating thermonuclear weapons as he approaches the planet.

Rumours of a planned *Dr. Strangelove* sequel have circulated over the years. According to blogger Todd Brown, Kubrick had asked Terry Southern to write a sequel for *Dr. Strangelove* and nominated Terry Gilliam to direct.[1] As Gilliam notes the story may have been credible:

> I was told after Kubrick died – by someone who had been dealing with him – that he had been interested in trying to do another *Strangelove* with me directing. I never knew about that until after he died but I would have loved to.[2]

According to Brown the project was to be titled *Son of Strangelove*. No script exists 'but index cards laying out the basic structure of the story were found among Southern's papers after his passing'; the plot was set largely in 'underground bunkers where Strangelove has taken refuge with a group of (at least mostly, possibly entirely) women'.[3]

Irrespective of any sequel proposal, real or imagined, the film certainly has its fans amongst cinema practitioners and industry cognoscenti. For example, Pablo Ferro, the title designer for *Strangelove* (and *A Clockwork Orange*), was hired by Barry Sonnenfeld to replicate the style in the 1997 science fiction comedy *Men in Black* and sequels *Men in Black II* (2002) and *Men in Black III* (2012). The cineaste Coen brothers gestured to *Strangelove* in *Raising Arizona* (1987) when a bathroom has 'POE' and 'OPE' conspicuously scrawled across a wall. Displaying such inter-textual 'knowing', *Dr. Strangelove* is perpetually referenced in film to provide an abbreviated cultural context in order to signify the Cold War logics of annihilation and/or the feeble systems of deterrence marshaled to prevent a holocaust. From Slim Pickens' cameo role in Spielberg's *1941* (1979) and Steve Buscemi straddling a nuke in *Armageddon* (1998) to *Mars Attacks!* (1996), post-9/11 science fiction thrillers such as *Next* (2007), and *Watchmen*'s (2009) elaborate war room scene, multiple aspects of *Dr. Strangelove*'s narrative and characterisation are portrayed, often in homage, transcending pastiche to embrace culturally indebted satire.[4] The influence is apparently everywhere. As George Case has suggested, a quick Google search of the phrase 'how I learned to stop worrying and love...' will demonstrate the currency of the film's subtitle, resulting in over a half-million hits, mostly as non-nuclear variations on the theme.[5]

In Steven Spielberg's version of *A.I. Artificial Intelligence* (2000) remnants of Kubrick's abiding concerns with nuclear energy – from both *Dr. Strangelove* and *2001* – are evident. The non-human perspective that prefaced and concluded the early draft of *Dr. Strangelove*, sardonically narrated as part of a series 'Dead Planets of Antiquity', is alluded to by the post-human world of the drowned planet presented at *A.I.*'s conclusion. As Kubrick foreshadowed in 1970:

> After all, what could be more absurd than the very idea of two mega-powers willing to wipe out all human life because of an accident, spiced up by political differences that will seem as meaningless to people a hundred years from now as the theological conflicts of the Middle Ages appear to us today?[6]

As the filmmaker's wife Christane and daughter Katharina recall, Kubrick remained concerned with geopolitics, militarism and the fate of the world's nuclear arsenals throughout his life, and his personal library contained later books on the subject decades after *Strangelove* was completed. Marvin Minksy remembers with some amusement that, years after he had advised Kubrick on machine intelligence for *2001*, and during the development of the *A.I.* project, upon news of the superpowers agreeing to halve their nuclear warheads, Kubrick felt the announcement was really pathetic because it can't really make any difference as long as they have enough to destroy the world. I wish... Can't anybody get through to them, to make them realise that they've got to do something much more effective than that.[7]

The MIT scientist observed that many years earlier Kubrick had *himself* 'made a movie called *Dr. Strangelove*' which explained that very point 'more clearly than anybody could possibly do'. Minsky reminded the director that, if a masterful work like *Dr. Strangelove* couldn't 'get through' to the right people then he 'didn't know what possibly could'. Minksy concludes his anecdote with a chuckle by recalling that Kubrick replied – after a long silence – 'Oh ... I forgot about that.'[8]

While the director may have momentarily lapsed in memory, feigned or otherwise, elsewhere *Strangelove* had clearly entered the public lexicon. The film and its eponymous character were being referenced in seemingly endless ways. In one a truly bizarre apparition, before a combined global television audience in the billions, masses of American citizens gathered in Washington DC for Barack Obama's inauguration during a frigid January morning in 2009. A sinister looking figure soon joined dignitaries on the podium. Dressed in black, wearing dark gloves and hunched over in a wheelchair the figure appeared, according to multiple commentators, 'Strangelovian'. That incongruous presence was none other than the departing Vice President of the United States, and chief architect of the Bush Administration's 'war on terror', Dick Cheney.

Numerous political media pundits glibly described Chaney as Strangelovean, invoking this now familiar, and instantly recognisable popular culture icon. Cheney was notorious for reorienting the US defence agenda after 9/11, known as the 'Bush doctrine', which foregrounded the option of American nuclear pre-emption.[9] For the Strangelove attribution to resonate so strongly, and immediately, with the American public 45 years after Peter Sellers' screen rendition, the invocation signified a number of things. Firstly, it acknowledged the deep cultural penetration of the Strangelove trope and iconography into the globalised twenty-first century. Secondly, the appellation connoted a sinister dread of a suppressed and latent tendency towards fascism (still) at the margins of American political establishment. Thirdly, the Cheney/Strangelove association suggested an almost robotic and inhuman tendency towards zero-sum calculus in government policy where ends justified any means.

Yet Cheney was only a recent target of such pejorative political brandishing. Also reflecting the film's cult status, during the Iraq War former Texas Governor and then sitting US President George W. Bush, was depicted in several online memes, Stetson in hand, straddling a nuclear bomb akin to Major Kong. Under the earlier Reagan Administration, as an uncompromising advocate of the Strategic Defense Initiative ('Star Wars'), the Defense Department's Richard Pearle was similarly targeted as a malevolent technocrat

A twenty-first century parody of neo-conservative Strangeloves as a mock DVD cover.

40TH ANNIVERSARY SPECIAL EDITION
WWW.INTERNETWEEKLY.ORG

Richard Perle   Dick Cheney
IN WILLIAM KRISTOL'S

Dr. Strangelove
Or: How I Learned To Stop Worrying And Love The Bomb

and policy wonk in an online fan mash-up. Hence, the imaginary figure of Dr. Strangelove remains a dynamic and plastic one. Other Presidents have been tarnished by both the film's allure and satirical opprobrium. Upon occupying the White House, President Reagan is said to have impatiently asked his aides to be shown the 'War Room'.[10] Apocryphal or not, this story expresses the film's cumulative suggestive power by rendering such an imagined space *normative* and anticipatory. Earlier, as Lyndon Johnston escalated US troop deployments into Vietnam, a popular protest badge depicted LBJ wearing sunglasses and smirking, next to psychedelic text displaying 'Strangelove Lives'.

The complex associations with 'Strangelove' resonated further. Within months of the movie's release, *Time* magazine's 'Nuclear Issue' featured Sellers in his Strangelove guise as part of a cover collage representing trends in American nuclear policy. Rod Serling's post-*Strangelove* script for a United Nations/ABC television special, *A Carol for Another Christmas* (1964), produced and directed by Joseph L. Mankiewicz, updated Dickens' narrative by featuring Sterling Hayden as an embittered American industrialist name Grudge. This modern-day Scrooge is reminded of the horrors of Hiroshima and shown projections of a future nuclear holocaust, where Peter Sellers (as the 'Imperial

Me'] egomaniacally rules over a diminishing band of survivors. Philip K. Dick's Nebula Award-nominated novel, *Dr. Bloodmoney, or How We Got Along After the Bomb*, was released in 1965. It was an informal and canny literary extension to *Strangelove*'s logic, set twenty years in the future, where a scientist's atmospheric nuclear experiment creates global fallout and catastrophic mutation.[11] The same year Peter George followed his *Strangelove* novelisation with *Commander-1*, featuring a crazed submarine commander who annoints himself leader of a world devastated and depleted by nuclear warfare.

Another key indicator of *Dr. Strangelove*'s dominant cultural impact was the honouring of the film by the Library of Congress in 1989, selected for official preservation in the National Film Register alongside other classics. The American Film Institute and other screen culture institutions regularly list *Strangelove* as one of the ten best film comedies of all time. Strangelovean imagery circulates widely within other mass culture products, such as *The Simpsons*' epistemology – whether inside Mayor Quimby's War Room with Professor Frink in a wheelchair wearing dark glasses, or Sideshow Bob whistling 'We'll Meet Again' (season seven), or Homer indulging in the fantasy of riding a nuclear bomb, waving a Stetson, and plummeting towards the Springfield Nuclear Power Plant (season five), or the entire Simpsons family doing likewise, straddling their sofa, in an opening montage across several seasons. The film is cited further in an episode titled '$pringfield (Or, How I Learned to Stop Worrying and Love Legalized Gambling)' (season five), and on a marquee for the Springfield X-rated cinema, shown playing 'Doctor Strangepants'.[12] Katharina Kubrick has confirmed that her father was chuffed by such references and was quite a fan of *The Simpsons*.[13]

Outside of popular culture, the apocalyptic fantasy of a Doomsday weapon continues to find currency. *The New York Times* magazine recently ran a sensationalist cover feature article headed 'The Doomsday Scam'. It concerned the purportedly decade-long quest by 'aspiring bomb makers – including ISIS' who have been desperate 'to get their hands on a lethal substance called red mercury'.[14] New scholarship in the *Bulletin of*

Screen frame captures of *Strangelove* homages from episodes of *The Simpsons*.

the *Atomic Scientists*, reports on a post-Perimeter Russian 'doomsday' drone, capable of causing a massive radioactive tsunami, something US physicists researched during the Cold War, and even a pre-Hiroshima American comic (*Bill Barnes, America's Air Ace*) forecast in 1942! Author Edward Moore Geist notes the Russian undersea drone, named Status-6, can carry a cobalt bomb, a 'conjectural device, which served as the basis of the "doomsday machine" [in] the classic 1964 film *Dr. Strangelove* [that] would employ radioactive cobalt to create unusually intense long-lived fallout'.[15] Concerns not only rest with Russian nuclear developments. In the lead up to the 2016 US Presidential election Republican candidate Donald Trump has reportedly asked a foreign policy adviser during a national security briefing – three times during the session – why he could *not* use nuclear weapons: 'If we have them why can't we use them?'[16] Fears mount over perceptions of Trump's 'thin skin' as Democratic candidate and former Secretary of State Hillary Clinton warns 'a man you can bait with a tweet is not a man we can trust with nuclear weapons', echoing the successful 1964 campaign by LBJ against Republican maverick Senator Barry Goldwater.[17]

Perhaps the greatest legacy of *Dr. Strangelove* is that the film helped a generation to recognise the inherent, grotesque foundation of nuclear deterrence and, perhaps, to learn *not* to love the bomb. Kubrick and his collaborators collectively showed us how to stare, unflinchingly, right into Pandora's atomic box. The evocation of nightmare comedy was an inspired and courageous artistic approach to the subject matter. Satire and black humour enabled unconscious and instantaneous recognition of the paradoxes of the nuclear mindset, stripped bare and revealed for all its absurdity. As a cinematic dreamspace – the credible nightmare/prophecy of what may become – Kubrick's film can be read as one of the most potent forms of twentieth-century secular Revelation. By returning the gaze of the nuclear gorgon, audiences were neither immobilised nor frozen in fear. Nor were they compelled to look away and acquiesce to the political-military-industrial-entertainment complex that perpetuates a 'state of nuclear terror', as psychologist Joel Kovel has described our episteme.

Nevertheless, falling out of love with the Bomb has proven to be tough over recent decades. Attempts at meaningful arms control have limped along since the late 1940s. Multilateral treaties – ostensibly to reduce the systemic threat by nuclear weapons production, and aimed at minimising escalation or spasm wars using these arsenals – have been few and far between. Such moves are often perceived as opportunities to exercise strategic advantage and commonly meet resistance. While further weapons proliferation is decried by members of the nuclear club, little is done to minimise their own stockpiles. Entire economies rely on tax-payer-subsidised contracts to globalised corporations for weapons development and production, their continued 'modernisation', the infrastructure for multiple means of delivery (sea, air and land forces), the vast

nation-state surveillance apparatus to ensure safeguarded security, and the disman-
tling, stockpile storage and the inter-generational, ecologically-safe preservation of the
remnant toxic fissile materials for thousands of years into the future. Noble Peace Prize-
winning President Obama, having vowed in Prague to work at nuclear 'abolition', instead
committed future American administrations to a $1trillion nuclear weapons upgrade. He
then brought his nuclear command code 'Football' and personal authorisation 'biscuit'
into the Hiroshima Peace Park during the 2016 visit attended by Japanese *hibakusha*.

Today nearly two thousand nuclear weapons remain globally on ready alert – with
many on 'hair-trigger' alert – capable of being launched within five to fifteen minutes.
A fraction of this arsenal could not only initiate a cataclysmic war but also generate a
nuclear winter adding to the firestorms and radiological impact across the global bio-
sphere. Hence, there is some irony in Kubrick's use of stock footage at the conclusion of
Dr. Strangelove. While the archive of Pentagon and Atomic Energy Commission films are
merged into an experimental montage to evoke the Doomsday Machine's triggering –
and quite possibly, the follow-up volleys of nuclear strikes from both sides – it stands as
visible evidence of the nuclear war that was *already* underway, but largely unrecognised.

Throughout the Cold War and beyond over two thousand nuclear tests were conducted, and over a quarter of these occurred in the atmosphere. The detonations released
multiple billions of curies of radiation, with the largest explosions circulating carcino-
genic toxins into the upper atmosphere, encircling the globe, and crossing hemispheres.
As a result, a large proportion of the human population – and countless animal, insect
and plant species – have absorbed these radionuclides over time. Kubrick's Doomsday
montage serves as a reminder to us all, that not only have these genocidal weapons
remained poised for immediate use over decades, but during the Cold War they *had* been
used all around the world – in America, Japan, the Marshall Islands, Kazakhstan, Russia,
Australia, Kiribati, Algeria, China, French Polynesia, India, Pakistan and North Korea.[18]
These two thousand-plus nuclear tests have contaminated vast areas of the planet
and left a toxic legacy now imprinted in our individual biology and the entire ecosphere.
Hence, not only does *Dr. Strangelove* stand as historical testament to a malignant Cold
War mindset but also as a cultural talisman of the *anthropocene* – our newly identified
epoch indelibly marked with 'a radiological signature in the geological record'.[19]

NOTES

1   See http://twitchfilm.com/2013/10/stanley-kubrick-wanted-terry-gilliam-to-direct-son-
    of-strangelove.html
2   Ibid.
3   Ibid.
4   See Mick Broderick, 1991, *Nuclear Movies*, 45.

5   George Case, *Calling Dr. Strangelove*, ibid.,loc 2513. Case claims a result of '13 million' hits.

6   Kubrick interview by Joseph Gelmis, *The Film Director as Superstar*, New York: Doubleday, 1970; http://www.visual-memory.co.uk/amk/doc/0069.html

7   Kubrick quoted by Marvin Minsky at http://www.webofstories.com/play/marvin.minsky/96

8   Ibid.

9   Nancy Spannaus, 2006, 'Will Cheney's 'Strangelove' Bush Go for Nuclear War Against Iran?', 19 October; http://www.larouchepub.com/eiw/public/2006/2006_10-19/2006_10-19/2006–17/pdf/30-31_617_intiran.pdf

10 In fact, Reagan would have been doubly confused. The White House does have a 'situation room' but *Dr. Strangelove* depicted a fictitious 'War Room', clearly shown in the film as within the Pentagon, and modeled on the big boards of the Strategic Air Command headquarters in Nebraska.

11 See Paul Brians, 1987, *Nuclear Holocausts: Atomic War in Fiction, 1895–1984* (Kent, OH: Kent State University Press), 182.

12 Mick Broderick, 2003, 'Releasing the Hounds: *The Simpsons* as Anti-nuclear satire', in John Alberty, ed., *Leaving Springfield: The Simpsons and the Possibility of Oppositional Culture* (Detroit: Wayne State University Press), 244–272.

13 Katharina Kubrick, Skype interview with the author May 2016.

14 C. J. Chivers, 2015, 'The Doomsday Scam', *The New York Times*, 19 November; http://www.nytimes.com/2015/11/22/magazine/the-doomsday-scam.html?_r=0

15 Edward Moore Geist, 2016, 'Would Russia's undersea 'doomsday drone' carry a cobalt bomb?', *Bulletin of the Atomic Scientists*, July, 238–242.

16 Nick Allen, David Lawler and Ruth Sherlock, 2016, 'Donald Trump "asked why US couldn't use nuclear weapons if he becomes president"', *Daily Telegraph*, 3 August, http://www.telegraph.co.uk/news/2016/08/03/donald-trump-asked-why-us-cant-use-nuclear-weapons-if-he-becomes-president/

17 Gabriel Samuels, 2016, 'Hilary Clinton Burns Donald Trump', *The Indpendent*, 29 July. On LBJ v Goldwater, see Robert Mann, 2016, 'How the "Daisy" Ad Changed Everything About Political Advertising', *The Smithsonian Magazine*, 13 Aprl.

18 See 'The Global Hibakusha Project' at http://nuclearfutures.org/projects/integrating-projects-and-showcases/, and http://bojacobs.net/Bo_Jacobs/Global_Hibakusha.html

19 Richard Monastersky, 2015, 'First atomic blast proposed as start of Anthropocene', *Nature*, 16 January, http://www.nature.com/news/first-atomic-blast-proposed-as-start-of-anthropocene-1.16739

BIBLIOGRAPHY

Abrams, Herbert L. 'Sources of Human Instability in the Handling of Nuclear Weapons'. In *The Medical Implications of Nuclear War*, edited by Solomon F. Marston. Washington DC: National Academies Press, 1986.

Abrams, Nathan. 'An Alternative New York Intellectual: Stanley Kubrick's Cultural Critique'. In *New Perspectives on Stanley Kubrick*, edited by Tatljana Ljujic, Richard Daniels and Peter Kramer. London: Black Dog, 2014.

Adam, Ken. 'Dr. Strangelove: The Missing Pie Fight'. http://www.webofstories.com/play/ken.adam/86

Allen, Steven. 'The Smear against Sane'. *The Realist*, no. 15, February 1960.

Anderson, Matt. 'Chaplin and Agee'. *Movie Habit*, 2005. http://www.moviehabit.com/essay.php?story=chaplin_agee

Anon. 'The 36 Hour War: The Arnold Report Hints at the Catastrophe of the Next Great Conflict'. *Life*, 19 November 1945.

_____ 'Coming: The End of the World'. *Newsweek*, 3 April 1963.

_____ 'Here's What Could Happen to New York in an Atomic Bombing'. *PM*, 7 August 1945.

_____ 'Khrushchev Basks in New Surprises'. *Life*, 4 August 1958.

_____ 'King Kong Defense System'. *The Realist*, no. 13, 1959.

Aubrey, Crispin. *Nukespeak, the Media and the Bomb*. London: Comedia, 1982.

Baxter, John. *Stanley Kubrick: A Biography*. Cambridge MA: Da Capo Press, 1997.

Bellovin, Steven M. 'Permissive Action Links, Nuclear Weapons, and the History of Public Key Cryptography'. 2005. Published electronically 21 October. http://web.stanford.edu/class/ee380/Abstracts/060315-slides-bellovin.pdf

Beres, Louis Rene. 'Nuclear Errors and Accidents'. In *Search for Sanity: The Politics of Nuclear Weapons and Disarmament*, edited by Paul Joseph and Simon Rosenblum. Boston: South End Press, 1984.

Bernstein, Jeremy. 'How About a Little Game?' *The New Yorker*, November 12 1966.

Biller, Jose, and Alberto J. Espay. 'Alien Hand Syndrome'. In *Practical Neurology Visual Review*. Baltimore: Lippinott Williams & Wikins, 2013.

Blair, Bruce G. 'Russia's Doomsday Machine'. *The New York Times*, 8 October 1993, A35.

'Bomber Gap'. *Cold War Museum*. http://www.coldwar.org/articles/50s/bomber_gap.asp

Boyer, Paul. *Fallout: An Historian Reflects on America's Half-Century Encounter with Nuclear Weapons*. Columbus: Ohio State University Press, 1998.

Brians, Paul. *Nuclear Holocausts: Atomic War in Fiction, 1895–1984*. Kent, OH: Kent State University Press, 1987.

Broad, William J. 'Russia Has 'Doomsday' Machine, US Expert Says'. *The New York Times*, October 8 1993.

Broderick, Mick. 'Fallout on the Beach'. *Screening the Past*, no. 36. 2013. http://www.screeningthepast.com/2013/06/fallout-on-the-beach/

_____ ed. *Hibakusha Cinema: Hiroshima, Nagasaki and the Nuclear Image in Japanese Film*. London: Kegan Paul International, 1996.

_____ *Nuclear Movies: A Critical Analysis and Filmography of International Feature Length Films Dealing with Experimentation, Aliens, Terrorism, Holocaust, and Other Disaster Scenarios, 1914–1990*. McFarland, 1991.

_____ 'Reconstructing Strangelove: Outtakes from Kubrick's Cutting Room Floor'. In *Stanley Kubrick: New Perspectives*, edited by Tatjana Liujic, Peter Kramer and Richard Daniels. London: Black Dog, 2015.

_____ 'Releasing the Hounds: The Simpsons as Anti-Nuclear Satire'. In *Leaving Springfield: The Simpsons and the Possibility of Oppositional Culture*, edited by John Alberty. Detroit: Wayne State University Press, 2003.

Broderick, Mick, and Robert Jacobs. 'Nuke York, New York: Nuclear Holocaust in the American Imagination from Hiroshima to 9/11'. *The Asia-Pacific Journal* 10, no. 11/6. 2012.

Brodie, Bernard. 'Must We Shoot from the Hip?' In *working paper*: RAND corporation, 1951.

Burr, William. 'First Strike Options and the Berlin Crisis, September 1961'. 2001. Published electronically 25 September. http://nsarchive.gwu.edu/NSAEBB/NSAEBB56/

_____ 'Newly Declassified Documents on Advance Presidential Authorisation of Nuclear Weapons Use'. 1998. Published electronically 30 August. http://nsarchive.gwu.edu/news/predelegation2/predel2.htm

Burr, William, and Hector L. Montford. 'The Making of the Limited Test Ban Treaty, 1958–1963'. *National Security Archive*. 2003. Published electronically 8 August. http://nsarchive.gwu.edu/NSAEBB/NSAEBB94/

Burr, William, and Svetlana Savranskaya. 'Previously Classified Interviews with Former Soviet Officials Reveal US Strategic Intelligence Failure over Decades'. *National Security Archive*. 1999. Published electronically 11 September. http://nsarchive.gwu.edu/nukevault/ebb285/

Carter, Ashton B., John D. Steinbruner, and Charles A. Zraket. *Managing Nuclear Operations*. Washington, DC: The Brookings Institution, 1987.

Carter, Dale. *The Final Frontier: The Rise and Fall of the American Rocket State*. London: Verso, 1988.

Case, George. *Calling Dr. Strangelove: The Anatomy and Influence of the Kubrick Masterpiece*. Jefferson NC: MacFarland, 2014.

Castle, Allison, Jan Harlan and Christiane Kubrick. *The Stanley Kubrick Archives*. Cologne: Taschen, 2008.

'Castro-Khrushchev Letters on First Strike'. *American Experience*. http://www.pbs.org/wgbh/

americanexperience/features/primary-resources/jfk-attack/

Chen, Janet, Su-I Lu and Dan Vekhter. 'Von Neumann and the Development of Game Theory'. https://cs.stanford.edu/people/eroberts/courses/soco/projects/1998–99/game-theory/neumann.html

Chilton, Paul A. *Language and the Nuclear Arms Debate: Nukespeak Today*. London: Francis Pinter, 1985.

Chivers, C. J. 'The Doomsday Scam'. *The New York Times*. 2015. Published electronically 19 November. http://www.nytimes.com/2015/11/22/magazine/the-doomsday-scam.html?_r=0.

Ciment, Michel, Gilbert Adair and Martin Scorsese. *Kubrick: The Definitive Edition*. New York: Faber & Faber, 2001.

'Civilian Defender Clay'. *Time*, 2 October 1950.

'Claim 'Fail-Safe' 'Plagiarized' Brit. '2 Hours to Doom''. *Daily Variety*, 12 February 1963, 1, 4.

Clavin, Tom. 'There Never Was Such a Thing as a Red Phone in the White House'. *Smithonian Mag*. 2013. http://www.smithsonianmag.com/history/there-never-was-such-a-thing-as-a-red-phone-in-the-white-house-1129598/?no-ist.

Cocks, Geoffrey. *The Wolf at the Door: Stanley Kubrick, History, & the Holocaust*. London: Peter Lang, 2004.

Colitt, Leslie. 'Berlin Crisis: The Standoff at Checkpoint Charlie'. *The Guardian*. 2011. Published electronically 25 October. https://www.theguardian.com/world/2011/oct/24/berlin-crisis-standoff-checkpoint-charlie.

Comprehensive Nuclear-Test-Ban Treaty Organisation. 'Castle Bravo on 1 March 1954, Bikini Atoll: Largest US Test in Terms of Yield and Fallout'. 2012. https://www.ctbto.org/specials/testing-times/1-march-1954-castle-bravo/

Council, National Security. 'Report of the Net Evaluation Subcommittee'. Washington DC, 1962.

Day, Dwayne A. 'Of Myths and Missiles: The Truth About John F. Kennedy and the Missile Gap'. *The Space Review*. 2006. Published electronically 3 January. http://www.thespacereview.com/article/523/1

De Vore, Robert. 'What the Atomic Bomb Really Did'. *Collier's*, 2 March 1946.

Della Sala, Sergio. 'The Anarchic Hand'. *The Psychologist* 18, no. 10, October 2005: 506–601.

Department of State. 'U-2 Overflights and the Capture of Francis Gary Powers, 1960'. *Office of the Historian*. https://history.state.gov/milestones/1953–1960/u2-incident

Downing, Taylor. 'War on Film - Dr. Strangelove'. *Military History*. 2014. Published electronically 20 February. http://www.military-history.org/articles/war-on-film-dr-strangelove.htm.

'Dr. Strangelove "Pie Fight" Alternate Ending (1963)'. http://lostmedia.wikia.com/wiki/Dr._Strangelove_%22Pie_Fight%22_Alternate_Ending_(1963).

Dunar, Andrew, and Stephen Waring. 'Power to Explore'. 1999] http://history.msfc.nasa.gov/vonbraun/excerpts.html

Dunaway, David King. *Huxley in Hollywood*. New York: Harper & Row, 1989.

Duncan, Paul. *Stanley Kubrick: Visual Poet 1928–1999*. Cologne: Taschen, 2003.

Early, Chris. 'February 25, 1956: Khrushchev Launches Surprise Attack on Stalin'. 2015. Published electronically 25 February. http://home.bt.com/news/world-news/february-25-1956-khrushchev-launches-surprise-attack-on-stalin-11363964039873

'The Einstein Letter - 1939'. Atomic Heritage Foundation, http://www.atomicheritage.org/history/einstein-letter-1939

'Fail-Safe Being Acquired by Col'. *The Hollywood Reporter*, 1 April 1963.

Farell, Robert H. 'Truman at Potsdam'. *American Heritage*, June/July 1980.

Federation of American Scientists. 'Nuclear Weapon Radiation Effects'. 1998. Published electronically 21 October. http://fas.org/nuke/intro/nuke/radiation.htm

Fowler, Harold. 'Survival'. *The Realist*, no. 3, October 1958.

Freuanfelder, Mark. 'George Dyson on Nuclear Weapon Scientists'. In *BoingBoing*, edited by Mark Freuanfelder, 2011.

Freud, Sigmund. 'The Uncanny'. 1919. http://web.mit.edu/allanmc/www/freud1.pdf

Geist, Christopher D. 'Arnold Marquis' 'the Fifth Horseman': Documentary Radio as Popular Criticism'. Bowling Green State University, 1975.

George, Peter. *Red Alert*. Ace Books, 1958.

Ghamari-Tabrizi, Sharon. 'The Think-Tank Man'. *Life*, 6 December 1968.

_____ *The Worlds of Herman Khan: The Intuitive Science of Thermo-Nuclear War*. Cambridge, MA: Harvard University Press, 2005.

Gooch, John and Amos Perlmutter, eds. *Military Deception and Strategic Surprise*. New York: Frank Cass, 1982.

Goodwin, James. 'Akira Kurosawa and the Atomic Age'. In *Hibakusha Cinema: Hiroshima, Nagasaki, and the Nuclear Image in Japanese Film*, edited by Mick Broderick. London: Kegan Paul International, 1996.

Grigorieff, Paul. 'The Mittelwerk/Mittelbau/Camp Dora'. http://www.v2rocket.com/start/chapters/mittel.html

Grossman, Karl. 'The Nuclear Cult'. *Counterpunch*. 2012. http://www.counterpunch.org/2012/06/18/the-nuclear-cult/

Guardian, The. 'Goldsboro Revisited: Account of Hydrogen Bomb near-Disaster over North Carolina – Declassified Document'. 2013. http://www.theguardian.com/world/interactive/2013/sep/20/goldsboro-revisited-declassified-document

Gusso, Mel. 'Terry Southern Literary Archives Go to New York Public Library'. *The New York Times*. 2003. Published electronically 3 April. http://www.nytimes.com/2003/04/03/books/03SOUT.html?pagewanted=all

Hargittai, Istvan. *The Martians of Science: Five Physicists Who Changed the Twentieth Century*. Oxford: Oxford University Press, 2006.

Haynes, Roslynn D. *From Faust to Strangelove: Representations of the Scientists in Western Literature*. Baltimore, MD: Johns Hopkins University Press, 1994.

Healy, Gene. *The Cult of the Presidency: America's Dangerous Devotion to Executive Power*. Washington DC: Cato Institute, 2009.

Heilman, Kenneth M. and Edward Valenstein, eds. *The Alien Hand: Terminology and Pathogenesis*. 4th ed. Oxford: Oxford University Press, 2003.

Heims, Steve J. *John Von Neumann and Norbert Wiener: From Mathematics to the Technologies of Life and Death*. Boston: MIT Press, 1980.

Hellman, Martin. 'Fifty Years after the Cuban Missile Crisis: Time to Stop Bluffing at Nuclear Poker'. *Federation of American Scientists*. 2012. www-ee.stanford.edu/ffhellman/publications/76.pdf

Hilgartner, Stephen, Richard C. Bell and Rory O'Connor. *Nukespeak*. London: Penguin, 1983.

Hill, Lee. *A Grand Guy: The Art and Life of Terry Southern*. New York: Harper, 2001.

Hill, Rodney and Gene D. Phillips. *The Encyclopedia of Stanley Kubrick*. Facts on File. New York: Checkmark Books, 2002.

Hirano, Kyoko. 'Depiction of the Atomic Bombings in Japanese Cinema During the US Occupation Period". In *Hibakusha Cinema*, edited by Mick Broderick. London: Kegan Paul International, 1996.

History Channel. 'Hotline Established between Washington and Moscow'. Published electronically 30 August. http:// www.history.com/this-day-in-history/hotline-established-between-washington-and-moscow.

Hitchens, Christopher. *The Trial of Henry Kissinger*. London: Verso, 2002.

Hoffman, David. *The Dead Hand: The Untold Story of the Cold War Arms Race and Its Dangerous Legacy*. New York: Anchor Books, 2009.

Horton, Robert. *Frankenstein*. London and New York: Wallflower Press, 2014.

Howard, James. *Stanely Kubrick Companion*. London: B. T. Batsford, 1999.

Howard, Jane. 'A Creative Capacity to Astonish'. *Life*, 12 August 1964.

Huxley, Aldous. *Ape and Essence*. Chicago: Elephant Paperback, 1992 [1948].

'John Von Neumann'. Atomic Heritage Foundation, http://www.atomicheritage.org/profile/john-von-neumann

Johnson, P. Anna. *Australia Years: the Life of a Nuclear Migrant*. Raleigh NC: Lulu.com. 2006.

Johnston, Robert. 'The Largest Nuclear Weapons: Multimegaton Weapons'. 1999. Published electronically 9 April. http://www.johnstonsarchive.net/nuclear/multimeg.html

'Joint Intelligence Objectives Agency. Foreign Scientist Case Files 1945–1958'. *US National Archives and Records Administration*. http://www.archives.gov/iwg/declassified-records/rg-330-defense-secretary/

Jones, Thomas. 'A Full Retaliatory Response'. *Air & Space*, November 2005.

Kagan, Norman. *The Cinema of Stanley Kubrick*. 3rd ed. New York: Continuum, 2000.

Kahn, Herman. *On Thermonuclear War*. Princeton: Princeton University Press, 1960.

Kaplan, Fred. *The Wizards of Armageddon*. Stanford University Press (ebook), 1991.

Kennedy, John F. 'Address at U.N. General Assembly, 25 September 1961'. http://www.jfklibrary.org/Asset-Viewer/DOPIN64xJUGRKgdHJ9NfgQ.aspx

_____ 'National Security Action Memorandum Number 160: Permissive Links for Nuclear Weapons in Nato'. (962. Published electronically 6 June. http://www.jfklibrary.org/Asset-Viewer/DOwYUab4bOmVeDyLvL58jQ.aspx

Kenny, Glenn. '"Mein Führer! I Can Walk!': Dr. Strangelove' Editor Anthony Harvey on the Lost Ending'. (2009). Published electronically 24 June 2009. https://mubi.com/notebook/posts/mein-fuhrer-i-can-walk-dr-strangelove-editor-anthony-harvey-on-the-lost-ending

Kissinger, Henry. 'Strains on the Alliance'. *Foreign Affairs*. 1963. https://www.foreignaffairs.com/articles/cuba/1963–01-01/strains-alliance

Knaack, Marcelle. *Post-World War II Bombers, 1945–1973*. Washington DC: Office of Air Force History, 1988.

Krämer, Peter. 'Complete Total Final Annihilating Artistic Control'. In *Stanley Kubrick: New Perspectives*, edited by Tatjana Liujic, Peter Krämer and Richard Daniels. London: Black Dog, 2015.

_____ *Dr. Strangelove*. London: British Film Institute, 2014.

_____ '"The Greatest Mass Murderer since Adolf Hitler': Nuclear War and the Nazi Past in Dr. Strangelove'. In *Dramatising Disaster: Character, Event, Representation*, edited by Christine

Cornea and Rhys Owain Thomas, 120–35. Newcastle: Cambridge Scholar Press, 2013.

_____ "To Prevent Heat from Dissipating': Stanley Kubrick and the Marketing of Dr. Strangelove (1964)'. *InMedia* 3 (2013).

Krassner, Paul. 'Yes, Virginia Is a Sanity Clause'. *The Realist*, no. 5, December 1958.

Kristensen, Hans M. 'Secrecy on a Sliding Scale: US Nuclear Weapons Deployments'. 1999. Published electronically 20 October. http://oldsite.nautilus.org/archives/nukepolicy/ Denmark/index.html

Kubrick, Stanley. 'How I Learned to Stop Worrying and Love the Cinema'. In *Films and Filming*: June, 1963.

Laurence, William L. 'Now Most Dreaded Weapon, Cobalt Bomb, Can Be Built'. *The New York Times*, 7 April 1954.

Leitch, Alexander. *A Princeton Companion*. Princeton, NJ: Princeton University Press, 1978.

Lemmer, George F. 'The Air Force and Strategic Deterrence 1951–1960'. *USAF Historical Division*. 1967. Published electronically December. http://nsarchive.gwu.edu/nukevault/ebb249/ doc09.pdf

Lewis, Roger. 'Some Sunny Day - My Autobiography: Dame Vera Lynn'. *The Daily Express*. 2009. Published electronically 21 August. http://www.express.co.uk/entertainment/ books/121730/Some-Sunny-Day-My-Autobiography-Dame-Vera-Lynn

Littell, Robert. 'What the Atom Bomb Would Do to Us'. *Reader's Digest*, May 1946.

Lobrutto, Vincent. *Stanley Kubrick: A Biography*. New York: D. I. Fine Books, 1997.

MacRae, Norman. *John Von Neumann: The Scientific Genius Who Pioneered the Modern Computer, Game Theory, Nuclear Deterrence, and Much More*. American Mathematical Society, 1999.

Marchetti, Celia and Sergio Della Sala. 'Disentangling the Alien and Anarchic Hand'. *Cognitive Neuropsychiatry* 3, no. 3. 1998: 191–207.

Marovitz, Sanford E. 'Aldous Huxley and the Nuclear Age: 'Ape and Essence' in Context'. *Journal of Modern Literature* 18, no. 1. 1992: 115–25.

Mather, Philippe. *Stanley Kubrick at Look Magazine: Authorship and Genre in Photojournalism and Film*. Bristol: Intellect, 2013.

McElroy, Gil. 'Amateur Radio and the Rise of Ssb'. *QST*. 2003. Published electronically January. http://www.arrl.org/files/file/Technology/pdf/McElroy.pdf

McGilligan, Patrick. *Backstory 3: Interviews with Screenwriters of the 60s*. Berkeley, CA: University of California Press, 1997.

McQuiston, Kate. *We'll Meet Again: Musical Design in the Films of Stanley Kubrick*. New York: Oxford University Press, 2013.

Menand, Louis. 'Fat Man: Herman Khan and the Nuclear Age'. *The New Yorker* (2005). Published electronically 27 June 2005. http://www.newyorker.com/magazine/2005/06/27/fat-man

Monastersky, Richard. 'First Atomic Blast Proposed as Start of Anthropocene'. *Nature*. 2015. Published electronically 16 January. http://www.nature.com/news/first-atomic-blast-proposed-as-start-of-anthropocene-1.16739.

Nasar, Sylvia. *A Beautiful Mind*. New York: Faber & Faber, 2012.

National Security Archive. 'The Berlin Crisis 1958–1961'. http://nsarchive.gwu.edu/nsa/publi-cations/berlin_crisis/berlin.html

_____ 'The Berlin Wall, Fifty Years Ago'. (2011). http://nsarchive.gwu.edu/NSAEBB/NSAEBB354/.

_____ 'Declassified Pentagon History Provides Hair-Raising Scenarios of US Vulnerabilities to

Nuclear Attack through 1970s'. 2012. Published electronically 19 November. http://nsar-chive.gwu.edu/nukevault/ebb403/

_____ 'First Documented Evidence That US Presidents Predelegated Nuclear Weapons Release Authority to the Military'. (1998). Published electronically 20 March. http://nsarchive.gwu.edu/news/19980319.htm

_____ 'Instructions for the Expenditure of Nuclear Weapons in Accordance with the Presidential Authorisation Dated May 22, 1957'. (Revised as at 28 January 1959). nsarchive.gwu.edu/NSAEBB/NSAEBB45/doc3.pdf

_____ 'New Details on the 1961 Goldsboro Nuclear Accident'. http://nsarchive.gwu.edu/nukevault/ebb475/

_____ 'Summary of Population Fatalities from Nuclear War in 1966'. 1962. http://nsarchive.gwu.edu/nukevault/ebb281/

Naylor, David. 'Inside Dr. Strangelove'. 2000.

Nornes, Abé Mark. 'The Body at the Center — the Effects of the Atomic Bomb on Hiroshima and Nagasaki'. In _Hibakusha Cinema_, edited by Mick Broderick. London: Kegan Paul International, 1996.

Nuclear Weapons Archive. 'The B-41 (Mk-41) Bomb: High Yield Strategic Thermonuclear Bomb'. http://nuclearweaponarchive.org/Usa/Weapons/B41.html

_____ 'Principles of Nuclear Weapons Security and Safety'. 1997. http://nuclearweaponar-chive.org/Usa/Weapons/Pal.html

PBS. 'Operation Alert, Race for the Superbomb'. _The American Experience_. http://www.pbs.org/wgbh/amex/bomb/peopleevents/pandeAMEX64.html

Phillips, Gene D. _Stanley Kubrick: Interviews_. Conversations with Filmmakers. Jackson, MI: University Press of Mississippi, 2001.

Plait, Phil. 'The 50th Anniversary of the Starfish Prime: The Nuke That Shook the World'. _Discover Magazine_. 2012. http://blogs.discovermagazine.com/badastronomy/2012/07/09/the-50th-anniversary-of-starfish-prime-the-nuke-that-shook-the-world/ - .V0fsuauG_FI

Poundstone, William. _Prisoner's Dilemma_. Anchor, 2011.

RAND Corporation. 'History and Mission'. http://www.rand.org/about/history.html

Reston, James. _The New York Times_, 12 August 1945.

Rhodes, Richard. _Dark Sun: The Making of the Hydrogen Bomb_. Simon & Schuster, 1996.

Rose, Kenneth D. _One Nation Underground: The Fallout Shelter in American Culture_. New York: New York University Press, 2001.

Rosin, Armin. 'A Spherical Bunker in Russia Was the Most Secure Place in the Entire Cold War'. _Business Insider_. 2015. Published electronically 10 March. http://www.businessinsider.com.au/a-spherical-bunker-in-russia-was-the-most-secure-place-in-the-entire-cold-war-2015–3?r=US&IR=T

Ross, Michael. 'Glenn Urges Probe for Toxic Experiments: Health: Senator Says US Should Disclose If Any Patients Were Unwittingly Exposed to Any Hazardous Substance in Tests Like Those for Radiation'. _Los Angeles Times_, 7 January 1994.

Sandia Laboratories. _Command and Control Systems for Nuclear Weapons: History and Current Status_. 1973.

Savranskaya, Svetlana. 'Cuba Almost Became a Nuclear Power in 1962'. _Foreign Policy_. 2012. http://foreignpolicy.com/2012/10/10/cuba-almost-became-a-nuclear-power-in-1962/

Savranskaya, Svetlana, Thomas Blanton and Anna Melyakova. 'New Evidence on Tactical Nuclear Weapons - 59 Days in Cuba'. *National Security Archive*. 2013. http://nsarchive.gwu.edu/NSAEBB/NSAEBB449/

Schlosser, Eric. *Command and Control: Nuclear Weapons, the Damascus Accident, and the Illusion of Safety*. Penguin Press, 2013.

'Scientist with Nazi Past Removed from Nm Space History Museum Hall of Fame'. *Anti-Defamation League*. 2006. Published electronically 17 May. http://archive.adl.org/NR/exeres/2D6AAE8C-3DE8-4E5E-9A51-B530031786D0,0B1623CA-D5A4-465D-A369-DF6E8679CD9E,frameless.htm

Sellers, Michael. *P.S. I Love You*. London: Collins, 1981.

Sellers, Peter. 'The Steve Allen Playhouse'. 1964.

Server, Lee. *Now Dig This: The Unspeakable Writings of Terry Southern, 1950–1995*. New York: Grove Press, 2002.

Shurkin, Joel. 'Edward Teller, 'Father of the Hydrogen Bomb', Is Dead at 95'. http://news.stanford.edu/news/2003/september24/tellerobit-924.html

Sikov, Ed. *Mr. Strangelove: A Biography of Peter Sellers*. New York: Hyperion, 2002.

'Slave Labor Built V-Weapons'. http://www.nationalmuseum.af.mil/factsheets/factsheet.asp?id=8093

Smith, Peter D. *Doomsday Men: The Real Dr. Strangelove and the Dream of the Superweapon*. London: Penguin, 2007.

'Southern Exposure'. *Time*, 12 June 1964.

Southern, Nile. 'Strange Loves'. *Written By*, 16 January 2016.

Southern, Terry. 'Notes from the War Room'. *Reprinted from Grand Street*, no. 49. 1996. http://www.visual-memory.co.uk/amk/doc/0081.html

Spannaus, Nancy. 'Will Cheney's 'Strangelove' Bush Go for Nuclear War against Iran?'. 2006. Published electronically 19 October. http://www.larouchepub.com/eiw/public/2006/2006_10-19/2006_10-19/2006–17/pdf/30-31_617_intiran.pdf.

Stark, Graham. *Remembering Peter Sellers*. London: Robson Books, 1990.

Stein, Peter and Peter Feaver. *Assuring Control of Nuclear Weapons: The Evolution of Permissive Action Links*. Lanham, MD: Harvard University, 1987.

Stimson, Thomas E. 'Is Our Atomic Stockpile Dangerous?'. *Popular Mechanics*, no. Annual Auto Issue. 1961.

Stix, Gary. 'Infamy and Honor at the Atomic Café: Edward Teller Has No Regrets About His Contentious Career'. *Scientific American*. October 1999.

Strategic Air Command. 'Atomic Weapons Requirement Study for 1959'. 1956.

Suid, Lawrence H. *Guts and Glory: The Making of the American Military Image in Film*. Lexington, KY: University Press of Kentucky, 2015.

'Suit Won't Stall 'Fail-Safe' Filming, Youngstein Avers'. *Daily Variety*, 14 February 1963, 1, 4.

Sylvester, Derek. *Peter Sellers*. London: Proteas Press, 1981.

Tagg, Lori S. *Development of the B-52: The Wright Field Story*. Dayton, OH: History Office Aeronautical Systems Center, Air Force Materiel Command, Wright-Patterson Air Force Base, United States Air Force, 2004.

Thompson, Howard. 'Movie Company to Be Dissolved'. 6 April 1963.

Tully, David. *Terry Southern and the American Grotesque*. Jefferson NC: McFarland, 2010.

Unger, Craig. *The Fall of the House of Bush*. New York: Scribner, 2007.

US Air Force. 'Operation Headstart'. *Film 242.FR.33* (1959). https://www.youtube.com/watch?v=GDWS_9uS9IM

US Department of Energy Office of Declassification. 'Restricted Data Declassification Decisions 1946 to the Present (Rdd-7)'. (2001). Published electronically 1 January. http://www.fas.org/sgp/othergov/doe/rdd-7.html-l49

Vandebilt, Tom. *Survival City: Adventures among the Ruins of Atomic America*. New York: Princeton Architectural Press, 2002.

Vandenberg, General. 'Transcript of the Commanders Conference'. 4–7, 1950.

Walker, Alexander. *Stanley Kubrick, Director: A Visual Analysis*. London: Widenfeld & Nicolson, 1999.

Wellerstein, Alex. 'Edward Teller's 'Moon Shot''. *Nuclear Secrecy*. 2011. http://blog.nuclearsecrecy.com/2011/12/12/edward-tellers-moon-shot/

_____ 'Nagasaki: The Last Bomb'. *The New Yorker*, 7 August 2015.

_____ 'Trinity at 70: 'Now We Are All Sons of Bitches''. *Nuclear Secrecy*. 2015. http://blog.nuclearsecrecy.com/2015/07/17/now-we-are-all-sons-of-bitches/

'Werner Von Braun'. *Operation Paperclip*. http://www.operationpaperclip.info/wernher-von-braun.php

'Werner Von Braun'. http://www.newworldencyclopedia.org/entry/Wernher_von_Braun

Wheeler, Harvey. 'Fail-Safe Then and Now'. *The Idler* 2, no. 32. 2000. Published electronically 29 May. http://www.the-idler.com

Wigley, Samuel. 'Rare Images of the Dr Strangelove Custard Pie Fight Rare Images of the Dr Strangelove Custard Pie Fight'. (2014). Published electronically 30 January. http://www.bfi.org.uk/news-opinion/news-bfi/features/rare-images-dr-strangelove-custard-pie-fight

''Winston' to 20th, 'Fail-Safe' to Col. As Eca Fold Nears'. *Daily Variety*, April 5 1963.

Wohlstetter, Albert. 'The Delicate Balance of Terror'. *P-1472*. 1958. http://www.rand.org/about/history/wohlstetter/P1472/P1472.html

_____ 'The Delicate Balance of Terror'. *Foreign Affairs* 37, no. 2. 1959: 211–34.

Wohlstetter, Albert and Henry Rowen. 'Objectives of the United States Military Posture'. *RM-2373*. 1959. http://www.rand.org/about/history/wohlstetter/P1472/P1472.html.

Wolfram, Stephen. 'John Von Neumann's 100th Birthday'. 2003.

Wranovics, John. *Chaplin and Agee: The Untold Story of the Tramp, the Writer, and the Lost Screenplay*. New York: Palgrave McMillan, 2005.

Wright, Mike. 'The Disney-Von Braun Collaboration and Its Influence on Space Exploration'. *Marshall Space Flight Center History Office*. http://history.msfc.nasa.gov/vonbraun/disney_article.html

Young, Ken. 'A Most Special Relationship: The Origins of Anglo-American Nuclear Strike Planning'. *Journal of Cold War Studies* 9, no. 2. 2007.

Zellen, Barry. 'Bernard Brodie and the Bomb: At the Birth of the Bipolar World'. 2015.

_____ 'Bernard Brodie: A Clausewitz for the Nuclear Age'. *Strategic Thinkers*. 2009. http://securityinnovator.com/index.php?articleID=15954&sectionID=43

PRODUCTION CREDITS

Stanley Kubrick Producer, Director, Writer
Terry Southern Writer
Peter George Writer (based on the book: *Red Alert* by Peter George)

CAST

Peter Sellers Group Captain Lionel Mandrake / President Merkin Muffley / Dr. Strangelove
George C. Scott Gen. 'Buck' Turgidson
Sterling Hayden Gen. Jack D. Ripper
Keenan Wynn Col. 'Bat' Guano
Slim Pickens Maj. 'King' Kong
Peter Bull Russian Ambassador Alexi de Sadesky
Tracy Reed Miss Scott/ 'Miss Foreign Affairs' (centerfold)
Frank Berry Lt. Dietrich
Glenn Beck Lt. Kivel
James Earl Jones Lt. Lothar Zogg
Shane Rimmer Capt. 'Ace' Owens
Paul Tamarin Lt. Goldberg
Jack Creley Staines
Robert O'Neil Adm. Randolph
Gordon Tanner Gen. Faceman
Roy Stephens Frank
John McCarthy Burpelson AFB Defense Team Member
Hal Galili Burpelson AFB Defense Team Member
Laurence Herder Burpelson AFB Defense Team Member
Victor Harrington War Room Aide (uncredited)
Burnell Tucker Mandrake's aide (uncredited)

PRODUCTION

Victor Lyndon associate producer

Leon Minoff executive producer (uncredited)

Laurie Johnson music

Gilbert Taylor director of photography

Anthony Harvey film editor

Ken Adam production design

Peter Murton art direction

Stuart Freeborn makeup artist

Barbara Ritchie hairdresser

Clifton Brandon production manager

Eric Rattray assistant director

John Aldred dubbing mixer

Richard Bird recordist

John Cox sound supervisor

Leslie Hodgson sound editor

Wally Veevers special effects

Kelvin Pike camera operator

Bernard Ford camera assistant

Vic Margutti travelling matte

Bridget Sellers wardrobe

Geoffrey Fry assembly editor

Ray Lovejoy assistant editor

Pamela Carlton continuity

Pablo Ferro main title design/trailer

John Crewdson aviation advisor (as Capt. John Crewdson)

Alan Bryce special effects (uncredited)

Brian Gamby special effects (uncredited)

Garth Inns special effects (uncredited)

Mike Shaw special effects (uncredited)

Jim Body visual effects camera operator (uncredited)

Bob Cuff matte painter (uncredited)

Peter George technical advisor (uncredited)

Jean Bernard pilot: outside bomber views (uncredited)

Arthur (Weegee) Fellig still photographer/special effects advisor (uncredited)

Bob Penn still photographer (uncredited)

INDEX

Printed in Australia
AUHW022039310123
374050AU00030B/146

9 780231 177092